MARTIN EBON

presents the often startling facts, and exposes the fakes, in his vivid exploration of the poles of prophecy. Revealing little-known investigations in this area by Freud and Jung, the author also takes a new look at the old faithfuls, Edgar Cayce and Jeane Dixon, surveys economic and business prophecies, and presents the latest developments in university experimentation as well as the major, well-documented, individual case histories of prophetic experiences in this century.

Also included is the astonishing evidence for precognition surrounding the sinking of the Titanic . . . previewed in extraordinary detail fourteen years earlier in a book entitled The Wreck of the Titan.

But your own discovery will be even more tantalizing:

PROPHECY IN OUR TIME.

SIGNET Books of Special Interest

- ☐ **TEST YOUR ESP edited by Martin Ebon.** Now you can test your ESP capacity right in your own home. The contributors to this unique volume, mainly staff members of the Institute for Parapsychology at Durham, N.C., tell you in simple terms how to set up tests for clairvoyance, telepathy, precognition and general ESP. (#Y7854—$1.25)
- ☐ **MYSTERIOUS PYRAMID POWER edited by Martin Ebon.** A message left by the gods? The storehouse of earth's past and future history? Or a mechanism for concentrating unseen psychic energies . . . ? This book explores it all, turning the key that could open the door to the storehouse of ancient knowledge and power which has long been lost in the mists of legend. (#E8110—$1.75)
- ☐ **REINCARNATION IN THE TWENTIETH CENTURY edited by Martin Ebon. Revised edition.** In this startling book about one of the most fascinating and controversial subjects of the century, a noted scholar has assembled the compelling testimony of those who claim to remember former lives. (#W8479—$1.50)*
- ☐ **DEMON CHILDREN edited by Martin Ebon.** Terrifying but true case histories of children suddenly transformed by demonic forces into creatures of evil, documented by leading psychic investigators. Stories range from the original incident on which *The Exorcist* was based to the tragedy of a young child enslaved by a Tahitian god. (#E7986—$1.75)
- ☐ **THE WORLD'S WEIRDEST CULTS edited by Martin Ebon.** From around the world, from the earliest dealings with the forces of evil to the terrible tragedy of the Jonestown death cult, here is a shocking but true look at the various strange beliefs which have flourished in the past and the bizarre groups which are still actively recruiting members today. (#J8767—$1.95)*

*Price slightly higher in Canada

Buy them at your local bookstore or use this convenient coupon for ordering.

THE NEW AMERICAN LIBRARY, INC.,
P.O. Box 999, Bergenfield, New Jersey 07621

Please send me the SIGNET BOOKS I have checked above. I am enclosing $_____ (please add 50¢ to this order to cover postage and handling). Send check or money order—no cash or C.O.D.'s. Prices and numbers are subject to change without notice.

Name _____

Address _____

City_____ State_____ Zip Code_____

Allow 4-6 weeks for delivery.
This offer is subject to withdrawal without notice.

PROPHECY IN OUR TIME

Martin Ebon

A SIGNET BOOK
NEW AMERICAN LIBRARY
TIMES MIRROR

COPYRIGHT © 1968, 1979 BY MARTIN EBON

All rights reserved. This book or any part thereof must not be reproduced in any form without the written permission of the publisher.

This is a reprint of a hardcover edition published by The New American Library, Inc., The hardcover edition was published simultaneously in Canada by General Publishing Company, Ltd.

SIGNET TRADEMARK REG. U.S. PAT. OFF. AND FOREIGN COUNTRIES
REGISTERED TRADEMARK—MARCA REGISTRADA
HECHO EN CHICAGO, U.S.A.

SIGNET, SIGNET CLASSICS, MENTOR, PLUME AND MERIDIAN BOOKS
are published by The New American Library, Inc.,
1633 Broadway, New York, New York 10019

First Printing, November, 1968

4 5 6 7 8 9 10 11 12

PRINTED IN THE UNITED STATES OF AMERICA

Acknowledgments

Writing this book has been a thoroughly enjoyable task. The cooperation of friends, acquaintances, and strangers was a source of continuous encouragement. My interest in the subject grew, of course, from more than a decade of work with the Parapsychology Foundation of New York, of which Mrs. Eileen J. Garrett and the Hon. Frances P. Bolton were, respectively, President and Vice-President. I am further indebted to the cooperation of Dr. J. B. Rhine and Dr. Louisa E. Rhine, of Durham, N.C., and to the staff of their Foundation for Research on the Nature of Man.

Mrs. Laura A. Dale, editor of the *Journal* of the American Society for Psychical Research, New York, not only prepared the index but was generous with helpful editorial suggestions. Others, whose names may be found in various chapters or in the bibliography, checked all or parts of the book's contents; they include Professor Hans Bender (Freiburg i. Br.), Mr. Hugh Lynn Cayce (Virginia Beach, Va.), Dr. Jan Ehrenwald (New York), Dr. Julie Eisenbud (Denver, Colo.), Mrs. Rosalind Heywood (London), Miss Aniela Jaffé (Zurich), Dr. Gardner Murphy (Topeka, Kan.), Dr. Emilio Servadio (Rome), Dr. Ian Stevenson (Charlottesville, Va.), Professor W. H. C. Tenhaeff (Utrecht), and Miss Rhea White (Huntington, N.Y.). I am, of course, solely responsible for any errors or other shortcomings.

M. E.

Contents

1. Can We Know the Future?   9
2. Disaster at Sea: The *Titanic*   17
3. Can Time Flow Upstream?   26
4. Cayce: The Seer of Virginia Beach   37
5. Hitler's Prophets   50
6. Croiset's Prophetic Chairs   67
7. Exotic Prophecy   76
8. Freud: Oedipus Without Oracle   88
9. C. G. Jung: Searching Healer   99
10. Premonition on the Couch   107
11. Beyond Freud   119
12. From New Jersey to the Grand Canyon   133
13. Can You Change Destiny?   148
14. Precognition in the Laboratory   158
15. Prophecy and Youth   167
16. Prophecy Involving Animals   176
17. Toward the Year 2000   184
18. The Washington "Seeress"   194
19. "Who Is Dead in the White House?"   204
20. Ever Since Dodona   216

Author's Note   228
Selected Bibliography   229
Index   234

1 Can We Know the Future?

On the morning of November 22, 1963, President John F. Kennedy acted out his own assassination. In a Dallas hotel room, with his wife Jacqueline and White House aide Kenneth O'Donnell as his audience, the President imitated the action of the barrel and hammer of a gun, pointing his index finger and thumb at his own head. Later, although Mrs. Kennedy preferred to have the bubble top put on the presidential car, Kennedy ordered that the top be left off. He thus assured the very death he had imagined two hours before.

On February 21, 1967, the Freedoms Foundation of Valley Forge, Pennsylvania, honored the memory of a soldier who had prophesied his own death on the battlefield. He was Pfc. Hiram D. Strickland of Graham, North Dakota, who had written to his parents from Vietnam: "I'm writing this letter as my last one. You've probably already received word that I'm dead and the Government wishes to express its deepest regret. Believe me, I didn't want to die, but I know it was part of my job. . . ."

On October 2, 1966, 4 A.M., Mrs. Sybil Brown of Brighton, England, awoke from a nightmare. She told her husband, "Something terrible's going to happen." In her dream, she had seen a six-year-old girl walking down the street toward her, while a black, menacing mass kept moving closer, to the right of her. At the same time, Mrs. Brown heard a voice in her dream, saying, "The whole family is in the house." Later that day, an avalanche of coal waste killed 116 children and 28 adults at Aberfan, Wales. Hundreds of people claimed that, like Mrs. Brown, they had either "felt" the disaster at the time it occurred, or had precise premonitions of it.

The following January, the Scottish motor-boat racer, Donald Campbell, died when his boat, "Bluebird," overturned on a lake. Two hours before his death, playing solitaire, he had turned up the ace of spades and the queen. Campbell then told his friends that "someone" in his family would die soon, because "Mary Queen of Scots did the same thing before she died."

These are examples of prophecy, premonition, precognition, foreknowledge—call it what you like—that have occurred with striking accuracy in our own time. They are not stories handed down from past centuries, although the history of prophecy goes back to the beginning of recorded time. Nor are these isolated examples. In the Institute for Parapsychology, Foundation for Research on the Nature of Man, the file of cases recording unusual experiences of this kind totals more than 14,000 and the largest single category is precognitive, most often involving dreams of imminent suffering or death in accurate detail.

Ever since man became conscious of his destiny and identity, death and disaster have usually been the subjects of prophecy. This ranges from prophets of the Bible and the Delphic Oracle to case histories of our own day, evaluated with the tools of statistics and psychology. These are now being recorded, documented, classified, and analyzed. This research was first methodically begun by the Society for Psychical Research (London) before the turn of the century. At present, reports of prophetic experiences in the dreaming or waking state are being carefully sifted by the American Society for Psychical Research, New York, and by similar organizations all over the world.

Prophecy fascinates and influences much of mankind. Interest ranges from the general to the intimate, from the profound to the superficially amusing. Among the age-old and modern questions that men and women ask are these: What will my future bring? Will it be good fortune or failure? Does it hold prosperity or economic trouble? Are there, in this future, romance, wedding bells, divorce, delinquency, the death of a loved one, the murder of a Prime Minister, a Hollywood scandal, spectacular stock-market actions, new health-giving drugs or poisoned foods, invasions from outer space, earthquakes and landslides, war or peace, a long life, or death for me?

No less than in past centuries, there are those today in all parts of the world who claim to know the future. Often they can point to prophecies that have come true. Their devices are many. They range from palm-reading at a neighborhood gypsy tearoom to the calculations of Wall Street chartists. The questions asked of ancient Greek oracles differ little from those addressed to men and women who today write astrological forecasts for the daily press of the United States, the popular Sunday papers of Britain, and the illustrated weeklies of Germany, France, Italy, Scandinavia, or Japan.

Powerful twentieth-century leaders in Asia and Africa consult soothsayers, just as royal rulers checked their plans with court astrologers years ago. Motion-picture actors in Hollywood or London want to be sure that the stars favor their new contracts at present, just as a royal wedding in Nepal and a teakwood deal in Thailand await the favorable nod of an astrological consultant.

Chemistry and physics have grown from the occult make-believe of alchemy. Witch doctors and herb dispensers of older civilizations were the pioneers who cleared the path for today's medicine. Is the flash of human insight, that mysterious split second of prophetic vision, the mental essence of computerized forecasts in technology, warfare, medicine, economics, and possibly all of human life?

Yesterday's intuition often has a way of becoming today's statistic. The elusive qualities of man are, increasingly, subject to experiment and documentation in the laboratory. But the search is far from completed. Many questions remain unanswered, and therefore doubly fascinating. If we can know the future, can we also influence it? How much can we reasonably guess on the basis of conscious or unconscious knowledge? Where does an imaginative or knowledgeable calculation end, and where does "pure" prophecy begin?

The very task of defining prophecy or precognition is subject to cultural differences, available data, or scientific methods. Boundaries between one form of forecast and another are blurred. Individuals who have successfully anticipated an event do not, for the most part, know exactly how they arrived at their image of the future. Many, baffled themselves, say rather helplessly that they simply "saw" a given event, just as a dream image appears in the mind, without going through retinal channels. Seen, as the phrase goes, in "the mind's eye," these visions elude easy categorization; and it would be premature to restrict the sweep of open inquiry, to establish categories that may prove too narrow to hold potentially significant material.

Prophecy is viewed differently, depending on a man's time and place in history and civilization. Yesterday's bewilderment may seem naive today and today's supposedly well-established standards may appear inadequate tomorrow. But the underlying phenomenon is not to be denied. And even if one or another document is doubted, if a particular eyewitness may fail to convince—what can never be in doubt is man's at least occasional authentic prophetic experience, psychologically valid whether it be called "subjective" or "objective" in the vocabulary of contemporary science.

We cannot always tell whether an experience of this kind is, strictly speaking, telepathic (from mind to mind), clairvoyant (from event or object to the mind), or whether it is concurrent or truly precognitive. The Delphic Oracle of ancient Greece may have been either clairvoyant or telepathic when she was tested by the fabulously wealthy Croesus, King of Lydia. Five other oracles had failed to state correctly what odd task Croesus was performing at the time. But the Delphic Oracle said accurately, "Croesus is boiling a lamb and a tortoise together, in a copper vessel with a copper lid." When he later checked with the Oracle on whether or not he should make war on the Persians, he was told that if he crossed the Halys River—in other words, marched against Persia—he would destroy a great empire." He did just that—but was badly defeated; he had destroyed his own empire.

Among Biblical prophets, Amos, who lived about 800 B.C., correctly, and without Delphic ambiguity, forecast the downfall of the Northern Kingdom of Israel under Jeroboam II: "For Amos saith, Jeroboam shall die by the sword and Israel shall surely be led away captive out of their own land."

In our own time, spectacular forecasts, such as those of the assassination of President Kennedy, have renewed public interest in prophecy. Few people remember that President Abraham Lincoln had a premonitory dream shortly before his own assassination, seeing himself in his bier in the East Room of the White House.

Probably the most solid, modern two-pronged research in precognition is being undertaken at the Institute of Parapsychology, under the direction of Dr. J. B. Rhine and his wife, Dr. Louisa E. Rhine. At the same time, though, daring psychologists, psychoanalysts, and psychiatrists, throwing aside Sigmund Freud's idea that prophetic dreams are mere imaginative wish-fulfillments, are studying apparently prophetic dreams reported by their patients—and finding them puzzling, convincing, and enlightening.

Even Nostradamus, the most self-assured but also one of

the most obscure prophets of our civilization, was baffled by the philosophic implications of prophecy. Modern philosophers, who have given this matter extensive and profound thought, in many instances find nothing to prevent the occurrence of prophecy. And the latest frontiers of theoretical physics are studied with questions about cause and effect, about the nature of time—can it, so to speak, run backward?

The former Parapsychology Laboratory of Duke University has recorded experiments, going back some thirty years, whereby subjects named cards correctly well beyond the odds of chance, in a deck that had not yet been shuffled; thousands of tests, piled up since then, provide statistical evidence that correlates with qualitative cases of prophecy reported since the days of Babylon.

Prophecy embraces man's ancient hope and fear. We want to know the future, hoping that it will bring happiness and satisfaction; if it contains pain or disaster, we want to try to change it. And, indeed, some premonitory dreams have caused people to change their plans and, apparently, avoid catastrophe. Still, even in such cases, more questions are raised than answered. If a woman in Detroit had not called her brother in New Jersey at 5 A.M., having dreamed that he would have a car accident—just as he was getting ready to leave on a trip—would the accident actually have occurred?

This raises profound religio-philosophical questions about man's free will, determination, fate, and destiny. Are our lives prescribed? Or are only patterns set, within which we are free to act? Are we, by our individual natures, prone to certain experiences? Can others, gifted with extrasensory perception, read our personality pattern and thus anticipate events correctly for us?

Did President Kennedy, by ordering that his car remain without a protective top, invite a fate that he expected? Did others sense this, and, in the atmosphere of general anxiety, express their impressions as prophecy? Did Lincoln, after his premonitory dream, virtually invite his own assassination? He was, after all, quite ineffectually guarded when John Wilkes Booth crashed into his theater box.

Are we to such a degree "captains of our fate" that some of us can sense the actions others are likely to take—can foresee a specific act by looking into a crystal ball, examining the palm of a hand, or using other devices that free the mind from distraction? Or, further, do basic emotional needs at times crash through the barriers of space and time, in moments of anxiety or panic, setting free visions of the future, in response to primeval desires?

Fear and greed, disaster and delight, and, over and over, death. These seem to be major elements in prophecy. When the *S.S. Titanic* hit an iceberg and the allegedly unsinkable ship went to the bottom of the Atlantic Ocean, taking more than 1,500 passengers with her, numerous premonitory dreams and hunches were recalled, including those of people who had canceled tickets and could cite the supporting testimony of others to whom they had expressed their prevision of the disaster.

And then there are present-day events that, if correctly reported, utterly defy analysis. A Dutch clairvoyant has, time after time, described with startling accuracy the personalities and key experiences of men and women who, days later, occupy certain chairs in meetings—although the very seating arrangements remain secret always until a few minutes before the meeting hall is filled. A trick? Two professors of psychology, in Holland and Germany, testify that they have supervised these experiments repeatedly and with utmost care.

Oh, yes, we know all about the psychology of testimony! Every psychology student knows that if a professor arranges for an incident within the classroom—a quarrel, perhaps—students will write down utterly disparate descriptions of it. We are, all of us, forever coloring stories, playing down certain elements, dramatizing others. Memory is notoriously unreliable. Witnesses are not to be trusted. Evidence can be manipulated.

True. Agreed. This applies to all facets of life. Perhaps it is even more true in areas that have retained a touch of the magical, of which prophecy is perhaps the outstanding, the most fascinating, elusive, primitive, and awe-inspiring. I spent some twelve years as Administrative Secretary of the Parapsychology Foundation, Inc., of New York, which stated in 1965 in a report on its *Ten Years of Activities* that modern parapsychology, which includes the study of precognition, "deals with phenomena that, because of their unusual character, have traditionally aroused a relatively high degree of emotionalism." The report adds:

"It is easy to see that phenomena which, in past centuries and other civilizations, carried magical connotations, continue to create reactions that range from near-superstitious total acceptance to defensive total disbelief. In our time, ancient dreams of the magical have been translated into a vast array of technological realities. Still, there remains a vast expanse of those unexplored, difficult-to-observe phenomena which constitute the field of parapsychology."

But it is simply not enough either to believe or to scoff. We cannot swallow whole every claim of prophecy that comes in the mail. Yet, we cannot, on the basis of available evidence —of which this book reviews only a part—close our eyes to the implications, either. Certainly we can go right ahead and disbelieve half of it, or two-thirds of it, or three-quarters, or nine-tenths—but not, if we are honest with ourselves, all of it. There is too much of it; it follows patterns too similar to be disregarded; it falls into categories that cut across the geography of the whole globe, and across all recorded time.

To believe blindly, knowing that conscious or unconscious distortions are always scattered through our lives, would be foolish. But to disbelieve with equal blindness is just as foolish, particularly in an era when each year's discoveries— studies of the human brain, for instance—illuminate the vastness of our ignorance.

It isn't even humility that should cause us to suspend judgment until we review the evidence; it is just good common sense. Our generation has experienced too much that our ancestors and other civilizations would have regarded as miraculous—to the degree, in fact, that Church authorities find it necessary to redefine their concept of the "miraculous" itself—to ignore claims that might go against traditional concepts of time and space. Just as we know that gravity loses its pull once a space vehicle reaches a certain height, so should our concepts of the past, present, and future remain open to reexamination.

The range of prophecy extends from conscious fraud and charlatanry-for-profit to precognition in the laboratory under strictly controlled conditions. The modern scientist engaged in quantitative ESP card experiments draws a clear line between historical or anecdotal material and his own efforts. But the public annoys the scientist intensely when it associates his experiments with such carnival side-show features as palmistry ("Your Fate Is in Your Hands!") or astrology ("Your Fate Is in Your Stars!"), crystal gazing, and "readings" by means of playing cards and other devices. Astrologers, in fact, fall into many categories; some of the best-established shy away from all forecasting, while others hedge their prophetic observations with the time-worn saying that "the stars impel; they do not compel...."

The only order into which prophecy can logically be put is a chronological one. And it is only in the past half-century that efforts have been made to collect and categorize prophetic dreams or waking hunches, to record events that bear them out, and to devise laboratory methods that guard against delusion or self-delusion. What remains is a strong residue of case material, with optimum documentation, together with mounting data from the ESP laboratory which supports the precognition hypothesis.

Prophecy is difficult to accept because it threatens to pull the ground right out from under our illusions of security. The so-called realities of space and time are the principles with which we feel we must live; in everyday life we cannot do without them. But the future often has a way of crashing unannounced into the present, in a dream, a hunch, a vision. Only someone who has personally experienced a psychic phenomenon can testify to the impact that such a perception can have. Someone who has actually dreamed of a blue sedan crashing into a red convertible just as the big clock over the bank entrance says ten minutes to eleven—and then sees such an accident at just that time—has come to know, secretly and with trembling, that the world is not what it seems to be.

Then, why not leave well enough alone? Why probe and poke into the future—the present gives us trouble enough—and confuse and upset people, raise doubts, and pose a lot of unanswerable questions? Well, you don't have to read this book. But, believe me, it deals with a dimension that is all around you. Modern society *has* adopted means of prophecy that were considered divination in ancient times. The soothsaying of Wall Street is often not too different from that of traditional oracles. Every day of the week, a number of security analysts are likely to say, in so many words, that the market, if it does not go up or down, is certain to remain stable.

Yet scientific methods of collecting and computing information are becoming more and more accurate. Only where human psychology is concerned—as in the fear or greed of the market place—is oracular hedging a preferred technique. There are many who stand, rightly, in awe of what appears to be mystical language; in poetry, it is designed to convey meanings which only certain forms of art or music may also be able to communicate. But where such language for practical purposes is consciously opaque, where grandiose phrases coil around elusive symbolism, concerning the future, we are not dealing with true communication; more likely, if this be the language of prophecy, past or present, we are facing a

Rorschach test in words, rather than an ink blot, onto which we may read anything at all, delighting in the mirror of our hopes.

Computers are pushing the frontier of accurate forecasting ever forward. From a small sampling, they now calculate nation-wide election results or public-opinion trends with amazing accuracy. Still, vast areas of knowledge remain hidden behind the curtain of the future, and man would not be man if he did not seek to lift that curtain every so often.

As the following pages show, the future intrudes on us in unexpected, dramatic, or trivial ways; it will not leave us alone in the microcosm of our existence, while laws exist that we cannot yet fathom. It is not enough to say that we are, in many ways, forever children who believe in their omnipotence and crave knowledge of the future as well as of the present. It is not enough, in fact, to maintain any sort of hypothesis about prophetic experience at this time. We know too little to form final judgment. But we also know too much to ignore the challenge of the intrusive future.

2   Disaster at Sea: The *Titanic*

Within this century, prophetic experiences were first systematically recorded. Verification and documentation were added. The basis for a scientific approach was established. In the annals of modern psychic research, the sinking of the *S.S. Titanic* stands unchallenged as a provocation for precognitive dreams and hunches. The reason for this may be found in the nature of the event itself.

Mass death is impersonal. Overall casualty figures from the Vietnam battle fronts, the record of more than 40,000 deaths from car accidents in the United States each year, all become virtually mere statistics in the public mind. Even gigantic, life-consuming military events, such as the battle of Verdun in World War I and the bombing of Hiroshima in World War II, have deep symbolic significance, but fail—

except to those directly or indirectly involved—to impart a personal emotional experience.

Plane crashes, too, which sometimes cause the deaths of more than a hundred persons, are little more than one-day sensations. The sinking of the *Titanic*, however, was unique in terms of a direct, public, yet intensely personal, shock: on her maiden voyage in the North Atlantic, at 11:40 P.M. on April 14, 1912, the ship struck an iceberg and sank within three hours. More than 1,500 of the 2,207 passengers and crew members drowned.

With the *Titanic* perished an early-twentieth-century dream, a mixture of hope, arrogance, self-assurance, much touted technological skill, and the notion that man was truly making himself master of the elements. The boat's flamboyant first voyage symbolized turn-of-the-century luxury and security; in the era of relative stability and wealth that characterized the decades before the First World War, the wealthy or wellborn grandparents of today's "jet set" and parents of yesterday's "café society" seemed immune to common danger. The *Titanic* had been described by its builders as "unsinkable." Many of the passengers were so convinced of the accuracy of this claim that they failed to arrange for their escape and thus assured their own death.

An American psychiatrist and psychical researcher, Dr. Ian Stevenson, has stated that "as an illustration of human folly compounded of ignorance and arrogance, few events could exceed the sinking of the *Titanic*." He also believes that "this general conviction of unsinkability, extending almost up to the actual moment of sinking," makes it particularly unlikely that the disaster was generally, "normally," anticipated. Dr. Stevenson contrasts the public attitude toward the *Titanic* with that surrounding the *Lusitania:* obvious expectations of danger enveloped the *Lusitania*'s last voyage, whereas almost complete outward confidence accompanied that of the *Titanic*.

An astonishing literary coincidence relates to the *Titanic*, too. In 1898, a novel by Morgan Robertson was published entitled *The Wreck of the Titan* (New York: *McClure's*), which anticipated the 1912 disaster in remarkable detail. It dealt with the early voyage of a giant ocean liner, the *Titan*, which, although it had been regarded as unsinkable, sank during the month of April; the fictional ship carried only a few lifeboats, so that most of those on board drowned. In Robertson's novel, the number of persons aboard was given as 3,000; the number of those on the *Titanic*, fourteen years later, was 2,207; in the novel, the lifeboats numbered twenty-four, those in the actual sinking totalled twenty; the boat's speed on hitting the iceberg was, in Robertson's story, twenty-five knots, while the *Titanic's* was twenty knots; in the novel, the liner's displacement tonnage was 75,000, and in the real-life disaster it was 66,000; the ship's length in the story was 800 feet, and the *Titanic's* was 882.5 feet; in fiction and in fact, the ship had three propellers. And then, of course, there is the remarkable coincidence of the name of the ship.

Dr. Stevenson, who, incidentally, is one of the world's leading authorities in the study of reincarnation—his book, *Twenty Cases Suggestive of Reincarnation,* was published by the American Society for Psychical Research (New York, 1966)—has brought together known data of parapsychological experiences concerning the sinking of the *Titanic* in two papers published in the Society's *Journal:* "A Review and Analysis of Paranormal Experiences Connected with the Sinking of the *Titanic*" and "Seven More Paranormal Experiences Associated with the Sinking of the *Titanic*" (the first in the Society's *Journal* for October 1960, the second in July 1965). The author was Chairman of the Department of Neurology and Psychiatry, University of Virginia, Charlottesville; he is now Alumni Professor of Psychiatry and engaged in full-time research.

Dr. Stevenson is a quiet, tenacious researcher, a meticulous man in his forties, who for years has combined clinical and administrative tasks as a psychiatric physician with extensive studies in psychic phenomena. In spite of his professional background and setting (the University of Virginia's School of Medicine), he does not emphasize psychological aspects of extrasensory phenomena as readily as do some of his colleagues. Yet, when surveying the *Titanic* cases, he asked, "What did this tragedy have that others just as large lacked?" One possible underlying cause was the very unexpectedness of the disaster, generating greater than usual individual emotion which, in turn, created stronger psychic "agency" or transmittal impetus. Dr. Stevenson notes that life and laboratory evidence suggest that "strength of emotion is an important feature" in making extrasensory perception possible.

The cases Dr. Stevenson collected came, in the first article, from published material; in the second, they were supplemented by letters or personal testimony. The *Titanic* material included apparently telepathic or clairvoyant as well as precognitive cases. We shall cite examples from the latter category, although there is some overlapping. Dr. Stevenson noted "a relative increase in the number of precognitive perceptions as the time of the disaster approached."

An English businessman, J. Connon Middleton, booked passage on the *Titanic* on March 23. But, ten days before the sailing, he dreamed of the ship "floating on the sea, keel upwards and her passengers and crew swimming around her." He had the same dream the next night. The dreams made him "uncomfortable" and "most depressed and even despondent," as he stated in a letter to the Society for Psychical Research, published in its *Journal* (London, 1912). Four days after his first dream, Mr. Middleton cancelled his reservation, after a cable from the United States advised him that, for business reasons, he should postpone his departure anyway for a few days. Only after he had canceled his trip did Mr. Middleton tell members of his family and friends of his prophetic dreams, and they later confirmed that he had done so. Two of them stated that he had dreamed of "floating in the air just above the wreck." Mrs. Middleton testified that her husband had never had a dream of this kind before.

Several days before the disaster, on April 10, Mr. and Mrs. Jack Marshall and their family stood on the roof of their home, opposite the Isle of Wight, watching the *Titanic* move out on its maiden voyage. Suddenly, Mrs. Marshall clutched her husband's arm and cried, "That ship is going to sink before she reaches America." Mr. Marshall tried to calm his wife with the information, so widely believed, that the boat was unsinkable. But Mrs. Marshall became angry and said, "Don't stand here staring at me! Do something! You fools, I can see hundreds of people struggling in the icy water! Are you all so blind that you are going to let them drown?" The incident was related by the Marshalls' daughter, Joan Grant, in her book *Far Memory* (New York, 1956). She had witnessed the incident as a child, and added: "During the next five days everyone was careful not to mention the *Titanic*, but Mother was nervy and Father looked harassed. It must have been almost a relief for her when everyone knew that the *Titanic* had struck an iceberg; not nearly so lonely as waiting until it happened."

A recent authoritative account of the ship's disaster, Walter Lord's *A Night to Remember* (New York, 1955), contains the precognitive impressions of one of the first-class passengers. Charles M. Hays, President of the Grand Trunk Railroad. A few hours before the *Titanic* struck the iceberg, Mr. Hays said that the time would soon come for "the greatest and most appalling of all disasters at sea." Later on, however, a little after the ship had actually struck the iceberg and was listing slightly, he seemed unconcerned and is quoted as having said, "You cannot sink this boat." But he apparently changed his mind at 12:45 A.M., after the crew had begun to lower the lifeboats. He is said to have remarked at this time, not too accurately, "This ship is good for eight hours yet." It sank one and a half hours later.

A British medium, Mr. V. N. Turvey, said on the day of the sailing that "a great liner will be lost." Three days later he forwarded this prediction in a letter to Mrs. I. de Steiger, with the additional forecast that the liner would be lost in two days. Mrs. de Steiger received the letter the following Monday, April 15.

One prominent passenger on the *Titanic* was the British editor and journalist W. T. Stead, a follower of spiritualistic ideas. When serving as editor of the *Pall Mall Gazette* in the 1880's, he published a fictional account, written as if narrated by a man who had managed to survive the sinking of a large ocean liner. Stead appended a note that stated. "This is exactly what might take place, and will take place, if liners are sent to sea short of boats." Stead, in 1892, wrote an article for the *Review of Reviews* in which he pictured the sinking of a liner in collision with an iceberg and the rescue of its sole surviving passenger by the *Majestic*, which, like the *Titanic*, was operated by the White Star Line. In actual fact, the captain of the real *Majestic* was Captain Smith, who later became the *Titanic's* captain and went down with the ship. In 1909, Stead gave a lecture at the Cosmos Club in which he pictured himself as shipwrecked and calling for help. In the book *Has W. T. Stead Returned?* (London, 1913), J. Coates stated that Stead consulted a sensitive, or medium, from time to time; this sensitive, Count Hamon, said in 1911 that any danger to his life "would be from water, and from nothing else." On June 21, 1911, Hamon advised Stead in a letter that "travel would be dangerous" to him in April 1912. Although Stead consulted several sensitives from time to time, he was occasionally quite caustic about their forecasts. One of them, Mr. W. de Kerlor, made several forecasts for Stead, beginning in September 1911. In the first interview, he said Stead would go to the United States, although he had no such plans at that time. He also said that he saw "the picture of a huge black ship," but only half of it, which "may mean that by the time this ship will be completed—when one will be able to see it in its whole length—it is perhaps then that you will go on your journey." Mr. de Kerlor also related a dream he had experienced, and that he regarded as applying to Stead: "I dreamt that I was in the midst of a catastrophe on the water; there were masses (more than a thousand) of bodies struggling in the water, and I was among them. I could hear their cries for help." In narrating this dream to Stead, he linked it with his earlier warning about the "black ship," which "meant limitations, difficulties and death." Stead brushed these predictions aside: "Oh, yes; well, well, you are a very gloomy prophet. . . ." Stead lost his life in the sinking.

Dr. Stevenson also reports that one first-class passenger, Edith Evans, recalled that a fortune-teller had once told her to "beware of the water." Miss Evans gave her place in a lifeboat to another passenger and was herself drowned.

One crew member deserted the ship when it stopped at Queenstown. Stevenson says that while foreknowledge, "perhaps unconscious," might have been a reason, so may have been several other motives.

Major Archibald Butt, military aide to President William Howard Taft, wrote to his sister-in-law, Mrs. Clara Butt, on February 23, 1912, that he was going to Europe: "Don't forget that all my papers are in the storage warehouse, and if the old ship goes down you will find my affairs in shipshape condition. As I always write you in this way whenever I go anywhere, you will not be bothered by presentiments now." He wrote this letter before leaving for Europe on the *S.S. Berlin,* not knowing that he would book return passage on the *Titanic.* He drowned.

Dr. Stevenson's comments on this letter are significant as a general observation: "When someone frequently predicts that a particular event will occur and it ultimately does, his apparent success may derive only from coincidence. Major Butt's warning to his sister-in-law loses strength as a precognition because of his habit of making such gloomy forecasts. At least he thought he had this habit, but perhaps he did not. On three previous occasions when he was planning, or was actually on, a voyage, his letters to his sister-in-law contained no predictions of disaster such as he subsequently claimed (in the passage quoted) he 'always' made. Some persons may deny the singleness and accuracy of their premonitions, just as others (probably more numerous) forget after a fulfillment that they have repeatedly predicted disaster and finally achieved only a coincidental matching of prediction and event."

One percipient of a precognitive experience concerning the sinking of the *Titanic* was Mrs. Charles Hughes of 19a Shelton Old Road, Stoke-on-Trent, England. Dr. Stevenson states, in his second paper on the *Titanic* cases, that she gave him a written account of the prophetic impressions she had had as a fourteen-year-old child. Mrs. Hughes recalled that on the night of Friday, April 12, 1912, she experienced "the most vivid dream I ever had." She saw herself on a road at Hanford and observed "a very large ship a short distance away as if in Trentham Park" with "figures walking about on it, and I just stood wondering what it was doing there and suddenly it lowered one end and I heard a terrific scream."

She awoke and frightened her grandmother with the story of her dream. The grandmother told her, "No more suppers for you, lady; dreams are a pack of daft." Mrs. Hughes recalls, "After a while I must have gone to sleep again and saw the very same scene and when the people screamed I must have done. Gran was real livid with me this time and said I wasn't stopping with her again at night."

Mrs. Hughes, then a child, told her mother about the dream the next morning. On Monday, the 15th, a man who came into the grandmother's shop for tobacco opened a morning paper and said, "Hey, old woman, is this your son?" As the grandmother's sight was not good, the granddaughter looked at the picture. It was of the crew of the *Titanic* and showed a picture of her uncle, the grandmother's son. The girl took the paper next door to her mother, and recalls that the mother said, "Oh, your dream!"

Dr. Stevenson visited Mrs. Hughes in August 1963 for additional information. As her mother and grandmother had died, he was unable to obtain corroborative statements. The uncle who had been lost on the *Titanic* was Leonard Hodgkinson, the ship's fourth engineer. He was sixty-five in 1912 and due to retire after the *Titanic* trip. Neither Mrs. Hughes nor her mother or grandmother knew that he was on the *Titanic*, although his wife, who lived elsewhere, did know about it. Why did she associate the ship with Trentham Park, when there were other parks in Stoke-on-Trent? Dr. Stevenson wondered whether there might be a lake in this particular park, which Mrs. Hughes had overlooked, one on which children sailed toy boats. He wrote to the Town Clerk of the City of Stoke-on-Trent, who sent him information that showed that the park itself contained lakes and that the adjoining Trentham Gardens contained a mile-long lake with boating facilities; children can sail toy boats in the garden. Dr. Stevenson observed that "a study of the map of the area shows that from the position the dreamer seemed to be in (on the Stone Road at Hanford looking south toward Trentham Park), the large lake in the adjoining Trentham Gardens would be included in the field of vision so that a boat in the lake might well seem to be 'as if in Trentham Park.'"

Another percipient who was a child at the time of the *Titanic* disaster, Mrs. Norah K. Mathews, gave Dr. Stevenson an account of her experience, together with a covering letter dated October 30, 1964. She recalled that she was eleven years old when she heard that her mother, Mrs. Mary Keziah Roberts, was going to sail on the *Titanic*. At one point, when her mother was combing her hair and singing, "Yip-i-addie-i-aye . . . I don't care what becomes of me . . ." the child felt sad and said, "Mama, why do you sing like that? . . . I don't want you to sing that song again; I don't want you to sail on the *Titanic*."

Mrs. Mathews placed her impression as "very close" to the time of the *Titanic's* departure, but could not give the exact time interval. She also said she had felt that "something was going to happen both to my mother and also to the fine new boat she was shortly going to sail on." Dr. Stevenson confirmed that Mrs. Roberts, the mother, was a stewardess on the ship and survived the sinking. Both the mother and father are dead now, and no corroboration by them was possible.

One crew member who refused to sail on the *Titanic* did ascribe his decision to a "hunch." He was Colin Macdonald, whose daughter, Mrs. Isabel Fernsworth, Dr. Stevenson interviewed on October 10, 1964. Mr. Macdonald was thirty-three years old in 1911, a marine engineer with a good deal of experience in Atlantic crossings. When the *Titanic* signed up its crew, he was offered a job as second engineer three times. He declined each time. His position was taken by J. Hesketh, who drowned. As Mrs. Fernsworth recalled it, her father had no specific perception of the boat's fate, but merely a strong impression that something was going to happen to it. Dr. Stevenson quotes her as saying that her father had had "other experiences of nonrational foreknowledge of events affecting himself and his family."

What does all this add up to? We may assume, to begin

with, that these reported incidents—and the emphasis here is on "reported"—make up only a small segment of the presentiments, or actual precognitive experiences, in the dream or waking stage, concerning the *Titanic* disaster. Some people like to talk about their presentiments while others prefer to forget them; few get into print; still fewer can be corroborated.

The *Titanic* cases are a mixed bag, ranging from aparently unconscious impressions to vivid hunches, dreams, and direct precognitions. They are paralleled by a variety of telepathic experiences. Stevenson listed nineteen such recorded experiences in all, related to the *Titanic*, of which ten fell into the precognitive category. Of these, six were experienced several months or longer before the event, four were within ten days or less of the sinking; the rest were telepathic or postcognitive. Stevenson feels that "accurate precognitions occur too rarely (probably) to form a reasonable basis for action in everyday life," and he notes that his case histories include numerous experiences "which the percipients ignored (at least with regard to action) until the events foretold had taken place."

Dr. Stevenson would like to see more research in the "motives which separate those who act upon premonitions from those who do not." He feels that "a cultural climate hostile to psychical experiences may influence percipients not to act on perceptions when a more favorable climate might encourage them to do so." It might be added that, even in acknowledging to themselves that they have had prophetic experience, people are likely to reflect the attitude of their environment. Stevenson notes also, in passing, "the occurrence of the opposite extreme in primitive societies and in some superstitious or mentally ill persons who act upon the vaguest hints or supposed premonitions."

Aside from the nature of the *Titanic* disaster as the most striking event of this character during the century thus far, the "cultural climate" of the period should also be considered. The event occurred at a time when the materialistic optimism of the nineteenth century, of which earlier study of psychic phenomena was an outgrowth, coincided with an upswing in technological achievement; Lindbergh's transatlantic flight was similar in symbolic impact, later on. The *Titanic* event was unique in many ways. Nothing quite like it had ever happened. Nothing like it will ever happen again. As a target for prophecy, too, it stands alone.

3 Can Time Flow Upstream?

One of the oddest phenomena known to biologists is the salmon that swims upstream, scaling rock-studded falls if need be, to make its way to the spawning grounds. Can time, similarly, flow upstream?

Following World War I, as scientific thinking began to force stricter codes of observation and recording on prophetic experiences, efforts were made to study them under controlled conditions. The time-space continuum presents several problems to physicists and philosophers alike; a pioneer researcher in this area was an utterly unphilosophical aircraft pioneer, the man who built the first British army airplane in 1907. His name, J. W. Dunne, is that of a Fellow of the Royal Aeronautical Society, a soldier in the Boer War, an adventurous engineer who had no truck with extraordinary matters—until they caught up with him.

Dunne was egocentric, given to grandiose ideas about himself, and possessed by a somewhat messianic streak. But he is impossible to ignore. His book, *An Experiment in Time*, first published in London in 1927, is still going strong. The British writer J. B. Priestley has called it "one of the most fascinating, the most curious, and perhaps the most important books of this age."

Oh yes, Dunne has since been "demolished" by some. The records of his own premonitory dreams have been weighed by psychical researchers and found badly wanting; his mélange of physical and philosophical ideas, his novel concept of "serial time," have been flayed to bits on the distinguished pages of the *Journal* of the British Aristotelian Society. Nevertheless, when a famous aeronautical engineer makes a splash in a way-out field, the waves do not die down for decades to come.

Like many writer-researchers who have a deep emotional concern for psychical phenomena, Dunne approached the subject of his own prophetic dreams with exquisite academic caution. He told his readers that he was merely presenting them in "the customary form of a narrative of the actual proceedings concerned, coupled with a statement of the theoretical considerations believed to be involved." Actually, Dunne was elated and alarmed by the incidents that, as he put it, "happened, one and all, to myself."

It started one night, when Dunne stayed overnight at a hotel in Sussex and dreamed that he had an argument with a waiter. He claimed that it was half-past four in the afternoon, while the waiter insisted that it was half-past four in the early morning. "With the apparent illogicality peculiar to all dreams," Dunne tells us that, in the dream, "I concluded that my watch must have stopped; and, on extracting that instrument from my waistcoat pocket, I saw, looking down on it, that this was precisely the case. It had stopped—with the hands at half-past four. With that I awoke."

Dunne lit a match and fumbled for his watch. He found it lying on a chest of drawers; "sure enough, it *had* stopped, and the hands stood at half-past four." He rewound the watch, without guessing at the hour, and went back to bed. When he came downstairs the next morning, Dunne went straight to the nearest clock, assuming that his own watch "was likely to be out by several hours." He figured that "it was extremely unlikely that I should have dreamed of half-past four at precisely half-past four." He was amazed, thereafter, when he found that the hands of his watch had lost only some two or three minutes, or "about the amount of time which had elapsed between my waking from the dream and rewinding the watch." This suggested to him that the watch had stopped at the actual moment of the dream. Dunne admitted he would normally have thought that he had dreamed the whole puzzling episode, including his getting up and winding the clock, but he knew differently. It was a weird story, but worth no more than mention to a friend over a tankard of ale at a congenial pub.

Next, Dunne was visiting in Sorrento, on an Italian trip. He woke up one morning wondering what time it was, but feeling too lackadaisical to struggle with the mosquito net and make his way over to his watch. He closed his eyes, went into a "semi-doze," and promptly envisioned the watch in a thick, whitish mist, the hour hand exactly at eight o'clock and the minute hand wavering between the twelve and the one. Dunne decided that it was two and a half minutes past eight. He woke up and took the watch out from under the mosquito curtain; the hands stood at two and a half minutes past eight.

"I was driven to the conclusion," Dunne wrote, "that I possessed some funny faculty of *seeing*—seeing through obstacles, across space, and round corners." But, he added, "I was wrong." It was more than that: he could, it soon appeared, look ahead in time.

Even if one were to assume that J. W. Dunne was given to self-deception, his dreams cannot be easily dismissed. In one, Dunne found himself on the sun-drenched Italian Riviera at Alassio, in January 1901. He was recovering from wounds contracted during the Boer War, and this is how he describes his experience:

"I dreamed, one night, that I was at a place which I took to be Fashoda, a little way up the Nile from Khartoum (Sudan). The dream was a perfectly ordinary one, and by no means vivid, except in one particular. This was the sudden appearance of three men coming from the South. They were marvellously ragged, dressed in khaki faded to the colour of sackcloth; and their faces under their dusty sun-helmets were burned almost black. They looked, in fact, exactly like soldiers of the column with which I had lately been [trekking] in South Africa, and such I took them to be.

"I was puzzled as to why they should have travelled all the way from that country to the Sudan, and I questioned them on that point. They assured me, however, that this was precisely what they had done. 'We have come right through from the Cape,' said one. Another added: 'I've had an awful time. I nearly died of yellow fever.'"

Dunne, keeping in touch with events in the world at large, received the *Daily Telegraph* from London even on the Riviera. The morning after the dream, he opened the paper at breakfast and ran smack into a prominently headlined news item, under a Khartoum dateline, reporting that the paper's own "expedition has arrived at Khartoum after a magnificent journey." The *Daily Telegraph* expedition, headed by Lionel Decle, had made a gruelling overland trip from the Cape; one of the three men in the expedition had died, not of yellow fever, but of enteric. The expedition had arrived in Khartoum long before the paper reached Alassio from London. So far, not much: maybe clairvoyance from the pages of the paper as it arrived at Dunne's hotel; maybe he'd overheard word the day before and forgotten it consciously.

Next, we find the peripatetic Dunne, in the spring of 1902, encamped with the Sixth mounted Infantry, near the runs of Lindley, in what was then the (South African) Orange Free

PROPHECY IN OUR TIME

State. There had been only intermittent mail and newspapers. One night, Dunne had "an unusually vivid and rather unpleasant dream." He found himself standing on hilly ground, made up of white rock that showed little cracks from which "jets of vapour were spouting upward." It was an island of which Dunne had dreamed before, but now "in imminent peril from a volcano."

When, in this dream, Dunne saw the vapor rising, he gasped: "It's the island! Good Lord, the whole thing is going to blow up!" He wanted to save the four thousand inhabitants who, he thought, lived on this island; they must be taken off in ships. Dunne describes as "a most distressing nightmare" his efforts to mobilize the skeptical authorities of a neighboring French-administered island to "despatch vessels of every and any description to remove the inhabitants of the threatened island." He found himself entreating a certain "Monsieur le Maire," shouting, up to the moment of waking, "Listen! Four thousand people will be killed unless—"

When the next batch of newspapers came, there was the *Daily Telegraph*, with a dispatch on its center sheet, which read:

VOLCANO DISASTER IN MARTINIQUE

Town Swept Away

An Avalanche of Flame

Probable Loss of Over 40,000 Lives

British Steamer Burns

The dispatch stated: "One of the most terrible disasters in the annals of the world has befallen the once prosperous town of St. Pierre, the commercial capital of the French island of Martinique in the West Indies. At eight o'clock on Thursday morning, the volcano Mont Pelée which had been quiescent for a century. . . ." and there followed further details of the disaster.

Dunne admits: "The number of people supposed to be killed was not, as I had maintained throughout the dream, 4,000, but 40,000. I was out by a nought. But, when I read the paper, I read, in my haste, that number as 4,000; and, in telling the story subsequently, I always spoke of that printed figure as having been 4,000; and I did not know it was really 40,000 until I copied out the paragraph fifteen years later." Being no fool, shrewdly, Dunne suspected himself of having had no dream at all, that "on reading the newspaper report, a false idea had sprung into my mind to the effect that I had previously dreamed a dream containing all the details given in that paragraph," and that the vision of the trek from the Cape to Cairo "might very well have been of the same character." But there was also the business of the watches to account for. In any event, he felt that if anything psychic was involved, he hadn't received the impulses by "astral wanderings" or telepathic messages "from the actors in the actual episodes," but that his dreams had been induced "either by the reading of the paragraphs" in some unknown way, "or else by telepathic communications from the journalist in the *Daily Telegraph* office who had written those accounts."

The next dream eliminated the possibility that Dunne had, retrospectively, made up his dreams after reading the newspaper dispatches. In this one, he found himself standing on a wooden platform, facing a deep gulf filled with heavy fog. Some sort of awning arched overhead. Just beyond, slowly visible in the fog, splayed the jet of a fire engine's hose, "playing a stream of water upon the smoke-hidden, railed structure where I stood." Then, he recalls, "the dream became perfectly abominable." Wooden planks were crowded with people, dimly visible through the smoke: "They were dropping in heaps; and all the air was filled with horrible, choking, gasping ejaculations. Then the smoke, which had grown black and thick, rolled heavily over everything, hiding the entire scene. But a dreadful, suffocated moaning continued—and I was entirely thankful when I awoke."

This time, Dunne was taking no chances. He carefully recalled every detail of the dream after waking—although he does not say that he wrote it down—and did not open the morning papers until he had revisualized the dream in his mind. But there was no news in that morning's newspapers which corresponded to his dream of fire, suffocation, and mass death.

The news was in the evening paper. The fire had taken place in a rubber factory, or a similar plant, near Paris. A number of working girls, cut off by the flames, had made their way onto a balcony. However, the fire ladders were too short to reach them. While the firemen went to get longer ladders, they directed streams of water onto the balcony to keep it from catching fire. But through broken windows behind the balcony, Dunne wrote, "the smoke of burning rubber or other material came rolling out in such dense volumes that, although the unfortunate girls were standing in the open air, every one of them was suffocated before the new ladders could arrive."

This series of dreams had rendered Dunne a greatly puzzled and frightened man. What was all this? Was he going mad? But then came a dream which, as he put it, somewhat simplified matters in that "it ruled out definitely: insanity, clairvoyance, astral-wandering, spirit-messages, and telepathy." But, he says, "it left me face to face with something much more staggering than any of these."

What he was left with, of course, was precognition.

It came with a dream in 1904. Dunne was staying at the Hotel Scholastika, a lakeside hotel in Aachensee, Austria. He dreamed he was walking down a narrow road between two fields with high iron fences on each side. Suddenly, in the field to his left, a horse acted as if it had "gone mad, was tearing about, kicking and plunging in a most frenzied fashion." Dunne was worried and looked over his shoulder to make sure there was no gap in the railings, and that he was safe from the rampaging animal. Everything looked quite safe.

"A few moments later," Dunne writes, "I heard hoofs thundering behind me. Glancing back, I saw, to my dismay, that the brute had somehow got out after all, and was coming full-tilt after me down the pathway. It was a full-fledged nightmare; and I ran like a hare. Ahead of me the path ended at the foot of a flight of wooden steps rising upward. I was striving frantically to reach these when I awoke."

The very next day, Dunne went fishing with his brother on the Aachen Lake. As he was "flogging the water," the brother drew his attention to an odd scene on the shore. It was the scene in Dunne's dream, but, he says, "though right in essentials, it was absolutely unlike in minor details." The two fields with the fenced-off pathway running between them were there; so was the horse, and it was acting crazily. There were wooden steps at the end of the pathway, leading up to a bridge.

The fences dividing the path from the fields were low, made of wood. And while, in the dream, the fields had been wide and parklike, these were ordinary small fields. The horse, too, was no rampaging monster, but rather small, "though its behaviour was equally alarming." Finally, Dunne observed, the horse was "in the wrong field, the field which would have been on my right, had I been walking, as in the dream, down the path toward the bridge."

Dunne began to tell his brother about the dream, but stopped to see whether the railings were secure enough to contain even this rather small horse. He could see no gap, and told his brother, "At any rate, this horse cannot get out," and they went on fishing. Well, the horse did get out, after all, came "thundering down the path toward the wooden steps," but plunged into the water and started to swim toward their side of the river. They picked up stones and started to run away from the bank. "On emerging from the water on our side," Dunne finishes, "the animal merely looked at us, snorted, and galloped off down a road."

Dunne had, by then, been thinking about the nature of his dreams for several years. His conclusions were much along along the lines expressed today by psychoanalysts who have been examining the premonitory dreams of their patients, notably Dr. Jan Ehrenwald; see page 129. His dreams, Dunne concluded, were not views of "distant or future events" but "the usual commonplace dreams composed of distorted images of waking experience built together in the usual half-senseless fashion peculiar to dreams." If they had only happened on nights after the corresponding events. Dunne observed, "they would have exhibited nothing in the smallest degree unusual, and would have yielded just as much true, and just as much false, information regarding the waking experiences which had given rise to them as does any ordinary dream—which is very little." Dunne set down his conclusion coolly: "No, there was nothing unusual in any of these dreams as dreams. They were merely *displaced in Time*." He was up against "a simple, if mysterious, transposition of dreams."

One other dream from Dunne's collection at that time merits attention. He observed, asleep, in the autumn of 1913, a scene at a high railway embankment, obviously just north of the Firth of Forth Bridge in Scotland. People were walking on the open grassland below the embankment. Finally, the dream showed that a train had fallen over the embankment; several railroad carriages were lying near the bottom of the slope. Somehow, and now on the lookout for prophetic elements in his dreams, Dunne tried to "see" the time of its occurrence; it was vague, perhaps in March or April of the following spring. He told his sister about it the next morning. He adds:

"On April the 14th of that spring, the 'Flying Scotsman,'

one of the most famous mail trains of the period, jumped the parapet near Burntisland Station, about fifteen miles north of the Forth Bridge, and fell on to the golf links twenty feet below."

To an engineer and scientist of Mr. Dunne's imaginative interests, the mere recording of premonitory dreams was not enough. First, he wanted to make them the subject of an experiment; next, he wanted to explain the conditions that made them possible. The task was formidable, but he began it in modest ways. Dunne urged his friends to keep an immediate record of their dreams, and to review them later for precognitive or other unusual elements.

This was more easily said than done. He found that his friends, and even he himself, were quick to miss clues and otherwise to deviate from the experimental procedure as well. He started with the hypothesis that contrary to the views he ascribed to psychical researchers of his generation (whom he called the "supernaturalists"), prophetic dreams were a normal occurrence—people just forgot them or failed to associate them with subsequent events. He warned against taking one's own alertness for granted. Soon, he found, in studying a dream record for precognitive elements, "one is apt to read straight on through the very thing one is looking for, without even noticing its connection with the waking incident."

Dunne caught himself being entirely too casual toward his own experiment. One afternoon he had been hunting in rough country, and had inadvertently trespassed on private land. Two men shouted at him from different directions, and they were "urging on a furiously barking dog." Highly embarrassed, Dunne ambled toward the nearest gate, "trying to look as if unaware of anything unusual." As the shouting and barking came nearer, he hurried "through the gate before the pursuers came into view." He called it "a most unpleasant episode for a sensitive individual, and one quite likely to make him dream thereof." Of course, the normal way would have been to dream about the chase after the event, perhaps the following night.

That evening, Dunne read over the dream records he had made early the same morning. At first he noticed nothing, but then his eye caught a faintly written sentence that read, "Hunted by two men and a dog." He had completely forgotten the dream which prompted him to make this brief notation; he did not even recall having written it down. This only reinforced his conviction that people generally dream prophetically but forget their dreams or lose track of them in one way or another.

More determined than ever to pursue his experiments, Dunne continued to test himself and to coax his friends into the tests. One night he dreamed of exploring a large, mysterious, and secret loft, eventually escaping the house in which he was by way of the loft. During the following day, he had no such experience—a rather boyish bit of nonsense, anyway—but found himself reading a novel in which one of the characters hid in a loft in the roof of an old house. Later in the story, the character had to escape the house, through the loft and a chimney. (Certainly this could have been a clairvoyant reading of the book he was about to read later on "in real life," but these distinctions must be permitted to blur.)

Next, Dunne taught his precognitive dream-hunting methods to a young woman he identifies as "Miss B." After several unsuccessful efforts, she recorded on the sixth day of the experiment that she dreamed of finding herself at one end of a path before a gate of five or six bars. Just at that moment, a man passed on the other side of the gate, herding three brown cows before him; he was holding a stick over the cows rather oddly, like a fishing rod. The whole business, fishing-rodlike stick and all, was experienced later in the day at a major London railway station.

On another occasion, one of Dunne's cousins dreamed of meeting a mysterious German woman (it was during the last period of World War One) at a hotel, who wore a black skirt and a black-and-white striped blouse, her hair in a bun atop her head. Two days later, and after submitting the record of her dream to Dunne, the cousin ran into just such a "spy"-like person, bun and all.

There were many such experiments, all quite intriguing. Several involved people who had experiences that seemed to blend into dreams they had had several days earlier, or that contained striking individual prophetic elements scattered in unrelated material. Dunne, however, wanted to get on with the business of developing a hypothesis for all these goings-on. At one point, he set down his partial observations as follows:

"The images which relate to events a long way behind can be recognized and counted; but those which relate to events similar distances ahead cannot be identified [which makes statistical breakdowns just about impossible]. Hence, the only way to strike a balance is to confine the statistics to the

PROPHECY IN OUR TIME

range of a few days either way. Images which relate equally well to either past or future—such as those of friends, and of everyday scenes—should not be counted. Images which are apparently of the past should be submitted to the same severe scrutiny as are those which are apparently of the future, for coincidence will operate just as effectively in either direction."

Computing in this fashion, Dunne found that "the images which relate indisputably to the nearby future are about equal in number to those which pertain *similarly indisputably* to the nearby past." Dunne realized soon enough that busy people can't be expected to spend about forty minutes before each breakfast noting down dreams—they may do it for a few days, but shortly they find the whole thing too tedious. By 1932, he had devised a simple type of statistical experiment, in order to fix "the proportion of effects suggesting *precognition* to similar effects suggesting *retrospection*."

I won't try to summarize Dunne's concept of "serial time" with any degree of completeness. The reader, if he has the curiosity and the stamina, should read Dunne's book himself. He wrote well, and with a certain amount of passion. His ideas are of interest today, when theoretical physics finds itself in search of new ways of dealing with the space-time continuum, and when philosophers talk like physicists, physicists invade the *sancta sanctorum* of philosophers, and psychoanalysts of the prominence of Dr. Jan Ehrenwald borrow concepts off the shelf of atomic physics to develop such principles as "telepathic leakage."

Dr. Ehrenwald's "doctrinal compliance" concept can be applied to Dunne. It so happens that the Dunne experiments worked well with Dunne himself, and with his relatives and friends; they were, in the Ehrenwald sense, complying with "doctrinal" concepts. Efforts to repeat these tests elsewhere were for the most part unsuccessful. However, the experimenter's involvement and enthusiasm can certainly help an experiment along—in an entirely unfraudulent way, of course—while a skeptical experimenter comes up with dry-as-dust results. When the Medical Section of the American Society for Psychical Research brought together a group of congenial psychoanalysts a few years ago, telepathic or precognitive elements began to appear in their analytic sessions with delightful frequency. When the little band of parapsychological frontiersmen disbanded, the phenomena began to peter out.

We are all magnets for the objects, events, and people that interest us at any given time. Dunne was fascinated by prophetic dreams, so prophetic dreams began to inundate him.

But now to his theories. Why did he speak of "serial" time? Because, as he defined it, a series is "a collection of individually distinguishable items arranged, or considered as arranged, in a sequence determined by some sort of ascertainable law." Dunne abandons the idea of "unidimensional Time." He wants to get away from the limited view of the "observer" of Time, you and me, because we experience all events in a manner whereby they apparently "follow one another in a definite sequence"—"successive experience is the observer's true Time dimension." We see the past, present, and future; we are three-dimensional, but the universe is not made in our image. Dunne goes on, ingeniously, and not always clearly, with the kind of diagrams that engineers are prone to produce and with calculations that they tend to scribble, all too rapidly, on blackboards. He comes up with a neat, if not easily digestible phrase: "We shall have a single multidimensional field of presentation in absolute motion, travelling over a fixed substratum of objective elements extended in all the dimensions of Time." He wants us to step out of our own psychological, all-too-human selves and let a wider objective take over. Our habits, he says with a touch of pedantry, are, after all, not a "law." Alas, they are all we have, poor things that we are! Yet, he is a strict taskmaster and demands that we understand that events exist and that we move up and to them—and it is this that we call the "flow of time." Dunne has been criticized for his theories, notably by Professor C. D. Broad in his paper "The Philosophical Implications of Foreknowledge," presented to the Aristotelian Society in London on July 11, 1937. But the fumbling, hopeful effort for a better understanding of time continues, in physics most of all, and in philosophy as much as ever.

Dunne maintains that he could have developed his theory without the prophetic dreams that he and his friends experienced; that he might have brought them in as mere afterthoughts. I don't believe him. I think he was struck by the weirdness of his experiences, and that he had others of a hallucinatory-religious nature which prompted him to devise a theoretical superstructure to accommodate them. Whatever his motivation, his work stands as a daring pioneer study in the anecdotal and speculative aspects of prophecy in our time.

4 Cayce: The Seer of Virginia Beach

The name of Edgar Cayce has taken on a magical ring. In the two decades since his death, something very much like a Cayce cult has developed in the United States, and it is reaching abroad as far as Japan. This was a modest man, in many ways an unworldly man; a good man, possessing unusual insight when he had fallen into a trance-like state which, in itself, was difficult to define. Among his varied gifts, while in his "sleeping" state, Cayce sometimes spoke as a prophet, a seer. He placed himself into a state closely resembling autohypnotic trance, spoke clearly but in a somewhat mystical manner, and had no memory of his statements when he "awoke." His major contribution, though, was as a remarkable healer of singular reputation.

Prophecy, to Edgar Cayce, was incidental. It played a distinctively minor role in his remarkable life, an elusive one, at that. Yet, any work dealing with prophecy in our time must take Cayce's prognoses into account, and try to view them against the background of his total work and personality. This man, whom devotees have at times labeled "the seer of Virginia Beach," has been singularly blessed with the attention of able biographer-analysts, including Thomas Sugrue, who wrote *There Is a River* (New York, 1943), Gina Cerminara, whose several books dealing with Cayce include *Many Mansions* (New York, 1953), Hugh Lynn Cayce's *Venture Inward* (New York, 1964), and, most recently, Jess Stearn, author of *Edgar Cayce: The Sleeping Prophet* (Garden City, N.Y., 1966). His life's work has been carefully recorded and classified at the headquarters of the Association for Research and Enlightenment, and of the Edgar Cayce Foundation, at Virginia Beach, Virginia.

In the many years this writer devoted to parapsychology, there had seemingly never been time for a visit to Virginia Beach until the hot summer of 1966. As luck would have it, the visit coincided with a week-long meeting on "Time and Prophecy," one of several symposia making up an eight-week program. The Association for Research and Enlightenment headquarters, although just north of the hectic seaside atmosphere of downtown Virginia Beach, might easily be viewed as a shrine to the memory and work of Cayce. Certainly, he now has hundreds, and perhaps thousands, who can only be called devotees to his memory. Yet the white wooden rambling building that houses the Cayce records and library is unpretentious; there is an atmosphere of neighborliness, a relaxed air of American friendliness, in the best sense of these words, which makes nonsense of any cultist ideas.

If prophecy was, so to speak, a sideline with Edgar Cayce, what was his main work? It has been amply and well described in the books cited above, and in others as well. The unschooled Cayce, in his trancelike state, appeared able to diagnose illness even when the patients were not present and were unknown to him, and to suggest methods of alleviating or curing their conditions. The variety of subjects on which Cayce touched was wide, perhaps too wide for easy acceptance. It included reincarnation and references to the allegedly sunken continent Atlantis and to religio-philosophical concepts that included elements from all major faiths.

The Cayce Foundation has done an excellent job of classifying the 14,246 psychic readings that Edgar Cayce gave between 1901 and 1945, and they are available to any serious researcher. Of these readings, 8,976 referred to physical problems, 2,500 were in the category of so-called life readings (which might include references to past "incarnations" or patterns of future existence), 799 referred to business matters, 667 to dream interpretations, 401 had mental and spiritual implications, 24 focused on home and marriage conditions, and 879 fell into the miscellaneous category. There are sub-categories for "prophecy" and "precognition."

The careful organization of this material and the general administration of the Foundation and Association are in the hands of the "seer's" son, the white-haired, modest Hugh Lynn Cayce. Frankly, of all the prophecies I encountered at Virginia Beach, it was not one of Cayce Senior's that charmed me most, but one that marked a turning point in the life of his son, Hugh Lynn. So, let us start with that one.

Hugh Lynn Cayce recalled this dream as we were sitting in his compact, sun-filled office; he looked rather boyish in his open-necked shirt. He had, at his father's suggestion, been keeping a record of his dreams. This became a routine and eventually somewhat dreary task, calling for marking down dream details each morning, immediately on awakening. Each page was dated, signed, and witnessed by the signature of a second person—a prescribed procedure for anyone wishing to note dreams that may turn out to have been precognitive or telepathic.

During the two years when Hugh Lynn kept this record, he had one dream that pictured him taking a young woman to a building known as the Old Masury House. Although at the time of the dream the house was empty and closed up, young Cayce dreamed that it had been transformed into a restaurant and night club with subdued background music. The young woman in the dream had a blank face; he did not know her identity. Everything else was as clear as a picture on a color television screen: there were candles on the table, because a blown fuse had temporarily disconnected the electric current; a waiter came to take their order at the candle-lit table, dressed in a white jacket with brass buttons. A few moments later, Hugh Lynn Cayce turned toward the door and saw his family's good friend, Morton Blumenthal—the man who helped build what was at one time the Virginia Beach Hospital and is now the headquarters of the Cayce Foundation—entering the place.

Sometime after the dream, but in the same year, the Old Masury House was actually made into a night club. And one night, Hugh Lynn did take a woman companion there for dinner. As it happened, having recorded hundreds of dreams in the interim, he had just about forgotten the one about the Masury House. When they approached the porch of the restaurant, the headwaiter apologized for the darkness and the use of candles: a fuse had blown, but everything would soon be all right.

As they sat down at the table and a waiter in a white jacket with brass buttons came up to take their order, Hugh Lynn began to tell the young lady rapidly about his dream, and about what would come next. The setting, the music; everything fit. "Now," he said, "if I turn around and see Blumenthal coming in through the door I think I'll get up and run. It would be just too spooky!" He turned around, and there was Blumenthal, making his way into the darkened room. The young woman's name at that time was Miss Sally Taylor. Shortly thereafter, it became Mrs. Hugh Lynn Cayce.

When they went back to the dream diary of less than a year earlier, there, duly dated and countersigned, was the record of the original dream—blown fuse, brass buttons, and all.

Otherwise, Hugh Lynn Cayce has inherited none of his father's gifts. As a matter of fact, being the son of a man who at varying times had been admired, reviled, hounded, deified, denounced, and always embattled, Hugh Lynn went through all the usual stages of a young, maturing man living in the shadow of fatherly eminence or notoriety.

His dream, too, was very different from the type of prophecy that seeped out of Edgar Cayce's readings. While the dream of the Old Masury House was romantic and had a happy ending, Cayce's prophecies tended to deal with long-range geological changes of continental magnitude and disastrous implications.

An admission of personal prejudice is necessary at this point. In the years of working as an administrator and editor in parapsychology, I waded through millions of words of evasive language, pseudomystical circumlocutions, and just plain long-winded claptrap. Belonging to the school that thinks highly of the declarative sentence, I found that Edgar Cayce's writings at first made my hackles rise. Get this:

"Yes, we have the work here and that phase concerning the indwelling in the earth's plane of those who first gave laws concerning indwelling of Higher Forces in man. In giving such in an understandable manner to man of today, necessary that the conditions of the earth's surface and the position of man in the earth's plane be understood, for the chance has come often since this period, era, age of man's earthly indwelling; for then at that period, only the lands now known as the Sahara and the Nile region appeared on the now African shores; that in Tibet, Mongolia, Caucasie and Norway in Asia and Europea, that in the southern cordilleras and Peru in the southwestern hemisphere and the plane of new Utah, Arizona, Mexico of the northwestern hemisphere. . . ."

That is an excerpt from one of the first readings concerned with evolution on earth, spoken in Cayce's trancelike sleep on May 28, 1925. Writers dealing with Cayce's readings, and his prophecies in particular, have virtually had to decode or translate his special language. Jess Stearn had done so very ably, while searching diligently for events that might be those to which Cayce's neo-Aesopian language could have referred.

Two pamphlets published by the Association for Research and Enlightenment refer to Cayce's prophecies. The first, "Earth Changes: Past, Present, Future" (Virginia Beach, Va., 1949), written by an anonymous geologist, deals with his remarks concerning the development of our planet. The second, "Times of Crisis" (Virginia Beach, Va., 1947), is devoted to world affairs; here, the material is uneven, tantalizing, elusive, and badly in need of annotation and the supplementation by data that would show how it stacks up against objective developments.

Cayce's geological forecasts for the period from 1958 to 1998 read as follows:

"As to the changes physical again: The earth will be broken up in the western portion of America.

"The greater portion of Japan must go into the sea.

"The upper portion of Europe will be changed as in the twinkling of an eye.

"Land will appear off the east coast of America.

"There will be upheavals in the Arctic and in the Antarctic that will make for the eruption of volcanoes in the torrid areas, and there will be the shifting then of the poles—so that where there have been those of a frigid or semitropical will become the more tropical, and moss and fern will grow.

"And these will begin in those periods in '58 to '98, when these will be proclaimed as the periods when His Light will be seen again in the clouds."

These are quotations from Cayce readings made on January 19, 1934. The geologist-author of the pamphlet compares Cayce's observations with statements by a Japanese authority, N. Miyabe, who reported to a scientific congress in New Zealand in 1953 ("Vertical earth movements in Japan deduced from the results of relevelings") that displacements "along the tectonic median line of southwest Japan" had taken place, while two other authorities, K. K. Iida and T. Wada, in 1955 had calculated that "subsidence in the Ise Bay region, Honshu, on the east coast of south-central Japan, is progressing at the rate of from two to six centimeters annually."

While the author notes that such developments "might well be expected in such a geologically instable region as Japan," he also cites a report by Dr. I. Ishii in a Tokyo geographical journal concerning geological shifts along the coast of Toyama Bay, "which caused the submergence of a forest, due to movements of a block of the crust."

Finding evidence supporting Cayce's observations concerning Northern Europe, the author cites C. R. Longwell as having stated in *A Text Book of Geology* (New York, 1939) that "in the countries bordering the Baltic Sea an uplift has been under observation for a long period," so that "raised beaches and other shoreline features" indicate that "parts of Sweden and Finland are at least 900 feet higher than they were at the close of the Ice Age."

The geologist-author adds these comments:

"It is in the advocation of the very rapid acceleration of this that the psychic information [provided by Cayce] departs from the standard geological concept of gradual change. It is also perhaps possible that if land appears off the east coast of America, the upper portion of Europe could be changed in the twinkling of an eye by the sudden blockage or diversion of the Gulf Stream that brings warmth to upper Europe."

On August 13, 1941, Cayce made probably his most dramatic forecast, referring to the period from 1941 to 1998. He foresaw gradual changes in world geography, including disturbances on the east and west coasts of the United States, as well as in the "central portion." Specifically, he said, "in the next few years, lands will appear in the Atlantic as well as in the Pacific," while present coastlines "of many a land will be the bed of the ocean."

Cayce was detailed on the following points:

"Portions of the new east coast of New York, or New York City itself, will in the main disappear. This will be another generation, though, here; while the southern portions of Carolina, Georgia, these will disappear. This will be much sooner."

He added that the Great Lakes "will empty into the gulf," which was regarded as referring to the Gulf of Mexico. Cayce, apparently referring to the St. Lawrence Seaway, said that "it would be well if the waterway were prepared, but not for that purpose for which it is at present being considered."

During the same session, Cayce described the Virginia Beach area itself as "among the safety lands," together with "portions of what is now Ohio, Indiana, and Illinois and much of the southern portions of Canada, and the eastern portion of Canada," while a sizable portion of "western land" would be among the area that "is to be disturbed."

The Cayce-oriented geologist-author, who published his analysis of the seer's prognosis originally as a scholarly paper entitled "A Psychic Interpretation of Some Late-Cenozoic Events Compared with Selected Scientific Data," cited seismological findings by Dr. C. F. Richter with regard to the earthquake possibilities in the New York area; these were in the "average" category; only a shock affecting Long Island in 1884 confirmed "the presence of a local source of earthquakes" capable of producing a disturbance.

As far as the sweeping forecast of the Great Lakes emptying into the Gulf of Mexico is concerned—provided this forecast had really been correctly "decoded" from Cayce's elusively worded reference to "lakes" and "the gulf"—the geologist-author notes that here, once again, Cayce's prophecy would mean that "a general geological trend" would take place at a greatly accelerated "rate of geographic change."

E. Tillotson, in the British scientific journal *Nature* (1960), published his "Notes on the Agadir Disaster" which cited that "evidence of a tremendous submarine upheaval off the coast [thus, in the Pacific Ocean] was obtained by preliminary naval soundings." Richter suggests in his work that "an excellent example of tilting on a large scale is afforded by the Great Lakes." He was, of course, referring to past events which created these lakes, where "to the northeast the land has risen since the disappearance of the great ice sheet, and as a result the lake bases have been tilted southward." He noted: "The tilting movement is still in progress and has been accurately determined; it is at a rate of five inches per hundred miles per century. Small as this rate seems, in 1,600 years it would cause the upper Great Lakes to discharge by way of the Chicago River into the Mississippi drainage." The Mississippi, of course, empties into the Gulf of Mexico at New Orleans.

As for the "safety zones," of which the Cayce forecast speaks—including Virginia Beach itself, sections of Ohio, Indiana, Illinois, and much of southern and eastern Canada—these are sections of low seismic and quake activities.

So much for the geological forecasts which may have significance for present and future generations. In a century that has experienced the San Francisco earthquake, and which is used to frequent reports of quakes in Turkey, Japan, and Chile, the Cayce prophecies carry a sense of immediacy. This feeling is strengthened by the public's uneasy feeling that nuclear explosions, whether in U.S. deserts, Soviet Central Asia, Western China, or near South Pacific atolls, may well play havoc with the earth's crust—and possibly speed up geological changes all around us.

An area of prophecy that is of more short-range concern and more directly in man's own hands is the political-economic one. At this point, my predilection for the simple declarative sentence is reinforced by a lifetime of research, writing, and lecturing on political and economic affairs. Consequently, I cannot help but regard Cayce's "psychic discourses on national and world affairs" with a high degree of curiosity, eagerness, and some disappointment. There is, to begin with, this question of style.

Gina Cerminara, who has done much to popularize Cayce's ideas, particularly on reincarnation, has written with candor and wit on "The Language of the Cayce Readings" (The Association for Research and Enlightenment *Journal*, April 1966). Why, she asks, did he have to engage in "psychic double talk?" Why, instead of saying "this is a spade," did he have to pussyfoot around, something like this: "This is as we find has to do with not the consciousness in spirituality (as commonly conceived) but rather the consciousness of materiality, as condensed in what is known as, or called, in the present, an implement of spading, or a spade."

Dr. Cerminara, Mr. Stearn, and others, at times, fill the role of those priestly aides-de-camp who translated the utterings of Delphic Oracles into everyday Greek. Cerminara, kind and patient, thinks that Cayce sounded awkward because "he was speaking from a point of view infinitely vaster and more intricate than the point of view of earth-plane man," rather like "an individual educated far above the level of the person to whom he is talking." She urges the reader to use all his "faculties of discrimination and judgment with regard to the Cayce Readings," but not to "permit the clumsiness of language to deflect you from the genuine worth of their contents."

With this in mind, the various "discourses" on domestic and international affairs, sixteen delivered between 1932 and 1944, may be more generously evaluated. The Association for Research and Enlightenment pamphlet "Times of Crisis" states that Cayce's readings have "a direct bearing on the present and future, as well as the recent past." With Dr. Cerminara's cautionary remarks still ringing in one's ears, one begins to read, reread, and re-reread this curious mélange of preachings, allusions, evasions, circumlocutions, and forecasts.

On January 15, 1932, Cayce was asked this question: "What can be expected in the trend of events, as to political and economic conditions in Europe?"

He answered: "Europe is like a house broken up. Some years ago, a mighty people was overridden for the gratification and satisfaction of a few, irrespective of any other man's rights. These same people are going through the experience of being born again; and this is a political and financial thorn in the flesh for many nations in Europe and the world. But this rebirth will come to pass by the prayers

PROPHECY IN OUR TIME

and supplications of those who may pray—even as Abram or Abraham—'If there be fifty, will it not be spared? . . . or if there be ten faithful, will not these peoples be spared?' The hope of Europe, then, depends upon you! You, in your own home today! Not with the same experience as Lot's, but in the same manner as his and the other people in Sodom and Gomorrah."

The pamphlet notes that "a question and answer followed, indicating that Russia was the nation mentioned above."

Chapters Eighteen and Nineteen of Genesis contain Abraham's plea to the Lord, asking that Sodom and Gomorrah be spared, if he could find fifty, or even many fewer, good men. Eventually, Lot and his two daughters (the wife turned into the well-known pillar of salt) made their way to Zoar. What, keeping the state of the Soviet Union in 1932 firmly in mind, and Genesis as well, was the deeper meaning, if any, of this prophecy? That those to whom he made his prediction might, by acting righteously, soften the heart of Joseph Stalin, who held the fate of all Russia in the palm of his hand, and who was preparing the Great Purge of the 1930's? Or was this just one of Cayce's off days? It is, surely, as much a religious exhortation as a specific prophecy.

On February 8, 1932, Cayce was asked, "What should be the attitude of so-called capitalist nations toward Russia?"

He answered: "The greater hope of the world will come through Russia's religious development. The one nation or group which is closest in relationship with Russia may fare best during the gradual changes and the final settlement of conditions, as to the rule of the world."

Looking back at this time, "Russia's religious development" has not been notable, although a good many other startling events have taken place in the Soviet Union. As for the "one nation or group which is closest"—that, to this day, would be anybody's guess.

On October 7, 1935, two and a half years after the Nazi takeover in Germany, and on the eve of the Spanish Civil War, Cayce did foresee the Berlin-Tokyo alliance. He speaks of a "taking of sides" by various "groups, countries or governments," as "manifested by the Austrians and Germans (later on, the Japanese) joining this influence." But in which direction did he expect them to exert their influence? His very next sentence reads: "Thus an unseen force, gradually growing, must result in an almost direct opposition to the Nazi, or Aryan theme. This will gradually produce a growth of animosities." He added:

"And unless there is interference by what many call supernatural forces or influences—which are active in the affairs of nations and peoples—the whole world . . . as it were . . . will be set on fire by militaristic groups and people who are *for* power and expansion." This can, and has been, interpreted as a forecast of the Second World War.

Stearn is generous in his appraisal of Cayce's predictive powers. He writes that "the sleeping prophet" foresaw "wars and peace, depressions, racial strife, labor wars, even the Great Society, which he saw doomed to failure." He notes that "he saw things for individuals, as well as for nations, predicting that they would marry, divorce, have children, become lawyers, doctors, architects, sailors, and marines." According to Stearn, Cayie gained most of his "prophetic impressions" when he was doing his "sleep-readings," but he was spontaneously psychic in his waking state, and fled from a roomful of young people once because he saw instantly that "all would go to war, and three would not come back."

Again, according to Stearn, Cayce's "batting average on predictions was incredibly high, close to one hundred percent," although he may have "missed once or twice" on such matters as Adolf Hitler's motivations or the "eventual democratization of China." According to this enthusiastic appraisal, Cayce "not only foresaw the two World Wars, but picked out the years they would start and end. He not only saw the great world-wide Depression of 1929, outlining the stock-market crash with uncanny detail, but forecast when the Depression would begin to lift in 1933."

Well, whatever may have been Cayce's occasionally accurate general predictions, his answers to some quite specific social questions permitted considerable latitude of interpretation. When, on October 25, 1937, he was asked, "Can a detailed prediction be given about the probable trends of business activity, and trends of security prices during 1938, 1939, and 1940?" his answer closely resembled the appraisals sometimes put forward by cautious Wall Street security analysts. Here it is, in toto:

"Here again, as has been indicated, such trends must indeed depend upon the influence prompting activities of those in power—those in positions to dominate the purposes to be set before the people as a whole. If an ideal is held fast by those in power, then—as has been indicated—a general trend toward greater security will be maintained, as well as better economic consideration of the whole, and greater peace and harmony.

"Not that there don't exist those same influences which have ever sought to transform a beautiful condition into dross. Whenever selfishness is the prompting attitude, turmoils and strife may be expected as results. Where purposes are those of the Prince of Peace . . . I am my brother's keeper . . . I will do the right . . . these purposes will bring, will keep social security, financial security and peace of mind and body for those who propagate His purposes."

Admirable religio-economic sentiments, to be sure; but hardly a clear-cut answer to a specific question on business trends and stock-exchange developments. Other questions and answers, recorded on the same day, ran as follows:

Question: "Is the year 1939 or 1940 likely to usher in the beginning of another major business depression?"

Answer: "Again this depends upon consideration of conditions throughout; and upon the building of those unselfish purposes into provisions of the law now being constructed. We do not find the depression likely, unless selfish motives and purposes succeed in dominating the direction of these provisions (in the law) against such a depression. If selfishness is triumphant; and if the layman, or worker, or wage earner unites all his efforts against capital, then we may expect desperate situations. But what will you do about it?"

Question: "Certain writers have forecast the possibility of a war around 1942 to 1944, which will involve the United States. At the moment, does it appear that we are likely to be involved in such a war?"

Answer: "It will if this is held up as a propaganda! But not if an attitude of peace and harmony is continuously kept —if consideration for the rights of others exists."

Question: "What is likely to cause such a war?"

Answer: "Selfishness!"

On June 20, 1938, Cayce answered a series of questions on world affairs. Nazi Germany had occupied Austria, was putting pressure on Czechoslovakia (the Munich Pact was in the offing) and Poland, while the Spanish Civil War had ended with the victory of General Francisco Franco. France was unprepared, Britain hesitant, the United States uneasy and remote. Japan had occupied Chinese Manchuria and was growing increasingly belligerent. This was the eve of World War Two. Here are the questions and answers:

Question: "About the Japanese and Chinese situations."

Answer: "These speak for themselves, what is happening and has happened. But might does not make right. The principles of the Christian faith will be carried forward through the turmoils that are a part of events in both China and Japan. Without these cleansings and purifyings, tradition alone may not be destroyed. It is through purging that the strength and beauty of each country will come forth."

Question: "About the Spanish situation."

Answer: "This is the point where the real troubles are only beginning. For unless consideration is given to each factor, others will then come in and divide the spoils. This is the growth from seed sown in ages past; and from it man can ... as a whole ... and should take warning."

Question: "About the Russian situation."

Answer: "As we have indicated before, a new understanding has come and will come to a troubled people. Here, because of the yoke of oppression, because of self-indulgences, another extreme has arisen. Only when there is freedom of speech, and right to worship according to the dictates of conscience ... until these come about, turmoils will still be within."

Question: "About the German situation, within its own country, and in its relations with others."

Answer: "So long as there is class distinction and mass discipline, there must be turmoils and strife. But so long as powers are held by those whose purposes and ideals are 'I am my brother's keeper,' and not forcing this [all would be well]. Being my brother's keeper does not mean that I am to tell him what to do, or that he must do this or that, regardless. Rather, it means that all are free before the law and before God."

Question: "About the British situation in its own country and in relation to its colonies."

Answer: "Britain is the balancing power in Europe as well as in the Far East. When its activities are set in such a way as to bring consideration of every phase, Britain will be able to control the world for peace to an ever greater extent. We find that France is the country where an old debt must eventually be paid."

Now what—with all the respect due to a man who has done an immense amount of good to thousands of people whom he lifted up from sickness and despair—is one to make of all this? Even as contemporary political-military analysis, it was way off the beam—not to mention its elusive, though consistent and provocative, tone of religious-philosophic uplift.

Stearn recalls that "Cayce was perhaps the first to visualize the approaching racial strife in the land, sounding his original warning back in the 1920's." Impressive enough, within limitations. On July 16, 1939, Cayce was faced with the following question, "What should be our attitude toward the Negro, and how may we best work out the karma created in relationships with him?" He answered: " He is thy brother!' Those who cause or brought servitude to him, without thought or purpose, have created that which must be met within their own principles, their own selves. These [Negroes] should be held in an attitude of their own individual fitness —as in every other form of association. For He hath made of one blood the nations of the earth."

Another question, on the same date, was: "Is there a racial or social problem facing the United States?" To this Cayce answered: "As indicated, all these problems hinge upon the efforts of individuals to live together as brothers, one with another." It is an answer such as this one which might prompt a cynic to name Edgar Cayce "The Nostradamus of Virginia Beach," a two-edged compliment, though Cayce never touted himself as a prophet in the first place. Stearn states, without quotation, that Cayce gave the date on which World War Two would end. But when he was asked, on May 20, 1942, just about two years before the war ended in Europe, "Based on present conditions, when will the fighting stop?" he replied: "This is dependent on many things. It could be over, it is possible for it to be over, by the 30th of September. But this would require a united effort on the part of those who pray—more than those who shoot! And they are not ready for it yet."

The above quotes have been given in full, rather than by selection, because a man of Edgar Cayce's accomplishments, as Dr. Cerminara has put it, deserves the application of all our "faculties of discrimination and critical judgment." It does him no service to pick agreeable raisins out of the enormous pie of his thousands of readings, just because they are sweet to the taste of those who wish to believe at any price.

Although unique in many ways, Cayce shared the weakness of other sensitives to be put upon, to give in to the demanding questions of the True Believers, to those who wanted to see him as all-knowing. His astonishing health and life readings, though, demand further study and should be brought to the attention of much wider medical and lay circles. The medical profession owes it to its own integrity to initiate—yes, and finance—a completely open-minded research project into the diagnoses and suggested treatments that Cayce put forward in his lifetime. Nothing said in the preceding paragraphs should be used to detract from the effort to expand the study of Cayce's diagnosis-and-treatment insights.

The man's very empathy, his keen ability to feel himself into the physical and emotional existence of people who came to him for help, prevented him from turning down demands for readings that lead beyond the kindly, encouraging, religio-philosophical uplifting to which he was most oriented by experience and personality. If he was, as some of his followers believe, merely the instrument through which higher and more knowledgeable entities sought to communicate, then his own limitations—to which he referred, humbly, time and time again—were perhaps responsible for garbled transmissions.

No one is served, certainly not Cayce's memory, by overstating the case for his prophetic abilities. However, Cayce's healing "readings," which included diagnoses as well as suggested treatments, contained much seemingly precognitive detail concerning the patients' health and—at times—death. In many instances, these forecasts were proved correct by subsequent developments.

5 Hitler's Prophets

Adolf Hitler promised Germany a "Thousand Year Reich" of Nazi rule. He was his own worst prophet. His National Socialist doctrine, of course, was built around a concept of historic destiny, of inevitable events, of reawakened ancient Teutonic forces that were supposedly moving Nazi Germany "relentlessly" toward dominance over all of Europe and a trembling world.

During the months that decided Germany's fate, in late 1932 and early 1933, this theme of historic inevitability was hammered home by a heavy-set, ruthless, self-assured, self-styled clairvoyant who billed himself at Berlin's huge Scala Theater as "Hanussen, Prophet of the Third Reich." He toured the nation, gave fashionable personal consultations on everything from astrology to financial forecasting, and published a swastika-decorated tabloid, *Hanussens Bunte Wochenschau,* which forecasted events with a mixture of boulevard sensationalism and awe-inspiring mysticism.

Erik Jan Hanussen had staked his very survival on the triumph of Nazism. He gave lavish parties and lent vast sums to the Storm Trooper chief for Berlin—Brandenburg, Count Wolf Heinrich Helldorf, and his influential deputy Herbert von Ohst. While German politicians bargained with each other, hoping to buy off the Nazi movement with a temporary illusion of power, Hanussen wrote on November 24, 1932:

"Hitler is the only one whose directions will be decisive for every coming government, whether he will publicly appear himself, or whether it will be one of his deputies. Hitler's will is decisive."

As the day moved closer when the aged and senile President Paul von Hindenburg would appoint Hitler to the post of Chancellor, thus sealing Germany's and Europe's door, Hanussen emphasized "the inevitable victory of Hitler and his nationalistic concepts." Eventually, he mixed his prophecies with an egocentric personal declaration that committed him fully to the Nazi path:

"I have pledged to be the first, if necessary, to devote everything I own and am, when the time comes, to make a sacrifice at the altar of Germany. I have encountered the readiness for sacrifice among all those who stood behind the banner of the National Concept; I know that Adolf Hitler sacrificed his all for his national idea; I saw Storm Trooper veterans in torn shoes and in thin jackets standing in the icy winds for hours to perform their duty; I have observed selflessness, integrity, and true patriotism among the millions who back Hitler and Hugenberg [Alfred Hugenberg, the monarchy-oriented politician-publisher then allied with the Nazis]; and so I had no choice but to demonstrate my respect and gratitude, unhesitatingly, in spite of everything, to serve the truth."

Hanussen's sacrifices consisted not only of lending money to Berlin Nazi bigwigs and loaning his sleek Bugatti to drive local Storm Trooper leaders to their "assignments," but of playing his personal friendship with Count Helldorf to the hilt. The Storm Trooper chief had admired Hanussen's apparently incredible telepathic and prophetic stage performances, had met him at a party given by the actress Maria Portales, and had witnessed an orgiastic hypnosis session on a weekend cruise aboard Hanussen's yacht, *Ursel IV*. And it was Helldorf who had arranged for the meeting between Hitler and Hanussen in the lobby of Berlin's Hotel Kaiserhof.

To Hanussen, this encounter was of the utmost importance. He had gambled on Hitler's victory, but he could not be sure of the Führer's "appreciation" for his raucous, self-publicizing methods, which had already antagonized future Propaganda Minister Joseph Goebbels, editor of the biting, aggressive evening paper, *Der Angriff*. The Kaiserhof meeting went well. Hitler's inherent belief in his own "destiny," his own preordained place in history, prompted him to say that "mysticism and occultism will need our attention." He apparently went so far as to anticipate the eventual establishment of an "Academy of the Occult" in which Hanussen would play a decisive role.

The Hitler-Helldorf-Hanussen alignment had taken place in 1931, when Nazi victory was far from assured. From then on, Hanussen spread the gospel of the Nazi movement's destiny not only in his weekly, but also in the series of "experimental demonstrations" in telepathy and prophecy that took him across Germany, as well as on less successful forays to Copenhagen and Paris.

Although he had bought his own publishing facilities, Hanussen continued to give "trance sittings" to writers. The Berlin *12 Uhr Blatt*, an afternoon paper, published his "trance" forecast that a Berlin-to-New York journey in the year 2500 would be impossible, as relentless "digging into the ground" would have brought about the destruction of New York—but, anyway, the trip would have been a mere one-hour rocket flight.

Other newspapers were less kind to the "Prophet of the Third Reich." The Communist-edited *Berlin am Morgen* ran a series, from May 25 to June 9, 1932, designed to expose Hanussen's background and conjuring tricks. Hanussen, furious, succeeded in obtaining an order from the 13th Civil Chamber of County Court I, Berlin, asking the paper to refrain from "referring to the activities of the petitioner as fake clairvoyance and from describing him as a charlatan, swindler, and crook who fleeces the public of its money." Adding to Hanussen's discomfort were the performances of an "anti-Hanussen," one Wilhelm Gubisch, who not only duplicated Hanussen's stage acts but proceeded to explain the man's extraordinary success in psychological terms, at a meeting of the Society for Scientific Psychology in the main hall of one of Berlin's leading hospitals, the Charité.

But as the Nazis began their final march to power, Hanussen became more self-assured and triumphant. A trial of the allegations against Hanussen, scheduled for February 21, was postponed by four weeks. On June 30, 1933, Hitler was named Chancellor. It must be remembered that the appointment of Hitler to the position of Chancellor was contingent on the holding of another election—and the Nazis had suffered sharp defeats at the polls of late. Hanussen's paper published an Election Extra containing such features as a "Horoscope of the New-Reichstag (Parliament)," "Germany's Future in Defense and Armament," and a general political "Prognosis by Erik Jan Hanussen." The latter article contained a postscript which cast doubt on whether the elections would actually be held. Hanussen wrote: "It will be a difficult task to avoid provocation, so that the elections will not be endangered at the last moment. More cannot be suggested at this point."

Under the circumstances, and coming from the "Prophet of the Third Reich," this was an inauspicious bit of forecasting. Yet, in the midst of the political churnings, with violence permeating the air of the German capital, Hanussen went on ahead with the opening festivities of his lavish "Palace of the Occult," taking up an entire floor at fashionable No. 16, Lietzenstrasse. All the magical paraphernalia, all the nouveau-riche extravagance, all the skilled showmanship of this extraordinarily charismatic, opportunistic, and hedonistic man were manifested in this super-shrine he had built for himself. Golden signs of the Zodiac looked down upon broad, low couches; hothouses containing exotic plants, snakes, and salamanders lined the walls. Together with lighting effects that could be centrally controlled, a system of hidden microphones enabled Hanussen to obtain valuable secrets from his visitors.

At the opening, at exactly midnight, when the actors and actresses, mingling with Nazi bigwigs, had been sufficiently awed by the grandeur of Hanussen and otherwise prepared by his champagne, the "Prophet of the Third Reich" took his place in the center of his lit-up glass circle; everything else was thrown into darkness. His eyes shrouded by a black mask, he gave his prophetic vision in halting, deep-throated tones of fear and menace:

"I see a vast and distinguished room. . . . Portraits of prominent men of history hang on the walls. They are men who have led Germany through much agony. Are they not the chancellors of the Reich? Yes, this is the Conference

Room of the Chancellery. Noise penetrates through the windows. The Storm Troopers move down the Wilhelmstrasse. There has been a magnificent victory. The people want Hitler. Victory, Victory! Hitler is victorious. Resistance is useless. But the noise comes closer. Is there a struggle? Shooting? No . . . no . . . it is not that. . . . I see flames, enormous flames. . . . It is a terrible conflagration that has broken out. Criminals have set the fire.

"They want to hurl Germany into last-minute chaos, to nullify the victory. They are setting fire to a large public building. One must crush this vermin. They want to resist Hitler's victory. Only the mailed fist of an awakened Germany can hold back chaos and the threat of civil war. . . ."

That was on the 26th of February, 1933. On the evening of February 27, at about 9:30, the news-agency teletypes in London, New York, and throughout the world were reporting a flash: "The Reichstag is burning!"

Hanussen's spectacular prophecy had come true. With it, his own flamboyant success seemed assured, especially amidst the violence that was immediately loosed; the Nazis used the Reichstag fire as an excuse to cancel the elections and embark on the reign of terror that lasted until Hitler's suicide in his Berlin underground bunker, ending World War Two, a decade later.

Who was this man who had prophesied Hitler's victory, who had so dramatically "foreseen" the conflagration that would envelop the Reichstag and help to seal the fate of a generation? And what, indeed, would be the fate that Nazism had in store for this all-too-knowledgeable, all-too-egotistic man Hanussen?

He was born Hermann Steinschneider in Vienna at 9 Yppenplatz, Ottakring district, on July 2, 1889. He was a showman from birth. His father, Siegfried Steinschneider, who hailed from Prossnitz, had been a song-and-dance man in the provinces. Little Hermann was stage-struck from childhood, or so he wrote in his biography *Meine Lebenslinie* (Berlin, 1930). He joined a traveling troupe at the age of twelve. Show biz was his métier. According to his own not altogether trustworthy account, he served successively as a trapeze artist, lion tamer, stable boy, and folk singer.

Steinschneider had the colossal nerve of the born con man. Once, stranded in Istanbul, he wrote and produced a fake Franz Léhar opera. Then, in order to save the ship's-passage fare home from Turkey, he pretended to be a singer, one

Titta Ruffo, who would pay for his crossing by giving concerts; shortly, he developed a timely sore throat.

Back in Vienna, he made his headquarters at the Café Louvre on Praterstrasse and edited a news sheet called *Der Blitz*, which gained revenue in odd ways. Much of the society gossip it picked up was never printed, because the ladies and gentlemen who figured prominently in these articles were willing, or at least persuaded, to pay for their nonappearance. *Blitz* pioneered a unique form of advertising, a novel in installments with built-in "commercials." The hero of this story was forever patronizing shops, restaurants, and night clubs that gave financial favors to editors—not unlike a "plug" in present-day television or the much-denied "payola" for disk jockeys.

Steinschneider at that time paid frequent visits to one Janos Bartel's "magic shop" on Vienna's Friedrichstrasse. Various "guess the right number" tricks and stage bits of "prophecy" attracted him. Then came World War One, and service in the Austro-Hungarian Army. But Steinschneider could no more abandon his prophetic pose now, than the proverbial cat can stop chasing the equally proverbial mouse. He told fellow soldiers news from home that would not reach them until days later. Once, he told his company commander that his wife had given birth to a son. Five days later, a postal card confirmed the news. This prophecy was fairly simple; a friend in the field post office passed newsworthy items on to Hermann, and then held up delivery of the cards by three or four days.

Fed up with too-active service, Steinschneider soon developed a "trembling" condition. He was moved to Cracow, behind the lines. But his health did permit him to put on stage performances for the army's "Widows and Orphans Fund." To raise 4,000 Kroner for the War Ministry, the army gave him a six-week furlough to perform in various frontal sectors. Next, he helped the army locate water in crucial areas around Galicia and Bosnia. He practiced dowsing, and he found enough water, in spite of a number of failures that he quickly explained away, to raise his prestige.

In the midst of all this, he wrote a competent professional conjurers' book, *Worauf beruht das? Telepathie, ihre Erklärung und Ausübung* ("The Origin of Telepathy: Explanation and Practice"; Cracow, 1917). In April 1918 he spent a furlough in Vienna. As a soldier on leave, he could not very well give stage performances; certainly not under his own name. It was here that the stage name "Erik Jan Hanussen" was born. His performances were successful, establishing a pattern that he continued for many years. He gained much acclaim when he "telepathically" traced a pin—just a tiny pin, mind you—to the handbag of an Imperial princess.

A master of self-made press-agentry, Hanussen became the center of many post-war controversies and sensations. Once, when whole sheets of freshly printed currency were stolen from the Austro-Hungarian Bank, Hanussen claimed that he had traced the thief clairvoyantly. His version of this (that he had cornered the thief in the bank building: "There he is!") differed from that of the police, who maintained that *they* had tracked the man down before Hanussen managed to pounce on him. But Hanussen did collect a reward of 4,000 Kroner, the bank gave him credit for stating correctly from what spot the currency sheets had been removed, and for noting that the thief had hidden them in the building's plumbing network.

Then he got into a publicity-producing feud with a professional strong man, "Iron King" Breitbart, who was built like a wrestler and claimed the ability to bite through and tear apart enormous steel chains. Hanussen, by rifling Breitbart's trunks and bribing his helpers, was able to duplicate the conjuring mechanism that made this startling performance possible. But he gave his imitation performance an occult switch when he announced that he would "hypnotize" a slender, pale girl, Martha Farra, into performing all the "feats of strength" that Breitbart had mastered. (Martha, however, fell in love with another performer and ran off to Budapest, taking the precious equipment with her. Hanussen had to make new copies of these intricate mechanisms and hire several successors to the inconstant Martha.)

Back in Germany, for several years and with growing success, Hanussen worked with a secretary assistant whom he had hired in Prague, Adolf Erick Juhn. It was in 1927, Juhn revealed later, that Hanussen hit on just the right combination of showmanship and mass psychology that began to lift performances to new heights of popularity. The thought occurred to him in Karlsbad, where he and Juhn were watching a rather dull "prophetess," one Frau Dagma, who combined "Indian" stage settings with a deliberately monotonous, pseudotrance delivery. Hanussen's idea was to add to this drama speed, dazzling repartee, alternate rapid-fire gags, and the solemn assurance of supernormal factors.

The whole technique is known to stage magicians as

"billet reading." It involves the careful selection of dates and notes of inquiries from the audience, signals from a collaborator, and self-revelatory hints coming from the audience. Hanussen carefully selected "fully cooperative" subjects, preferably women. (When the author of this book, then a fairly naive teen-ager, went onto the stage of the UFA-Palast in Hamburg to serve as a volunteer subject, Hanussen, smiling, sent him back to his seat, in favor of a "member of the fair sex.")

Hanussen's proud ship of showmanship nearly broke up when it hit the iceberg of one Gendarme Havlicek, whose foolhardy sense of duty prompted him to arrest the performer on February 11, 1928, at a hotel in Teplitz-Schönau, for practicing fraud in his alleged clairvoyance. The proceedings that followed were chaotic. The charges against the man were odd enough. He was accused of milking thirty-four persons, described as "mentally weak," of from twenty-five to two hundred Kroner apiece in private consultations. Hanussen, who had always been cautious in hedging his claims, managed to avoid the major impact of these accusations.

The crucial part of the trial, though, came with a performance that Hanussen might have staged himself. He was asked, in the presence of experts who had been selected for their "open-mindedness" toward supernatural phenomena, to perform his standard feats. He was to find a hidden object, make an analysis of a handwriting sample on a blackboard, and answer five questions clairvoyantly. His performance, in spite of courtroom pressures, was masterful. He carried audience, experts, and judges along with his dazzling flow of words and charismatic powers of suggestion. On May 27, 1930, the Leitmeritz Court dismissed the case with a 131-page opinion.

Hanussen shrewdly and frankly confessed that the decision might well have gone the other way, had he not performed, undismayed, with his customary skill. "Imagine," he said, "what might have happened if Friedrich Smetana had been asked, with a gun pointed at his head, to compose *The Bartered Bride*."

From then on, he treated the Leitmeritz decision as an official-judicial confirmation of his "powers." Yet, he had done no more at Leitmeritz than to act out the principles laid down in one of his earlier conjuring instruction books, *Das Gedankenlesen: Lehrbuch der Telepathie* ("Thought Reading: A Primer of Telepathy"; Vienna, 1920). He emphasized in these instructions to students of stage magic that creation of the right atmosphere was essential to the conjurer's success: "The illusion of the supernatural must surround him in the eyes of his audience, which will be a thousand times more manageable when it has become a group of believers. With success, self-confidence rises, and with self-confidence the power of persuasion itself."

His excellent performances in finding hidden objects, his eyes bandaged to concentrate the better on small muscular clues from knowing subjects accompanying him to the objects by "thinking hard," Hanussen explained as follows: "If I were to strip away all that is mystical or supernatural, if I were to show thought reading for what it is, we would arrive at virtuosity in the knowledge of audience psychology, linked to the meticulous study of procedures concerning ideo-motor motions."

More than a decade passed after he wrote these shrewd observations and instructions. By 1933, his knowledge of mass psychology had become second nature—to a level of self-assurance so dangerously close to arrogance that he now seemed to lack normal human alertness to signals of impending danger, threatening even a man who claimed to know the future, even the "Prophet of the Third Reich." He had prophesied the Reichstag fire, and events that followed had put his Nazi terrorist friends firmly in control. They were moving into every segment of public life, particularly the media of mass communications, which is still mainly in private hands.

By asking Count Helldorf's intercession, Hanussen saved his friends at the daily *12 Uhr Blatt* from an official ban. Meanwhile he delighted in the severe difficulties of his journalistic critics; his published shouts of triumph over their misfortunes crossed the border into viciousness. On March 8, he rejoiced, "For years I have waited for this moment. . . ." He was riding very high indeed. Helldorf even assigned a special Storm Trooper bodyguard to Hanussen. He now used his influence to engineer deals and payoffs; his lavish style of living came to demand enormous sums during those early weeks of Hitler's reign.

Having heard that Hanussen had helped another paper, an executive of the respectable *Berliner Tageblatt* sought similar intercession. The director of the paper's publishing firm, Karl Vetter, approached Hanussen. A deal was negotiated. In return for the paper's continued existence, Hanussen's old friend and Helldorf's aide, Storm Trooper Commander von Ohst, should be given a well-paid supervisory job with the *Tageblatt*. Vetter and Ohst soon saw eye to eye. Their agreement was so complete that it left Hanussen financially out in the cold. Ohst owed him thousands; Hanussen decided that either Ohst should pay up, or Hanussen should be paid a commission for engineering the deal.

Hanussen had overplayed this hand. He had earlier made enemies of the caliber of Dr. Goebbels. After hearing of Hanussen's demands from Vetter, Ohst ostentatiously strapped on his shoulder holster and went out into the street on the evening of March 24, 1933; Hanussen was soon to appear for his scheduled performance at the Scala. Hanussen's secretary, Ismed Dzino, was waiting for him at the Café Dobrin on Kurfürstendamm. Hanussen never came. The Scala management was forced to announce that the "Prophet of the Third Reich" had fallen ill, and that the audience could have its money back at the box office.

Dzino telephoned Hanussen's housekeeper. What had happened? Well, some Storm Troopers had called on Hanussen, and he had gone with them. Had they been, Dzino said, from "our unit"? No, they had been others . . .

The morning papers published a short, inconspicuous item that was widely read:

"The clairvoyant Erik Jan Hanussen was arrested last night before his performance. He is accused of having inveigled himself into the National Socialist Party through the use of forged papers."

Ten days later, on April 8, the official police report contained a piece written with notable restraint. It read:

"On Friday, April 7, the body of a well-dressed man was found by highway workers in a small pine tree nursery on the road between Baruth and Neuhof, south of Berlin. On the basis of company labels in the suit of the dead man, it was concluded that his identity is presumably that of the former publisher Hermann Steinschneider, who has been active as a clairvoyant under the name of Erik Jan Hanussen.

"This assumption was confirmed by a former employee of Steinschneider, who unmistakably identified the dead man in the morgue as his former employer. Steinschneider's body showed several shot wounds, apparently inflicted by others. The district attorney's office has undertaken the task of clarifying this matter, and it is being aided by the Berlin homicide commission under the direction of Crime Commissioner Albert.

"As several items of value were found on the body, the suspicion of murder for purposes of robbery has to be eliminated. The police seek the criminal in underworld circles, with which Hanussen has, of late, been strongly involved. Apparently, the criminals shot the clairvoyant to death in Berlin, and then transported the body to Baruth. It must have remained in the woods for several days, as it was considerably decomposed."

Rumor had it that Ohst had gone from the *Tageblatt* offices directly to Hermann Göring. The two, together with Helldorf, allegedly had decided that Hanussen was getting out of hand and had to be eliminated. Another version suggested that the "Prophet of the Third Reich," having forecast its rise, might equally well be capable of prophesying its downfall. In any event, his usefulness had come to an end. He was lured into a car with the ruse that he was wanted urgently at the Ministry of the Interior. He was killed in the Storm Trooper compound on Motzstrasse. Ohst, who himself had been greedy and obviously knew too much, was never seen again.

The newspaper *Montag-Morgen* published the following medical police report concerning the incident on April 10:

"Medical examination has shown that death took place between ten and fourteen days ago. Just how long the body had been in the woods could not be ascertained. The body was relatively well preserved, but the face had been severely decomposed. One of the murder weapons was found. It is a large-caliber revolver, which had apparently been caught in the clothing and fallen off during the transport of the body. Police regard it as a coincidence that the body was found early. It had been hidden very skillfully and was difficult to locate. Clues of a struggle could not be found.

"There were also no indications that would make it possible to arrive at any conclusions concerning the criminal. It is well known that Hanussen had considerable influence on women and thus destroyed much marital happiness. This could offer one reason for the crime. The police are also investigating the twenty-three court actions in which Hanussen has been involved, in order to ascertain whether some clue toward the identity of the criminal might be found."

Police efforts "against person or persons unknown" were discontinued on June 1, as "clues toward the identification of the criminal or criminals could not be found." Hanussen was buried at the cemetery in Stahnsdorf. Creditors of the "Prophet of the Third Reich" sold his yacht, his cars, his palatial residence. When the creditors met in the Charlottenburg suburb on June 29, their combined demands amounted to 142,536 German Marks.

Aside from having become too difficult and overbearing for Nazi leadership to tolerate, there may have been more concrete reasons for eliminating Hanussen. Published anonymously in Zurich under the title *Ich Kann Nicht Länger Schweigen* ("I Can Remain Silent No Longer"), a book appeared in 1935 which alleged that Hanussen had actually hypnotized the Reichstag arsonist, Marinus van der Lubbe, enabling Helldorf to command him to go to the Parliament building by a specific route and then set fire to it. However, the hynosis had only been partially successful, and van der Lubbe had merely set a curtain afire, which had smoldered briefly. One of Göring's henchmen was supposed to have set the real fire. But Hanussen, according to this version of events—the anonymous author was later identified as Walter Korodi—had been a participant, with inside knowledge of the incendiary conspiracy that firmly established the Nazi régime. As long as he remained alive, his mere existence was a threat to the regime.

Erik Jan Hanussen survived less than two months of the "Thousand Year Reich" whose birth he had prophesied. The Nazi regime, no matter how totalitarian and authoritarian in its public posture, was far from monolithic. Behind the façade of ferocious single-mindedness hid the erratic hopes and fears of a leading clique whose individual members were beset by shifting obsessions. The single surviving member of the clique, once Hitler's devoted and trusted deputy, Rudolf Hess, was the key figure in Nazism's attitude toward the mystical. The Nazi vocabulary abounded with references to Germany's "destiny" and many aspects of an ordained national future. A vague Nordic, Teutonic mystique permeated much of the pseudophilosophy used by Hitler to rationalize his policies.

The original owner of the Nazi party's key newspaper, *Völkischer Beobachter,* was an astrologer who had adopted the fanciful name Rudolph Freiher von Sebottendorf, although on his birth certificate he was plain Adam Glandeck. He sold the *Beobachter* to the Nazi party, but continued to edit an astrological monthly, *Astrologische Rundschau.*

A contemporary of Sebottendorf, the woman astrologer Elsbeth Elbertin, had analyzed Hitler's birth date in 1923 and concluded that it would be unwise for him to take any hasty action in November of that year. Hitler took part in the Munich uprising of November 8, 1923, and wound up in jail, where he wrote his magnum opus, *Mein Kampf*. There is no evidence that this forecast made any particular impression on Hitler, nor that any astrologer who identified his own "destiny" with Nazism managed to attain a position of power as the Nazi regime's "court astrologer."

A tragic figure in the confused drama that followed Hitler's rise was Karl Ernst Krafft, a man so fantastically devoted to astrological forecasting that he gave up the safety of living in Switzerland to devote himself to his calling in the service of the Nazis. He then came to the attention of the Secret Police when he predicted that Hitler's life would be in danger during the first ten days of November 1939. He was devastatingly correct; a bomb went off at that time, near Hitler, in the Munich Hofbräuhaus, the beer cellar that had been the center of the 1923 uprising. Shortly after Hitler had left an anniversary celebration of the uprising there, the cellar was torn apart by the explosion.

Krafft, in his fanatical desire to prove astrological forecasting correct, sent a telegram to Berlin to remind the officials of his prediction. He added that according to the stars Hitler's life would remain in danger for several more days. For his eagerness, Krafft was arrested and taken to Berlin. The Propaganda Ministry of Dr. Joseph Goebbels decided that Krafft's specialty could be utilized in psychological warfare. He was put to work on the writings of Nostradamus, the famous sixteenth-century French prophet, selecting and angling them to forecast the inevitability of Germany's victory in World War II. Records of the secret conferences in the Propaganda Ministry, kept in Soviet archives for some twenty years but partially published in recent years, showed that Goebbels used Krafft's interpretations of Nostradamus mostly for distribution in occupied France.

Whether Krafft was ever actually used as an astrological adviser, rather than as a propaganda instrument, remains doubtful. However, he did become a tool in an ingenious attempt to influence Allied decisions. In 1940, while he was on leave in Bucharest, the Romanian Minister to London, Virgil Tilea, wrote to Krafft asking him for astrological forecasts concerning the course of the war. As reported by the late British poet Louis MacNeice, in his book *Astrology* (London and New York, 1964), Tilea had met Krafft in Zurich and had been impressed by his flair as a prophet. But when Krafft received the Romanian diplomat's request, he showed it to his superiors in Berlin, who insisted on drafting and redrafting a response several times, to suit their propaganda purposes. When Tilea at last received it in London, it reflected the Nazi line so clearly that he assumed Krafft must be working for Hitler. Tilea suggested that it might be useful for the British government to employ an astrologer who could develop forecasts virtually identical to those that Krafft was presumably preparing for Hitler, but pro-Ally. He even recommended a specialist, the former Hungarian-German film writer and novelist Louis de Wohl (Ludwig von Wohl).

De Wohl, a versatile and adaptable man best known for his popular biographies of Christian saints, went through the rest of the war, as MacNeice put it, "imagining he was countering Krafft in Berlin." MacNeice, who credits this information to Felix Nebelmeier of Switzerland, supposedly an Allied intelligence officer assigned to examine the Krafft episode, adds the following details:

"But Krafft did not spend the rest of the war in the way de Wohl assumed. On June 12, 1941, he was arrested. Like many other things, this was the fault of Rudolf Hess, another Nazi leader who, like Himmler, was generally thought to be under the influence of astrologers. Hess's unauthorized flight into Scotland precipitated a great deal of face-saving and scapegoat-finding in Germany. Among those who suffered, thanks to Hess's reputation, were the astrologers. After all, Hess had had one on his staff at the Brown House in Munich —a certain Ernst Schulte-Strathaus, who was officially an expert on art. Schulte-Strathaus denied that he had ever given Hess any astrological advice or that he had any idea that Hess was going to leave Germany, but the sheer fact of their association provided another weapon against the astrologers. The Gestapo went into action."

The Gestapo not only tried to trace astrological links with the Hess flight, but generally cracked down on astrologers and other occultists. Most of those arrested during the Operation Hess were released shortly afterward. Others, including Krafft, were retained in custody. But even while he was imprisoned in Berlin, Krafft's services were being used by the Propaganda Ministry. He seems to have rebelled against this treatment and his tasks. From a prison on Berlin's Lehrterstrasse, Krafft was later transferred to two concentration camps: first to Oranienburg, and then to Buchenwald, where he died on January 8, 1945.

One of those who were arrested during the Operation Hess was a veteran German parapsychologist, Dr. Gerda Walther.

This remarkable woman had earlier been the assistant of the German psychical researcher Dr. Albert Baron von Schrenck-Notzing, a Munich physician. The author of this book visited Dr. Walther most recently in 1965, in her book-crammed tiny apartment in the shadow of Munich's two-domed Frauenkirche Cathedral. She recalls that it was largely due to Schulte-Strathaus, who had known Schrenck-Notzing well, that Hess had prevented drastic measures against astrologers and related specialists. She regards it as a malicious distortion that Hess's flight "was prompted by the occultists and astrologers."

Dr. Walther summarized the events of this period and her own arrests and experiences in the article "Hitler's Black Magicians" (*Tomorrow*, New York, Winter 1956). She recalls therein that the Goebbels ministry used other devices of alleged prophecy to firm up the German war spirit. Krafft's version of the Nostradamus predictions was dropped behind the Maginot Line to undermine French morale, and distributed, at one time, in pamphlets as far away as Iran. Goebbels, according to Dr. Walther, encouraged the spread of stories relating to clairvoyance and precognition. One of them concerned a man who gave his streetcar-seat to an elderly woman; she promptly told him she knew the exact amount of change he had in his pocket. When he, and those around him, expressed amazement at her occult knowledge, she added that she knew many things, including the future and the certainty of a magnificent Nazi German victory! At the same time, a film made at the behest of the Propaganda Ministry featured a young man, known for his optimistic prophecies, who turned out to be consistently right; this, too, was linked with the German war effort. Dr. Walther adds that Goebbels' attitude was entirely cynical and pragmatic: "If prophecies and other occult phenomena proved useful to his propaganda, he used them; he was just as ready to disavow them completely, if he had to."

When Dr. Walther was taken to Munich's Gestapo headquarters, the former Wittelsbach Palace, as part of the Operation Hess, one fellow prisoner turned out to be a strange woman who refused to take off her overcoat, and simply sat on the prison bed, saying, "I'll soon be free again, I'll soon be called for. . . . If I say so, it's true!" She was, indeed, released, even though it was a Saturday, and prisoners were usually kept over the weekend. The woman's name was Elise Lehrer, and even her imprisonment did not prevent her from repeating her notoriously consistent prophecies of Hitler's downfall. She eventually died in the Ravensbrück concentration camp, having stated, over and over again, that the collapse of Nazi Germany was inevitable. These forecasts came as part of a chain of striking instances of precognition. Miss Lehrer, a Bavarian country girl, once refused to join a group of girls on an excursion because she foresaw a train accident. She persuaded two of her friends to stay home. Two others left on the trip, however, and were killed in a train crash. Elise Lehrer also foretold the fire in the Munich Palace of Glass, which destroyed priceless works of art.

Although it is usually assumed that Goebbels, as Dr. Walther notes, was a cynical pragmatist, there are other aspects of his personality that allow for the assumption that in dealing with prophecy he may have assumed that there was "something to it, after all."

That Goebbels did, perhaps even in some pseudo-occult fashion, believe Nazi Germany could make a last-minute comeback has been noted by the British historian Hugh Trevor-Roper, who relates in *The Last Days of Hitler* (New York, 1947) that Goebbels, during the second week of that fateful April in 1945, sent for two horoscopes: Hitler's and Germany's. Both had been "carefully kept in one of Himmler's research departments." Goebbels presented these horoscopes to Hitler in the light of a historical parallel with the Seven Years' War: when Frederick the Great, in his war with Russia, was facing almost certain defeat, the Tsarina died and the situation was reversed. Goebbels told Hitler that he saw in Roosevelt's death a parallel to the death of the Tsarina: "It is written in the stars that the second half of April will be the turning point for us. . . . This is the turning point!"

Trevor-Roper notes that the two horoscopes obtained by Goebbels "unanimously predicted the outbreak of war in 1939, the victories till 1941, and then the series of defeats culminating in the early months of 1945," to be followed by a reversal during the second half of April and Germany's triumph in 1948.

While prophets, astrological and otherwise, were thus relatively without honor—until the last moment—in Nazi Germany, except for propagandistic manipulation, Louis de Wohl eagerly engaged in imitating, countering, and anticipating Nazi astrologers from his position with the "Psychological Research Bureau" in London. De Wohl, who tended toward a dramatic view of his own importance, gives an account of these activities in *The Stars in War and Peace* (London, 1952). Commissioned into the British Army with the rank of captain, he wrote that it was his task to come "to the same interpretative results," though *for* England, as the German astrologers who were supposedly advising Hitler. The zenith of popular dramatization was reached in the magazine article "Why Churchill Had an Astrologer" (*This Week*, November 1, 1959), which claimed that de Wohl "had worked for years with Hitler's Chief Astrologer," whom the writer called "William," and "knew his formula." In addition, he was supposed to have known "personally all of the five astrologers who were then advising Hitler." Actually, of course, there were none.

At least in one respect de Wohl's task was not too different from that of his alleged German counterpart, Krafft: He, too, put astrology at the disposal of psychological warfare. As part of Britain's "black propaganda" against the Nazis, make-believe issues of the defunct German astrological magazine *Zenit* were circulated among German army units. As the "forecasts" were written by de Wohl—with the use of proper astrological vernacular—after the events had occurred (a fake date on the magazine's masthead facilitated all this), his prophecies were strikingly accurate, and the more general forecasts of the Nazis' defeat were, therefore, particularly convincing.

There remains some doubt to this day as to the origins of the alleged prophecies made by a Polish medium, Tegoborza. Her forecasts are said to have been made in 1893, during a spiritualistic seance in the house of one Wieloglowski, in southeastern Poland. According to the Polish Press Bureau in London, then a subdivision of the Polish Government-in-Exile, Tegoborza's prophecies were deposited in the archives of the Ossolinski Library at Lwow. When these predictions were circulated by the Allies in 1940, Poland was under the double occupation of Nazi Germany and the Soviet Union, and it was certainly in the interest of the Allies to keep the morale of the Polish people as sturdy as possible.

Among the Tegoborza prophecies, in verse in their Polish original, was this one: "The besmirched Cross [the swastika, supposedly] shall fall together with the Hammer [Communism], and the predatory powers shall be left with nought, while the Masurian Land shall return to Poland, and Danzig will be our port." And, "The Lion [Britain] of the west, basely betrayed by his freeman, shall unite with the Cock [France] and lead a young man to the throne. . . ." An excellent prophecy, on the whole. Should it be credited to the

British Ministry of Information, or perhaps to psychological warfare specialists of the Polish Government-in-Exile?

At any rate, the Hanussen episode, the dual roles of Krafft in Germany and de Wohl in England, as well as the mysterious Tegoborza prophecies indicate a public yearning, particularly in times of crisis, to gain some ritual certainty of the future. At various times this need is met by colorful individuals, whether sincere or fraudulent, and even by government agencies.

6 Croiset's Prophetic Chairs

Paranormal events seem to follow national cultural patterns. In Great Britain, they follow the tradition of haunted houses and ghostly appearances. In Germany, public interest in astrology is high, and poltergeist phenomena are reported with relative frequency. In France, unorthodox healing has many followers. Brazil is the world's newest stronghold of spiritualism. The Philippines report extensive "psychic surgery." The United States has pioneered in quantitative laboratory experiments. The Soviet Union tends toward physiological tests that confirm the tenets of dialectical materialism. And in the Netherlands, sensitives, known as "paragnosts," show themselves adept at helping the police and private individuals to locate missing persons; one unique Dutch sensitive has made modern psychical history: Gerard Croiset, a paragnost par excellence, healer, and prophet.

The hard-working, lean, intense Croiset has been the subject of a series of investigations by two of Europe's most prominent parapsychologists. They are Professor W. H. C. Tenhaeff, Director of the Parapsychological Institute, University of Utrecht, and Professor Hans Bender, Director of the Institute for Border Areas of Psychology and Mental Hygiene, University of Freiburg im Breisgau. Acting separately or as a team, Tenhaeff and Bender have supervised many precognition experiments with Croiset that reflect his particular inclinations and abilities. These curious—and really quite inexplicable—tests are known as "chair experiments."

The tests were developed in 1949 by Professor Tenhaeff to permit careful organization and fit Croiset's gifts. The experiments consist of two steps. First, Croiset gives a description of the characteristics and certain outstanding experiences of a person whom he expects to occupy a certain chair in a lecture hall—before the chair has even been booked. Next, the person who eventually occupies this chair is questioned to see to what degree Croiset's description fits or deviates from the personality and experiences of this individual.

These chair experiments have now been going on for a good number of years, and they have taken place in many parts of Europe. At first, Croiset's impressions were more or less spontaneous. As time went on, Tenhaeff and Bender tightened experimental conditions to guard against advance leakage of information to Croiset. And they have developed specific methods for weighing Croiset's descriptive statements against the later testimony by the chairs' occupants. In all this time, the experimenters have been keenly aware of the outward impression that some sort of conjuring trick might be involved—or at least some unconscious signaling by the participants or by persons on the periphery of these experiments.

By now, these baffling tests add up to thousands of pages of reports. Professor Tenhaeff's book *De Voorschouw* ("Precognition"; The Hague, 1961) contains about one hundred pages dealing with Croiset's chair experiments. In his outstanding anthology *Parapsychologie: Entwicklung, Ergebnisse, Probleme* ("Parapsychology: Development, Results, Problems"; Darmstadt, 1966), Professor Bender notes that these experiments are unique as "an example of the quantitative utilization of qualitative tests using statistical methods, especially adapted to the particular character of the experiment."

An example: In June 1953, Bender and Tenhaeff set up a series of experiments in three high schools in the German Palatinate. Neither of them had ever visited these towns before. On June 3, at 2 P.M., Croiset sat down with the two psychologists in front of a tape recorder in the small town of Neustadt and addressed himself to the task of anticipating what was to take place on the same evening in the city of Pirmasens. He picked chair No. 73, and this is what he recorded:

1. I see a lady, about thirty years old or younger, who often wears a vest made of angora wool.
2. She is wearing a white blouse.
3. With this lady I see a man who reminds me of a

movie actor, who some years ago played in the film "The Private Secretary" with Martha Eggert.
He also resembles Churchill.

4. Does this lady live near a red building, in front of which there are high column supports? I see steep steps. Does this lady visit the building frequently? I am under the impression that there is a fence in front of this building. It gives a rather dilapidated impression.
5. Has this lady suffered an upset in a delicatessen store? Did she buy a basket of fruit there, or did she look for one? I am particularly aware of a box of dates.
6. Did she recently read something about Upper Silesia, or has she had a conversation dealing with Upper Silesia?
7. Did she have a slight infection on her right big toe?
8. I see a kite that won't rise. Something remains unfulfilled. . . . Something to do with a man between twenty-eight and thirty-two years of age, gray suit, dark blond hair. He wears a pullover. This man had a plan, but this lady got in the way. (Because of this: the kite did not rise.)
9. I see the symbol of an "all-seeing eye"—an eye within a triangle.
10. I see a green cigaret box. The lady turns up her nose at it.

So much for Croiset's taped observation. Some 250 people attended the meeting at Pirmasens that evening. There were rows of benches, with folding seats, but additional chairs had been placed near them, which had not been recorded on the seating plan. After everyone had been seated, Croiset accompanied Tenhaeff and Bender into the room. He said that the woman about whom he had earlier recorded his impressions was present in the room; she did not sit in chair No. 73, but two seats away from it.

It was not possible, during the actual evening meeting, where Croiset's predictions were discussed, to clarify all the points Croiset had mentioned, as a number of them were too personal to state in public. However, the woman was interviewed the next day. Her answers were recorded. The places Croiset had mentioned were visited afterward and, when this was added to the documentation, photographed. Listed in numbered reference to Croiset's earlier impressions, the following statements were recorded:

1. and 2. The woman is thirty-two years old and wore a white blouse. As she was about to take this blouse from her wardrobe, she saw the vest of angora wool and considered whether it might not be wiser to wear the warmer garment.
3. The lady states that Croiset's description fits her boss, a jolly, hefty man.
4. She does not live near a building with column supports. She remembers that the only red building she knows with such architectural features is the cemetery chapel in Pirmasens, which she visited two days earlier when she attended a funeral. At the time, she vividly remembered another funeral, during her last visit to the cemetery chapel in 1942. At that time she was much concerned about a friend stationed in Russia from whom she had had no mail. On the day prior to the experiment she received a letter from this young man who, although he had married meanwhile, wanted to resume his relationship with her, and this had repelled and angered her. There is no fence before this building, and it does not give a dilapidated impression.
5. She recalls, in this connection, that there is a delicatessen across from the place where she works which always displays some fruit. She had not, she thought, particularly noted "a box of dates."
6. She points out that a book, a *Biography of the Landscape of Silesia,* has been on her table for the past three days, in connection with a visitor just arrived from Upper Silesia.
7. She had shortly before suffered an infection on her left foot (not on the right one); the tape recording did not reveal whether or not it was on her big toe.
8. Age and hair color would apply to the young man who had written her the letter mentioned earlier. She does not know whether he wears a pullover. Indeed, his plan did not succeed, because it had outraged her.
9. This symbol of the "all-seeing eye," interpreted by Croiset as illustrating a keen intelligence, was regarded by the participants as applicable to the personality of the woman in question.
10. At the time of their friendship, the young man had given her a green-yellow cigaret case. That she

should turn up her nose at it might symbolize her anger over the recent approach by this former friend.

The Pirmasens chair experiment was one of the earlier tests undertaken by Bender and Tenhaeff. Later experiments were tightened up, notably in the selection of chairs by drawing lots; these tended to make the experiments rather clumsy, but helped to guard against control errors and facilitated quantitative evaluation. Croiset, accompanied by Tenhaeff and Bender, later performed his chair experiments in the presence of other researchers at the Centro Studi Parapsicologici in Bologna, as well as in Verona, Zurich, and elsewhere.

Similar chair experiments were made by the Italian researcher V. Perrone, who worked with the sensitives Alesandra Bajetto and Tino Menozzi; he reported the results, which he found to be significant, in the *Bolletino della Società Italiana di Metapsichica* (1955).

Year by year, the methodological framework of the chair experiments was tightened up. On January 6, 1957, at 2 P.M., a preparatory session took place at the Utrecht Institute. Professor Tenhaeff was present, as were his assistant, Miss Nicolauda Louwerens, and two professors of the university: a biologist, J. H. Bretschneider, and a physicist, J. A. Smit. A seating plan was put before Croiset, showing the arrangement of chairs as they would be, twenty-five days later, at the home of a resident of The Hague, Mrs. C. V. T. The list of thirty guests who were to sit in the chairs had not yet been drawn up.

Having selected the future occupant of chair No. 9, Gerard Croiset listed the following twelve points in his tape-recorded description:

1. On Friday, February 1, 1957, in the home of a lady in The Hague, a cheerful, active, middle-aged little woman will sit in this chair. She is very interested in caring for children.
2. Between 1928 and 1930, I see many of her footsteps were taken near the Kurhaus and Strassburger Circus in Scheveningen [a seaside resort near The Hague].
3. When she was a little girl, she had many experiences in a district where there was lots of cheesemaking. . . . I see a farm on fire, where some animals are burned to death.
4. I also see three boys. One has a build like mine. He

has a job in some overseas area. It seems to me a British territory.
5. Has she been looking at a picture of a maharajah? I see somebody from India . . . he is wearing the dress of an inhabitant of that country . . . a turban with a large jewel.
6. Did she ever, as a girl, drop a handkerchief into a cage of wild animals—they look like lions—which tore the cloth to pieces?
7. I also see a scrap pad with the number "six" on top. At first it was a "five," but she changed it to a "six." This just happened, and she had many arguments about it.
8. Has she only recently soiled her hands on an old-fashioned paint box? I see a box with small tablets of paint. . . . Did she hurt herself slightly with that? The middle finger of her right hand?
9. Has she also recently been visited by a woman friend, about forty years old . . . not very tall, well-built, stout, with dark hair, and wearing a dress with several large pleats in front? Did this woman talk to her about sexual problems, and did she advise her friend to visit a psychiatrist?
10. Has she experienced a strong emotion about the opera *Falstaff?* Is this the first opera she ever saw?
11. Did her father receive a gold medal for services he rendered?
12. Has she taken a little girl to the dentist? And did this visit create a lot of commotion? I can almost say this will happen on Friday, February 1, 1957.

The recording was completed, spooled back, and then played for Croiset to hear. Did he, Professor Tenhaeff asked, have any supplementary observations? Yes; "Croiset felt, for instance, that when he spoke of the second point, the seaside resort," he "saw the picture of a man of about forty-five, very emotional and sensitive . . . his wife did not understand him. They were separated. . . . This man had affairs with other women. And his wife had affairs with other men."

Concerning the fourth point, where he saw three boys, Croiset got the impression that "one of these boys is dead," and that this death had something to do with the German wartime occupation of the Netherlands. On the sixth point, Croiset added that the impression of a wild animal, a lion, was probably symbolic. He said: "I once compared a mesmerist [hypnotist] to a lion tamer and the public to the lions. When the lion tamer gets too close to the lions, they devour him." Expanding on his remarks concerning the twelfth point, he said: "I suddenly saw my grownup daughter as a child. When she was five years old, I took her to the dentist. She refused to open her mouth and stayed with the dentist for several hours."

The next day, January 7, Professor Tenhaeff telephoned Dr. A. Tuyter in Utrecht, telling him that Croiset had taped his prophetic impressions for the February 1 meeting. He did not, of course, reveal what these remarks had been. Dr. Tuyter, in turn, telephoned the hostess and said, "You can mail out the thirty invitations now." Meanwhile, Croiset's twelve initial impressions were transcribed and typed on stencils, and forty mimeographed copies were made. The supplementary observations were not duplicated, awaiting verification.

To assure random selection of the chairs, two packs of numbered cards were especially prepared on January 31. On February 1, Tenhaeff, Miss Louwerens and her sister Annet, Dr. Tuyter, and a prominent Finnish parapsychologist, Dr. Jarl Fahler of Helsingfors, arrived at Mrs. T.'s home at The Hague at 7 P.M. One set of numbered cards was placed on the thirty seats, while a parallel list was kept; there were five seats in each of six rows. The meeting was to take place on the first floor. Meanwhile, the guests were assembling in a basement room. The method of the experiment was explained to them, and each one received Croiset's mimeographed impressions. "Please read these carefully," they were instructed; "if any of these points apply to you, state so in the space to the right of each point."

The second set of numbered cards was then taken out of its sealed wrapper. Miss Louwerens handed one card to each participant as they came up the stairs. Annet Louwerens saw to it that they were seated correctly, and they were cautioned not to touch a chair that was not assigned to them, as this might distort the experimental results.

As an additional precaution, Croiset himself did not arrive in The Hague until after the guests had been seated. He had driven the thirty-six miles from Utrecht to The Hague in order to appear after 8:30 P.M. and be unable to influence the seat selections—unless by long-distance telepathy, psychokinesis, or another form of extrasensory perception that could simply not be screened out.

The twelve mimeographed points were read out. One guest,

Mrs. M. J. D., who held card No. 9 and thus chair No. 9, was asked whether the statements applied to her. She said, "Yes, many of them do." Virtually none of the impressions Croiset had recorded nearly two weeks earlier seemed to apply to the twenty-nine other participants. In addition to giving testimony at the meeting, Mrs. D. was interviewed privately in Amsterdam on May 18. Also, she and her husband gave another interview at the office of Professor Tenhaeff's Parapsychological Institute in Utrecht on June 20. Here is a summary of her responses, again numbered from 1 to 12, including Croiset's hits and misses:

1. Mrs. D., forty-two years old and a cheerful, active, vivacious woman, said that she took great interest in child care. As a little girl, she had often said that she wanted to have a castle with a hundred babies in it.
2. Her parents were divorced. Her father, a highly strung and emotional man, worked in the Netherlands East Indies, now known as Indonesia. When he returned to the Netherlands on leave, from time to time, he often took his daughter to the Scheveningen Circus. Both her parents had had extramarital relations.
3. Mrs. D. had often visited farms when she was a child. However, the chief product of these farms was butter, rather than cheese. She did not have a direct experience with a burning farm, but her eldest son, while working on a farm, had seen a horse killed by lightning; this experience had profoundly affected him, and he had presumably transmitted these emotions to a certain degree to his mother.
4. There was no direct connection between Croiset's references to three boys with overseas jobs. However, her husband was one of three brothers. One had volunteered to fight in Indonesia in 1945; he was trained in England, but did not get beyond Singapore, then a British possession. The third brother, who died in a German concentration camp, resembled Croiset in build.
5. A few days before the meeting, Mrs. D. had seen a picture of a Yogi in a book and had spoken to her son about it and about Hinduism generally. Her husband added that his wife had at times said that she felt the presence of an "invisible helper" or

"protecting spirit" in her life, and that she had imagined this entity to be a Yogi.

6. Here, Mrs. D. could see no way in which the "lion" image applied to her, but Croiset said that the symbol would become clearer when Point 9 was discussed.

7. In reference to Croiset's having seen a "five" changed to a "six," Mrs. D. recalled that between January 26 and February 1, she had made a mathematical error in her housekeeping records, entering a "five" where there should have been a "six." As this created a mistake in her addition, her books failed to tally, and this led to a quarrel with her husband.

8. In early January, the children of the D. household had been "messing around" with an old-fashioned paint box containing small tablets of paint. Mrs. D. had cleaned their hands, but had managed to get paint on her own and on a towel. At about the same time, she cut the middle finger of her right hand on a vegetable can.

9. This was a fairly crucial and emotion-laden point, linked to the "lion image in Point 6. Mrs. D. said that she had discussed sex problems with a woman friend, who was not very tall, was rather well built, though stout, had dark hair, and often wore a dress with large pleats. When she mentioned this encounter at the February 1 meeting, Croiset told her she had been wrong in advising this woman to visit a therapist. When he heard the man's name mentioned at the meeting at the Parapsychology Institute on June 20, Croiset said, "This man is not trustworthy in sexual matters. A mesmerist or psychiatrist must know how to remain aloof from his patients. Otherwise the lions will devour him."

10. This was a solid hit. Mrs. D. was a professional opera singer. Not only was *Falstaff* the first opera in which she performed, but she had also fallen in love with a member of the company, a tenor.

11. While her father did not actually receive a gold medal, he was given, on his retirement, a gold cigaret case.

12. Three weeks following Croiset's prediction, on February 1, Mrs. D. took her daughter to a dentist to have a cavity filled. It was a very painful and frightening visit for the child.

Not all of Croiset's chair experiments show his apparent precognitive or telepathic gifts as clearly as does this case. But many cases *are* equally strong. Often Croiset's associations with a symbol or with his own experiences, notably during his childhood, show a strong emotional identification with the events in other people's lives.

Professor Tenhaeff ascribes part of Croiset's abilities to the sensitive's childhood deprivations and general emotional patterns. An American writer, Jack Harrison Pollack, in a recent biography, *Croiset the Clairvoyant* (New York, 1964), notes that he comes from a family of actors, in which exhibitionism is a strong factor, and that he must have felt abandoned at an early age—his father periodically deserted the family. Gerard himself was placed in foster homes, beginning at the age of eight; he had six different pairs of foster parents. One foster father chained his leg to a stake that had been driven into the floor. The child also suffered from rickets.

Croiset is very sensitive to anything that is painful to children: witness the little girl at the dentist's. As a healer, he is sought out by many parents who bring their children to him; often, his healing efforts are directed toward bone diseases, frequently in the legs and feet. Tenhaeff summarizes Croiset's almost-magnetic pull toward certain personalities and incidents with the apt observation that "he unconsciously searches for events in the lives of others that are associated with those in his own." The particularly striking aspect of this predilection is, however, that he seeks out these events not only in the past and present, but also in the future, and that he is accurate as often as he is.

7   Exotic Prophecy

"Give up your worldly goods and follow me!" This demand, implying that present sacrifice will assure future reward, is a basic theme of the human heritage. It is shared by primitive and modern man. It takes a variety of forms, ranging from sacrifices requested by the sun god to the emotional pitch of a life-insurance agent: "So that your Loved Ones may live without worry." Reincarnation believers regard poverty and suffering in the present as investment in a credit balance for future incarnations.

Civilizations, whether ancient or contemporary, "primitive" or industrialized, vary in their practice of prophecy. Where modern communications techniques have not substantially intruded, archaic forms of precognition or telepathy have survived in colorful and striking ways. At times, as in the cases cited on the following pages, primitive needs create caricatures of wish fulfillment on a grand scale.

Buying off the gods is an old and ever-present expression of man's anxiety, stemming from fears of the schemes of avenging ghosts, irascible ancestors, or jealous inhabitants of Olympus. Hell-fire sermons and the selling of indulgences belong to these guilt-riddled traditions. Throughout history, Western movements headed by prophets of doom have claimed that the world was coming to an end on a specific date unless man mended his ways, and that a few "chosen ones" might escape to a mountain top or other refuge.

World-wide parallels exist today, notably dramatized in the "Cargo Cult" practices of the South Pacific. In 1966, natives of New Ireland, a small Australian-administered island in the New Guinea area, attracted attention with their plan to "buy" President Lyndon B. Johnson, so that he might assure them of their rightful "cargo." The word "cargo" is used by the natives to describe all kinds of materials introduced by Europeans: "cargo" is pidgin English, more properly spelled "kako" or "kago." It includes such objects as steel axes, steel tools, clothing, cans of meat and tobacco, rice in bags, aircraft, rifles—just the kinds of goods likely to be unloaded from boats to the amazement of natives who have never seen anything like them, but who soon begin to appreciate their uses, and would like to have plenty more for themselves. President Johnson, in local pidgin English, was regarded as "namba wan man bilong gaman," or "Number One Man Belong Government," and thus able to practice powers known in much of Oceania as "mana." The Cargo Cult concept is an adaptation of earlier beliefs, developed during colonial rule and roughly based on the hypothesis that the white man's gods must be more powerful than native deities; all you have to do is look at his riches, his clothing, his vehicles, and other godlike displays of wealth!

When the first House of Assembly for Papua-New Guinea was elected, hundreds of people from the northern tip of New Ireland refused to vote for any of the listed candidates, and insisted that "Johnson bilong America" become their ruler. Following the typical sacrifice-for-the-future pattern, a nineteen-year-old "prophet," one Bosmialek, preached that if the people voted for Johnson, the Americans would return to New Guinea, bringing ample "cargo" riches.

The district leader from Kavieng, New Ireland, visited the northern section and came back with word from Bosmialek's followers that they had collected $1,000 in silver to buy President Johnson. The U.S. Air Force then sent a master sergeant to tell the natives officially that Mr. Johnson was too busy running the United States to come to New Ireland. Nevertheless, the Cargo Cult idea remained alive; the Bosmialek group even mobbed native policemen who had gone into the village of Lokono to collect long overdue local government head taxes. A larger police contingent was sent to Lokono. By then, the villagers had fled; but they returned later and paid their taxes.

Bosmialek, in a microcosmic illustration of classical Cargo Cult prophecy, urged that the natives engage in a huge feast "to assure" that an American ship would arrive to bring them the desired cargo. The local District Commissioner was particularly upset by the possibility that Bosmialek's prophecy might indirectly come true. The native prophet had given April 10 as the arrival date of the ship. On April 9, the District Commissioner received a radio message that a U.S. ship would land a geographic survey party close to Bosmialek's headquarters. If this happened, the prophet's influence would attain immense proportions, as would his potential for causing political unrest.

The Commissioner sent a radio message to the unsuspecting survey ship. At his request, the Americans put in at Kavieng, where they were briefed on the unusual impact which their visit might have. They agreed to change to civilian clothes and land on the crucial coastline in a small boat, unlikely to fit Bosmialek's grandiose prophecies.

Bosmialek's prophecies nevertheless continued on a grand scale. He told his followers of a dream prophesying that the liner *Queen Mary* was on its way with 600 U.S. Negro troops, who would help oust the Australian administration. At the same time, according to this dream, other soldiers would land by helicopter. Bosmialek ordered his followers to clear landing pads for the 'copters. True to the pattern of followers of prophets clinging to their hopes, up to and often beyond the moment of crucial revelation—be it joyful or disastrous— Bosmialek's adherents took new heart from the delivery of an outboard motor, displaying the brand name "Johnson," claiming that it was a gift sent directly by the U.S. President.

Tommy L. Fraser reported from Lae, New Guinea, in *The Washington Post* (April 24, 1966) that the Cargo Cult had taken on aspects that were "far from humorous." He noted that "one of its manifestations was the insistence of a local 'prophet' that the natives destroy their garden harvests and their valuable pigs as an 'act of faith' to induce their ancestors to deliver the goods," which never came. The dispatch added:

"These people, living a hand-to-mouth existence at hardly more than subsistence level, picture the white man as rich beyond their imagination and, furthermore, he seems to them to get his wealth without having to work for it." Disillusion sets in after a while, but new cults crop up.

New Guinea, where a Stone Age culture has, at times, felt the impact of Western civilian and military riches in extreme form, is a center of Cargo Cult traditions. Australian and Dutch anthropologists and ethnologists have studied its phenomena in Papua and New Guinea.

Dr. Peter Lawrence, of the Australian National University in Canberra, has done a detailed study of "The Cargo Cult and Religious Beliefs among the Garia," who number some three thousand people and live near the New Guinea town of Madang, in the foothills of the Adelbert and Finisterre Mountains. The study, published in the *International Archives of Ethnography* (Leiden, 1954), dealt with field work undertaken from April 1949 to July 1950, linking the Cargo Cults with Garia religious beliefs.

The study notes that such cults have been known since the last century throughout the Southern Pacific, including Fiji, the Solomon Islands, New Hebrides, and Torres. The "Vailala madness," which began in 1919, left traces that were visible up to 1931. Two coastal villages on the Gulf of Papua, Nomu, and Arihava, were swept with the prophecy that boats laden with food would arrive, brought by ancestral spirits. A local prophet, Evara, who had some knowledge of European and Christian cultures, stated that the ancestral spirits would drive out all whites—and that, in the past, all men had been white. These prophecies disrupted native life almost totally, creating widespread starvation and unrest and requiring large-scale relief as well as other countermeasures.

Dr. Lawrence writes that today "very few areas in New Guinea, especially those which have been in contact with Europeans for a long time, have remained wholly unaffected by the movement." Outbreaks were frequent before World War Two, but during and after the war, the author remarks, "they have become so numerous that they are causing considerable anxiety among missionary and administrative circles." Dr. Lawrence emphasizes that the Madang natives assume that Europeans or Americans who control such "cargo" do not make the items, but that they are "derived from a specific deity" over whom they have some means of control. The cult, Dr. Lawrence states, "aims to acquire supplies of cargo for the natives by means of ritual ordained by the prophecies of certain inspired leaders."

These prophecies of individual leaders cut across ethnic boundaries, prompting New Guinea's various tribes to unite in supporting the "particular prophecies and rituals" advanced by one leader. There have been ten different cult prophecies in the Kein area of the Madang district.

One Cargo Cult case bears a fascinating resemblance to prophecies recorded recently in the United States by a team of sociologists from the University of Minnesota, which will be analyzed shortly. In this one, though, in 1947, a woman by the name of Polelesi of the Garia village of Igurue claimed she had seen one of "God's angels" in a dream, warning her of the coming of a second flood. She told her fellow villagers that they would be saved, because God would send them a ship. Other Garia inhabitants were urged by her to come to Igurue, so that the ship could pick them up. Some obeyed her, but others refused to leave their homes.

Polelesi prophesied that those who refused to get ready for safe passage by the promised ship would be drowned or eaten by crocodiles. Dr. Lawrence reports: "In a clairvoyant moment, she proclaimed that she had seen God, Jesus Christ, angels, and the spirits of the dead in the clouds above the mountain. She had seen a storehouse built there as well, and in it was cargo which would soon be brought down to the survivors by the spirits. She ordained special prayers to God and the spirits, and later, when it began to rain, she announced that this was a divine sign of the imminence of the cargo's arrival. . . ."

Basic prophecy patterns of this type know no boundaries, and fit easily into specific cultural situations. The contemporary parallel to the Polelesi case was documented in this country by investigators of the Laboratory for Research in Social Relations at the University of Minnesota. The researchers examined the case of a woman in a Western university town whom they call Marian Keech. She had allegedly received messages from "spacemen" forecasting a widespread destructive flood. A small group of the woman's devotees were, she said, to be picked up by men from outer space, presumably landing in a UFO craft, before the flood struck.

The findings of this research team, published by Leon Festinger, Henry W. Riecken, and Stanley Schachter in *When Prophecy Fails* (Minneapolis, 1956) noted that Mrs. Keech's "automatic writings" had considerable impact on her followers up to and beyond the time of the prophesied UFO pickup, which was supposed to take the small band of devotees to a safe destination, perhaps on another planet. The team was particularly interested in the reaction of various followers as, step by step, each succeeding prophecy remained unconfirmed and was replaced by yet another one. When eventually even the flood itself did not come about, members of the group took refuge in "substitute confirmations" (just as the New Guinea natives had welcomed the "Johnson" outboard motor) before the movement disintegrated.

The researchers reported, without specifying the year, and guarding all identities by using substitute names, that the Lake City *Herald* carried a news report headlined: "Prophecy From Planet Clarion; Call to City: Flee That Flood. It'll Swamp Us on Dec. 21, Outer Space Tells Suburbanite." The newspaper story gave the following details:

"Lake City will be destroyed by a flood from Great Lake just before dawn, Dec. 21, according to a suburban housewife. Mrs. Marian Keech, of 847 West School Street, says the prophecy is not her own. It is the purport of many messages she has received by automatic writing, she says. . . . The messages, according to Mrs. Keech, are sent to her by superior beings from a planet called 'Clarion.' These beings have been visiting the earth, she says, in what we call flying saucers. During their visits, she says, they have observed fault lines in the earth's crust that foretoken the deluge. Mrs. Keech reports she was told the flood will spread to form an inland sea stretching from the Arctic Circle to the Gulf of Mexico. At the same time, she says, a cataclysm will submerge the West Coast from Seattle, Washington, to Chile in South America."

The report of the University of Michigan team, presented below in a combination of paraphrases and direct quotations, noted that Mrs. Keech felt she had been chosen as an agent to learn and transmit teachings from the "superior beings." In early October, two of the investigator-authors visited Mrs. Keech, and subsequently three members and some hired observers joined the group that had clustered around the seeress.

Mrs. Keech's interest in the occult had begun fifteen years earlier, in New York. In the interim, she had become attracted to a succession of esoteric doctrines, ranging from theosophy to dianoetics. At the time she began automatic writing, Mrs. Keech had become actively interested in reports of flying saucers. After receiving a variety of automatic writings, she recorded "messages" from a source called "Sananda" and identified as "the contemporary identity of the historical Jesus—his name having been adopted with the beginning of the 'new cycle' or age of light."

Mrs. Keech communicated her esoteric contacts to her husband, whom observers described as "a man of infinite patience, gentleness, and tolerance amounting almost to self-abasement; he never believed that his wife could communicate with other worlds, yet he never actively opposed her activities or sought to dissuade her from her writing." Her most important contact was a Dr. Thomas Armstrong, whom she had met through the Steel City Flying Saucer Club. Dr. Armstrong, a physician, lived in Collegeville, about one hundred miles from Steel City.

Armstrong and his wife Daisy played a major part in publicizing Mrs. Keech's prophetic exhortations. Both came from Kansas and had served as medical missionaries in Egypt. During July, August, and September, the Armstrongs and Mrs. Keech assembled their complex rationale. The first "Sananda" messages of prophetic content came on the second of August. It is characteristic of the indirect, "mystical" language:

"The Earthling will awaken to the great casting [conditions to be fulfilled, in the special language emerging from these messages] of the lake seething and the great destruction of the tall buildings of the local city—the cast that the lake bed is sinking to the degree that it will be as a great scoop of wind from the bottom of the lake throughout the countryside. You shall tell the world that this is to be, for such it is given. To you the date only is a secret, for the panic of men knows no bounds."

Ten days later, the Armstrongs and Mrs. Keech were able to receive the following "Sananda" message, and it can easily be imagined that, inasmuch as they accepted it as "gospel" from other-worldly entities, the impact was enormous:

"This is not limited to the local area, for the cast of the country of the U.S.A. is that it is to break in twain. In the area of the Mississippi, in the region of Canada, Great Lakes and the Mississippi, the Gulf of Mexico, into the Central

America will be as changed. The great tilting of the land of the U.S. to the East will throw up mountains along the Central States, along the Great New Sea, along North and South—to the South. The new mountain range shall be called the Argone Range, which will signify that the ones who have been there are gone—the old has gone past—the new is. This will be as a monument to the old races, to the new will be the Altar of the Rockies and the Alleghenies."

Other messages said that Egypt would be "remade," the desert would become a fertile valley, the legendary continent of Mu would rise from the Pacific, the Atlantic seaboard would be submerged, France and England would sink to the bottom of the Atlantic, and Russia would become one great sea.

As the time of the prophesied "flood" and expected removal by flying saucers neared, a coterie of followers emerged. Not unlike the followers of the Cargo Cult, they sacrificed worldly goods, gave up careers, endangered families, suffered loss of income. One peripheral member of the group was the originally skeptical Kitty O'Donnell; Bob Eastman, a sort of disciple to Armstrong, had brought her along to the Keech sessions. She became caught up in the prophecies, gave up her job, left her parents, moved into an expensive apartment of her own, and prepared to use up her life savings of some six hundred dollars, as she, too, expected to be picked up by flying saucers. On December 4 she said: "I *have* to believe the flood is coming on the 21st because I've spent all my money. I quit my job, I quit comptometer school, and my apartment costs me $100 a month. I *have* to believe." Fred and Laura Brooks, virtually engaged to be married, gave up their studies in anticipation of the flood. Laura threw away many of her personal possessions—soon she would not need them any longer.

On November 22, Dr. Armstrong was asked to resign his position on the college health staff. Parents had complained that he was using his position to teach "unorthodox religious beliefs." But Dr. Armstrong rationalized the event as "part of the plan" of the "Guardians," designed to shake him loose from the ties of the world, preparing him to leave it for a better one. On December 4, group members removed all metal from their clothing in preparation for the "pickup."

On December 17, news of Dr. Armstrong's dismissal had leaked out, and information on the plans for evacuation by flying saucers reached the information media. Reporters and photographers descended on the group. By the time the newspapers had their fun with Mrs. Keech, the group was more than ready to escape its hostile earth environment. At 4 P.M., the group gathered in Mrs. Keech's kitchen to await the saucer men. By 5:30 nothing had happened. Mrs. Keech then received a "message" instead, telling her that when the group was picked up later on, she would return to "the Father's house" and need not come back to earth again. After midnight, the group assembled quietly in the backyard, ready for a pickup once again. Mrs. Keech went into the house around one o'clock to "get a message." Departure, she then said, was imminent; the flying saucers would pick them up within the hour.

Once again, the group was elated. Once again, nothing happened. Mrs. Keech went into her car to write down another "message": everyone was being blessed for being patient and disciplined; they would all be appropriately rewarded; they should now go back and rest; at the proper, but unspecified, time a man would come to lead them to a pickup place. Mrs. Keech spoke reassuringly about the fact that it had all been splendid "basic training."

On the morning of December 20, Mrs. Keech received a message which said: "At the hour of midnight you shall be put into parked cars and taken to a place where ye shall be put aboard of porch [flying saucer]. . . ." As the authors of *When Prophecy Fails* put it: "This was the message everyone had been waiting for and it had come none too soon, for before another dawn the whole of Lake City was to be flooded. But the chosen ones would be safe." The remainder of the day was spent in more detailed preparations. As the clock struck twelve, the believers sat motionless. Midnight passed. The flood was seven hours away. Reporters telephoned. Dr. Armstrong told them, "No Comment. We have nothing to tell you."

Mrs. Keech then recorded a "message" that was a masterpiece; it read:

"For this day it is established there is but one God of Earth and He is in thy midst, and from His hand thou has written these words. And mighty is the word of God—and by His word ye have been saved—for from the mouth of death have ye been delivered and at no time has there been such a force loosed upon the Earth. . . ."

The Little Band of Believers, by their faith, had saved the earth! There it was, testimony from the highest authority. This "Christmas message" was relayed to the newspapers. Floods of publicity ensued: television, a big national magazine, many press and radio interviews. The Associated Press and the United Press told Mrs. Keech that there had been earthquakes that very day in Italy and California. She said, "It all ties in with what I believe." Yet the group still expected to be "picked up."

But within days, as the sensation gave way to other news, public interest slackened. Bob Eastman made a long-distance call to Kitty O'Donnell, who had left previously. She said, "You didn't get picked up, huh?" Reply: "No, we haven't had any positive action yet." Eventually Kitty said, "Well, I don't know, but I just regret it in a way, Bob. Of course, I learned a lesson, but I just regret that I made such an ass of myself, giving up my money and stuff . . . and I don't know. . . ."

On Christmas Eve, the pathetic band of believers caroled in front of the Keech home, hoping that spacemen might even then come to take them away. Crowds gathered. Police had to control the mob. On the 26th, neighbors filed charges against Mrs. Keech and Dr. Armstrong, accusing them of a variety of infractions ranging from disturbing the peace to contributing to the delinquency of minors. The police were reluctant to prosecute; they warned the Keeches—who left the community quickly and quietly. The Armstrongs also packed their bags and drove with their two younger children to Collegeville.

It would be quite unsatisfactory to speak of the foregoing events as a mere case of hallucination in one woman. Mrs. Keech's "messages" obviously fitted a mood of the period, aroused latent wishes on the part of a number of followers, and gave the participants a distinct feeling of belonging among the "chosen ones" of the earth. A psychologically oriented Italian anthropoligst, Guglielmo Guariglia, has pointed to the basic motivations that seem to underlie virtually all prophetic cults of this kind: "Expectation of salvation through a mythical personage or an extraordinary power, as well as of an earthly paradise." In the case of the Keech cult, the paradise was supplanted, in accordance with space-age expectations, by outer space or another planet.

Guariglia's unique analytic survey, linking nationalist ferment toward independence, the desire for economic affluence, and Cargo Cult prophecies, was published in Austria under the title "Prophetismus und Heilserwartungs-Bewegungen als völkerkundliches und religionsgeschichtliches Problem" ("Prophecy and Salvation Movements as a Problem in Ethnology and Religion"; Vienna, 1959). This account of prophetic movements throughout the world, mainly in what the author identifies as "contemporary illiterate societies and underdeveloped cultures," places scattered pieces of psychological and political significance into an imaginative mosaic. The author notes that natives of the Oceanic area in contact with Western civilization resent such intrusion, but "simultaneously wish to achieve the freedom of the whites and their living standards." He finds, as does Dr. Lawrence of Australian National University, that followers of prophetic movements generally prefer "an immediate earthly paradise to a future spiritual paradise." Guariglia traces nationalistically oriented prophecy movements to the "myth of the return of a Culture Hero," one who left in ancestral days because of a "sin committed by the group," thus creating "a yearning for his return and the re-establishment of the Lost Paradise." It is rare to find such a clear juxtaposition of Western monotheistic concepts of a Garden of Eden, lost because of "sin" (man's guilt, which modern psychology encounters), with the realities of politico-economic movements.

Some additional examples from the Oceanic areas help to illustrate these points.

One of the oddest prophecies from this area was repeated, seven years apart, in separate areas. In 1930, sections of northern and northeastern Papua saw scenes of pig killings and week-long feasts; in 1937, the same thing happened in a Papuan village, Kairaku. The explanation was a prophecy which claimed that "the Big Pigs" would come, eliminating all need for the tedious task of breeding pigs for food.

In northeastern Papua, the Assisi cult, practiced from 1930 to 1944, survived World War Two in a number of adaptations. Among the prophecies circulating in this area then was one stating that "Christ" would come with Cargo; that work would become unnecessary; that those who were white would become dark, and those who were dark would become white. Typically, local prophets prompted the Papuans to destroy their gardens as a sign of faith. One prophet practiced his own versions of Catholic communion and Protestant rites.

Students of Marxist splinter movements will find unique material in a prophetic movement that hit the island of Lifu, New Caledonia, in 1947. In this case, the Cargo was to be a richly laden ship sent by the Communist party of France for the benefit of native Communists. While only part of the island went along with this prophecy, landing and unloading facilities were built at one shore point to accommodate the expected Red riches. Jean Guiart, writing on " 'Cargo' Cults and political evolution in Melanesia" (*South Pacific*, 1951, No. 7), exempts Communist organizers from collusion, and voices "the opinion that the natives are entirely responsible for this 'deviation.' "

A calculated Communist effort to exploit Cargo Cult mentality was reported from the hill country of northwestern Thailand in 1966. Persuasive "Buddhist travelers," who had just crossed the border from Laos into Thailand, brought with them exciting tales of the wonders and riches they attributed to a Laotian messiah.

"He is waiting," they told the Thai tribesmen. "Plant no rice and kill your animals. Pack up and come!"

As related by correspondent Mark Gayn for the *Chicago Daily News* syndicate, the hill country is "a world of superstition and childlike faith," and twenty-three families were persuaded, rid themselves of their earthly possessions, and crossed the border into Laos. Nothing was heard of them for several months, until they returned, bitter, weary, and impoverished. "There is no messiah," they said.

Gayn added: "There were also many others who slaughtered their cattle and left their fields untilled but did not go to Laos. After a few months, they began to drift into small towns to beg Thai officials for food. An investigation was launched and showed that some thousand tribesmen had fallen under the spell of itinerant missionaries."

Six of the men who had presented themselves as Buddhist missionaries were arrested. Gayn reports that their testimony convinced officials that the stories of a Laotian prophet were not the expressions of a "weird cult but a deliberate effort to produce chaos and discontent in the hill country." Gayn added: "If this is so, then the 'messiah' provides merely another facet of the bitter and expanding conflict in which Bangkok now finds itself, pitted against malcontents at home and their Communist patrons abroad. Along with the 'messiah' there are the more familiar features of sabotage, terrorism, guerrilla ambush, espionage, and radio war."

Ancient oracles were accused of accepting bribes to give misleading military advice. The use of a Buddhist "prophet" to create an economically disruptive Cargo Cult movement in Thailand fits into the pattern of the not-so-cold war waged by Communist China in southern Asia. And while we are gaining knowledge of the validity of prophecy, we must be aware of its employment as a weapon of psychological warfare.

8 Freud: Oedipus Without Oracle

The scientific study of prophetic claims has made halting but notable progress with the advancement of psychology, notably in psychoanalysis. Sigmund Freud, who so greatly widened man's insight into his unconscious drives, was selective in his research and ideas; nowhere is this more striking than in his major concept of the Oedipus complex. Named after the legendary Greek King Oedipus, who killed his father and married his mother, Freud's concept postulated that just about everyone falls in love, at least briefly, with the parent of the opposite sex.

Examination of Sophocles' play *Oedipus Rex* shows that Freud accepted one key idea from this ageless tragedy but ignored the significance of another. He plucked the Oedipus complex from the plot and dialogue, but shunted aside Sophocles' classic acceptance of oracular prophecy. Freud could have noted the universal validity of Oedipus' predestined fate, while recognizing the fundamental psychological implications that relates man's longing to know the future, as dramatized in the play. In his *Interpretation of Dreams*, Freud wrote that the play was "known as a tragedy of destiny," and that "its tragic effect is said to lie in the contrast between the supreme will of the gods and the vain attempt of mankind to escape the evil that threatens them." But to him the play's impact on a modern audience, as on an ancient Greek one, "does not lie in the contrast between destiny and human will," but in "the particular nature of the material on which that contrast is exemplified."

According to Freud, we are moved by the fate of Oedipus "only because it might have been ours—because the oracle laid the same curse upon us before our birth as upon him." And he adds: "It is the fate of all of us, perhaps, to direct our first sexual impulse toward our mother and our first hatred and our first murderous wish against our father. Our dreams convince us that it is so." Freud added that we outgrow these emotions, unless we become psychoneurotic; for

PROPHECY IN OUR TIME

the mature audience watching *Oedipus*, "these primeval wishes of our childhood have been fulfilled, and we shrink back from him with the whole force of the repression by which those wishes have since that time been held down within us."

In summarizing the Sophocles play, Freud plays down the element of predestination but emphasizes the love-of-mother and hatred-of-father themes. He does note that the oracle warned Oedipus' father, Laius, that the still unborn child would murder him. In order to prevent the prophecy from coming true, the parents abandoned the newborn baby in the mountains, presumably to die. The child was found, of course, by a shepherd, who called him "Oedipus," which means "swollen feet."

Freud picks up the story when the rescued child, a grown prince at an alien court, wondering about his origin, "questioned the oracle and was warned to avoid his home since he was destined to murder his father and take his mother in marriage." Oedipus, believing the King and Queen of Corinth to be his parents, now flees to Thebes. On the way, he quarrels with an old man and kills him. Further on, he answers a riddle posed by a malevolent sphinx who has held Thebes in bondage. The grateful Thebans make him their King, replacing Laius, who had failed to return from his last trip. It was, of course, Laius whom Oedipus had killed on the road.

In the second scene of the play, Oedipus demands of an old high priest that he identify the murderer of Laius. Freud notes, with collegial satisfaction, that Sophocles developed the play in a series of dramatic steps "that can be likened to the work of the psychoanalyst," by "revealing, with cunning delays and ever-mounting excitement," that Oedipus is "the son of the murdered man and of Jocasta," who has become his wife. Freud summarizes: "Appalled at the abomination which he has unwittingly perpetrated, Oedipus blinds himself and forsakes his home. The oracle has been fulfilled."

Because of the wide attention that Freud's concept of the "Oedipus complex" has attracted in popular psychology, the implications of Sophocles' sequel to the play have been largely ignored. The eighty-nine-year-old philosopher-playwright had his final say in *Oedipus at Colonus*, completed shortly before his death and performed posthumously. In it, the aged Oedipus returns to Attica, accompanied by one of his daughters, at peace with himself but in rebellion against fate. As he had never known that Laius and Jocasta were his natural parents, destiny had virtually tricked him into his actions and into the partial self-destruction he committed by blinding himself. Oedipus, at the end of his life's journey, turns with contempt on those who took advantage of his misfortune. He acts out yet another oracular prophecy by going serenely to an all-forgiving death—a man purged of whatever curse he may have suffered, cleansed of a guilt that was never his. In the concluding scene of the play, Oedipus is freed of his "complex" by following a predestined fate that is no longer tragic, but that of a man sure of his essential purity and worth.

As translated by Robert Fitzgerald, in *Sophocles: The Oedipus Cycle* (New York, 1939), Oedipus comes to terms with his own fate in this soliloquy:

". . . The bloody deaths, the incest, the calamities
You speak so glibly of: I suffered them,
By fate, against my will! It was God's pleasure,
And perhaps our race had angered him long ago.
In me myself you could not find such evil
As would have made me sin against my own.
And tell me this: if there were prophecies
Repeated by the oracles of the gods,
That Father's death should come through his own son,
How could you justly blame it upon me?
On me, who was yet unborn, yet unconceived,
Not yet existent for my father and mother?
If then I came into the world—as I did come—
In wretchedness, and met my father in fight,
And knocked him down, not knowing that I killed him
Nor whom I killed—again, how could you find
Guilt in that unmeditated act? . . ."

Preparing for death, Oedipus settles in the groves of the Furies, at Colonus, about a mile northwest of Athens. Eagerly, he awaits word from the Oracle of Apollo. He welcomes his daughter Ismene, reminding her that she had once before acted as messenger, "Unknown to Thebes, bringing me news of all / The oracle had said concerning me. . . ." He questions her to find out whether the gods are "concerned with my deliverance." Ismene assures him, "I have, father, the latest sentences of the oracle." Oedipus asks, "How are they worded? What do they prophesy?" She replies, "That you shall be much solicited by our people / Before your death—and after—for their welfare." And further: "The oracles declare their strength's in you. . . . For the gods who threw you down sustain you now. . . ."

Clearly, these passages indicate a concern for the continuing theme of oracular power, the impact of destiny on man. Freud sought out and found the Oedipal tragedy in the work of Sophocles, but ignored its dramatization of the psychological dynamics underlying man's search of prophetic assurance, the desire to know, conquer, and possibly control a seemingly inevitable fate. The Oracle's roles in the Oedipus plays need be regarded as neither malevolent nor benign; they may simply stand for the yearning for knowledge of good and ill, beyond man's "normal" sensory range. The Oracle's key roles in the Oedipus legend correspond to human concern with future destiny, strong in man's emotions, in his daily existence as well as in his apparent premonitory dreams. At times, such dreams have a multiple impact: they not only picture events that seem to come true later on in defiance of orderly chronological concepts, but they may also reflect emotional states that bring about the events; the very strength of the dream experience may help to pave the way for these events. Freud never got around to studying closely, much less accepting, a number of the psychological implications of *Oedipus at Colonus,* but some of those who build their own ideas on the foundation of Freudian concepts, have done daring and fascinating research in precognition as well as in telepathy.

Sigmund Freud was a man who tried to be fair. He sought to be helpful to his patients, cooperative to his friends and colleagues. Psychoanalysis was, from the start, a controversial concept. Freud's probings into sexual elements of the human psyche made him a target for attacks from many directions. But he was tolerant; he knew, professionally, the vast variety of human foibles. Within the psychoanalytic movement itself, there were antagonisms, splits, doctrinaire arguments, politicking.

With all this going on, the last thing Freud needed was involvement with "occult" matters such as telepathy or, worse still, prophecy. But he was being pushed and pulled on these subjects as on so many others. For himself, he was fascinated by reports of psychic phenomena. His "ambassador" in Great Britain and eventual major biographer, Ernest Jones, knew that psychoanalysis was having a difficult time finding acceptance in its own right. Jones cautioned against any trucking with ideas that were even more suspect.

On the other hand, Freud was being badgered in Vienna by his brilliant and eccentric disciple, Sandor Ferenczi, to acknowledge psychic phenomena. And Freud's 1912 split with C. G. Jung was partly over the issue of the "occult," for which Freud expressed extreme aversion, but which Jung regarded as a fitting subject for exploration in the development of his own "open system" of analytical psychology.

A partial selection of quotations is a basic form of propaganda, as well as of scholarly oneupmanship. Interpretation, reinterpretation, or the supplementing of older ideas with newer research findings can be helpful or confusing. Freud wrote a great deal. Sometimes he could be quite dogmatic; at other times he would hedge, make a pronouncement but proclaiming that he had not, in fact, expressed his final thought or written his final words on that given subject. All this makes it possible to read Freud on precognition and telepathy in dreams from different viewpoints. And this is at least partially why some of those, who for want of a more suitable label are often known as neo-Freudians, may be classified—on the subject of prophecy, at least—in three ways:

(1) Those who emphasize Freud's early writings, in which he regards telepathy as unproven, and claims of precognition as just so much retrospective falsification.

(2) Those who have found telepathic and even precognitive material in the dreams of their patients, and who do not only regard this as significant, but as actually helpful in the therapeutic process.

(3) Those who feel that even when the actual, outward, dream material may lack telepathic, or precognitive content, parapsychological communication may be detected, by analysis, in the underlying symbolism.

The wish to know the future is alive in man today, as it has been since prehistoric times. It has a strong, basic emotional appeal. Certainly, an issue so old and fundamental cannot be cast aside by schools of psychology that seek to explore, understand, diagnose, heal, and guide modern man. But let the reader be warned; let him buckle his intellectual seat belt. The ride is going to be rocky.

First of all, Freud himself. His own dealings with prophecy were, of course, dominated by the contact he had with the dreams, hallucinations, and neurotic symptoms of patients. The case material he encountered had, therefore, a built-in bias. On November 10, 1899, he noted down and commented on a case, entitling it "A Premonitory Dream Fulfilled." It was a skimpy thing, which today wouldn't be given refuge in the files of the American or British Societies for Psychical Research, or in the files of Dr. Louisa E. Rhine of the Foundation for Research on the Nature or Man. But it was Freud's first recorded encounter with precognition in a dream, and it does illustrate his somewhat dogmatic position at the time.

Freud describes this patient, identified as "Mrs. B.," as an estimable woman of critical sense, who told him that "once some years ago she dreamt she had met Dr. K., a friend and former family doctor of hers" on Vienna's main shopping street, the Kärnterstrasse, "in front of Hiess's shop." She told Freud that the next morning "while she was walking along the same street, she in fact met the person in question at the very spot she had dreamt of."

Freud, in his essay, goes to great lengths to knock down the "importance of this miraculous coincidence" and to point out the excellent underlying reasons why she might have "felt convinced" of having had such a dream after the actual encounter took place. Dr. K. had been her lover, briefly, after the death of her first husband. She had, Freud surmised, "dreams of this kind quite often now," twenty-five years after their liaison, but "such dreams were put aside on waking," and "that was what happened to our ostensibly prophetic dream." Freud concluded:

"The content of the dream, the rendezvous—was transferred to a belief that she had dreamt of that particular spot, for a rendezvous consists of two people coming to the same spot at the same time. And if she then had an impression that a dream had been fulfilled, she was only giving effect in that way to her memory of the scene in which she had longed in her misery for him to come, and her longing had at once been fulfilled. Thus the creation of a dream after the event, which alone makes prophetic dreams possible, is nothing other than a form of censoring, thanks to which the dream is able to make its way through into consciousness."

This Freud paper was not published until after his death, in 1939. Yet he wrote it just six days after his major work, *The Interpretation of Dreams,* was first published. In this book, in fact, the less dogmatic, more tolerant Freud at times shows itself. He wrote, for instance, that "dreams are reputed to have the power of divining the future," and commented: "Here we have a conflict in which almost insuperable scepticism is met by obstinately repeated assertions. No doubt we shall be acting rightly in not insisting that this view has no basis at all in fact, since it is possible that before long a number of the instances cited may find an explanation within the bounds of natural psychology."

However, elsewhere in this book, Freud once again rules out (though he qualifies this) any actual prophetic elements in dreams; they become projections into the future of what has been derived from images of the past. He writes: "And the value of dreams for giving us knowledge of the future? There is of course no question of that. It would be truer to say instead that they give us knowledge of the past. For dreams are derived from the past in every sense. Nevertheless, the ancient belief that dreams foretell the future is not wholly devoid of truth. By picturing our wishes as fulfilled, dreams are after all leading us into the future. But this future, which the dreamer pictures as the present, has been moulded by his indestructible wish into a perfect likeness of the past."

There developed in Freudian circles a tendency to out-Freud Freud himself. But orthodox and purist Freudian excesses are rare today. Yet the traditional Freudian position is a respectable and important one. Eduard Hitschmann, writing in the *International Journal of Psychoanalysis* (October 1924) on "Telepathy and Psycho-Analysis," suggested bluntly that individuals who report such supernatural experiences as "so-called veridical dreams" might well be in dire need of psychotherapy.

A detailed review of premonitory dream experiences as they emerge in psychoanalysis was presented by the Swiss analyst, Hans Zulliger, in the leading Freudian journal, the *Internationale Zeitschrift für Psychoanalyse* (1932, No. 13), under the title "Prophetic Dreams." Dr. Zulliger cites a number of cases which he encountered in his practice, examining reported precognitive experiences against his knowledge of each personality and case history.

Zulliger's account begins with the plan of a group of mountain climbers to spend a weekend in the Bernese Alps. Three of them invited a fourth mountain-climbing enthusiast, whose fiancée had recently died. After a good deal of persuasion, this fourth man agreed. However, two days later he changed his mind: in a dream, he had seen himself falling to his death from the Jungfrau mountain. Nevertheless, the friends again persuaded him to climb the Gantrisch mountain with them; even children had climbed it, and it offered a superb view.

The fourth man disregarded his precognitive dream, stumbled during the descent, and fell to his death. Dr. Zulliger reports that the three mountaineers were shocked to find that their friend's dream had "come true." He observes that, in a case such as this, it is impossible to search for psychological factors and that "this dream and the subsequent accident are designed to support the belief that there are, indeed, prophetic dreams." For himself Zulliger agrees with Hitschmann that "the assumption of mystical powers is nothing but a psychological attitude, projected into the environment," often expressing antagonistic emotions in expectation of disaster. Zulliger writes that "such emotions may also be assumed to be the cause of all those 'prophetic' dreams which are concerned with the death of beloved family members or acquaintances."

Zulliger regards telepathic dreams as noteworthy because they appear to bridge gaps in space, while prophetic dreams "concern different sensory perceptions, because prophecy deals with prognosis in time." He observed that psychoanalytic treatment had recorded relatively few prophetic dreams, at that time, as it regarded them as secondary to diagnosis and treatment, whereas the general public considered them as "phenomena in their own right." Zulliger emphasizes in this essay that knowledge of specific psychological circumstances is essential for the evaluation of precognitive dreams, which cannot be gained from secondhand or thirdhand material; the latter is likely to be distorted in the retelling.

From his own files, Dr. Zulliger cites another example that could not be analyzed because the protagonist had died. In this case, a woman of twenty-four reported to a group of friends on the way home from a party that she had had a slight fever during the preceding night, which seemed to have caused the following dream: "She was walking cross-country with her fiancé. Suddenly, they encounter a huge wall. A heavy black door opens; she strides ahead and through the door. The wind bangs it shut before her future husband can reach it, while she falls into a bottomless depth." Zulliger felt that the dream suggested that the young woman's forthcoming marriage might be ill-advised. She was strongly attached to her father, making such remarks as "I'll only marry someone who is like Daddy!" and "I wish I could marry Daddy!" While these statements might have seemed childish or ridiculous, they came from an intelligent young woman whose father had prompted her to undertake the planned marriage. The woman accepted her future husband as if he had been handed to her, like a present, by her father. The wedding was supposed to take place four days later. The day after the dream, the young woman fell ill with pneumonia. She died on the day of the scheduled wedding.

Zulliger comments: "Considering these facts against the background of what we already know of the woman's attitude toward her father and her fiancé, we are justified to speculate. We may assume that the bride preferred death to this marriage. Possibly her fever during the night of the dream had indicated the beginning of pneumonia. And even viewing the dream itself, we may ask whether it does not indicate unconscious suicide intent."

The Swiss psychoanalyst saw a parallel between the two dreams. The young man in the first dream had not been able to come to terms with his fiancée's death; he wanted to die "in order to be united with her." The young woman who after her feverish night went to the party and failed to look after herself may have neglected her health and thus "succeeded in dying, rather than marry the man she did not love." However, Zulliger regards such analysis, after the fact, as unsatisfactory and preferred "to operate with such prophetic dreams as are available within psychoanalytic practice."

One of Zulliger's patients, a young man soon to be married, reported a visit in his future bride's kitchen, where he knocked a glass bowl to the floor. This reminded him of a dream he had had during the preceding night: He was supposed to open a glass container whose cover was tight and immovable; he concluded that there was no choice but to break the glass. Looking back, the man regarded this dream as prophetic. Zulliger says that, seen casually, the dream and the actual breaking of the glass bowl might be considered as just another coincidence. However, his analytic sessions revealed that the young man had worried a good deal about his forthcoming wedding and the challenge of deflowering his bride—all this was mixed up with fears of retribution through castration and the secret wish for a wife who had been previously deflowered by another man. The analysis developed in the direction of a classical Oedipus situation, wherein the young man was found to desire, subconsciously, his own mother, while fearing his father's revenge. All this, Zulliger finds, the patient acted out in his dream in a symbolic manner; he notes that "for the problem of the prophetic dream, this example is of particular interest, as it enables us to observe successive breakthroughs of the unconscious with particular clarity." Zulliger adds:

"The dream that comes true is actually not directed toward the future. It testifies to something that exists in the unconscious and reaches back into the dreamer's early past. Such Oedipal fantasies exist in early childhood, where they cannot be acted upon, and are thus activated when the boy has grown into manhood and faces a real marriage situation."

Another of Zulliger's women patients reported that she had previously told him that she had dreamed of holding a baby to her breast, a dream which had preceded her becoming pregnant. She then told the analyst that, once again, she had experienced such a dream and that it, too, had forecast a pregnancy. Zulliger, however, reports that this patient, who was about to finish her therapy, had not really recorded the first premonitory dream as she claimed, but had been "mistaken in her memory." And the second dream did not turn out to be prophetic. After a delayed menstruation, there was no second pregnancy.

Nevertheless, Zulliger felt that he had gathered a good deal of material on the psychodynamics of the prophetic dreamer from this woman patient. She was deeply satisfied to have gained knowledge of something unknown to the analyst; she saw in herself something like "mediumistic" abilities, which gave her the feeling of being exceptional; she hoped to forecast other happy events; and she thought herself capable of foreseeing dangers that she "might avoid, as she would be forewarned." Next, the woman became upset by the idea that she might then also be able to know in advance should her husband, she herself, or the analyst be in danger. This led to revulsion from the possible "power" of being able to foretell the death of those near her; but she found solace in the conclusion that, after all, her prophetic ability was not really that great.

The wish to look into the future, Zulliger writes, contributed to her false memory of the prophetic dream about the first baby. He says: "It is evident that someone who can foresee birth may also be able to foresee death. She became aware of this, when, during the same visit, I turned on the electric light. It reminded her of the immense pleasure she experienced when as a small child she was able to switch the light near her little bed on and off. The game with the light switch amused her more than anything else, because she felt that, like God, she was able to command day and night. We may, in the wish to possess 'mediumistic' abilities, recognize remnants of that phase in the child's development in which the narcissistic youngster sees himself as 'omnipotent.'"

Where Dr. Zulliger interprets the dream of the woman who later died of pneumonia in suicidal terms, others might see it as a diagnosis of the illness that was building up within her. This position has been taken by Havelock Ellis, who wrote in *The World of Dreams* (New York, 1925) that "a physical disturbance may reach sleeping consciousness many hours, or even days, before it is perceived by waking consciousness, and becomes translated into a more or less fantastic dream." Ellis regarded "prophetic" dreams, "in which the dreamer foresees, not a physical condition that is already latent, but an external occurrence" as "usually fallacious." He ascribes these to the "emotional preparation of the dream, and the concentrated expectation," which sets the stage for an event that can fit the prophecy. Havelock Ellis does, however, leave the door open to other conclusions, saying, "That there are other prophetic dreams, less easy to account for, I am ready to admit. . . ."

A similar position was taken by a veteran U.S. psychical researcher and writer, H. Addington Bruce, who reported on early work of the American Society for Psychical Research on December 11, 1911, in the *Outlook*, a weekly magazine which could cite Theodore Roosevelt among its contributors. Bruce, writing on "Dreams and the Supernatural," said that many people were reluctant to admit that they had dreams which dealt with "events of future occurrence," although he saw "no need to go beyond subconscious perception to explain premonitory dreams." Like Ellis, he felt that such dreams might take place when illness had "already so far progressed as to cause organic changes occasioning sensations too slight to be appreciated by the waking consciousness, but sufficient to stimulate the sleeping consciousness to activity." Bruce added that "when the dream relates to some one other than the dreamer, it is safe to assume that, consciously or subconsciously, an inkling of the other person's state of health had been obtained by the dreamer before the dream."

Bruce shows how undefined the frontier between an "inkling," some form of telepathic or clairvoyant knowledge, and prophetic conclusions really are. Delicate threads connect all these concepts: sensory or extrasensory clues of a present condition may indeed lead to unconscious conclusions about the future, and thus to some form of prophetic impression.

9   C. G. Jung: Searching Healer

Freud's most gifted disciple and later his most relentless antagonist, Carl Gustav Jung, brought emotional insight to many through his analytical psychology. This sturdy, pipe-smoking, white-haired man, who seemed to draw strength from the Swiss mountains to which he retreated from time to time, was deeply concerned with the meaning of psychic phenomena. This involvement hastened his break with Freud. Nearly a half-century later, in 1958, Jung wrote:

"It interested me to hear Freud's views on precognition and on parapsychology in general. When I visited him in Vienna in 1909, I asked him what he thought of these matters. Because of his materialistic prejudice, he rejected the entire complex of questions as nonsensical, and did so in terms of so shallow a positivism that I had difficulty in checking the sharp retort on the tip of my tongue. It was some years before he recognized the seriousness of parapsychology and acknowledged the factuality of 'occult' phenomena."

Freud and Jung broke irretrievably in 1912, and Jungian psychology then developed along its own distinct lines. Their disagreement on parapsychology dramatized fundamental differences in their views of man's psyche. Yet, while Jung bitterly resented Freud's description of "occultism" as a threatening "black tide of mud," he too, was for the most part carefully guarded in commenting on such psychic phenomena as precognition. When advancing daring concepts, Jung was, in the American vernacular, something of an Indian giver. No sooner did he advance a startling idea than he seemed to snatch it back for reexamination, or cushion it in multiple qualifications. It must be kept in mind, however, that in later life—notably after 1946, when he expanded his concept of the archetype—Jung no longer sought to fit his findings into the framework of existing psychology.

The reason for this seesawing between daring and caution can be found in Jung's concern for his professional status vis-à-vis his intense personal experiences with telepathy, precognition, hauntings, and other highly dramatic incidents. He felt so keenly on this overall subject that he seemed sometimes obliged to build walls around walls around walls in order to guard his scientific standing. As a result, he often *sounded* quite as cautious as Freud. For instance, in his paper "General Aspects of Dream Psychology" (in *The Structure and Dynamics of the Psyche;* Vol. 8, Collected Works) Jung first states blandly that "in the superstition of all times and races the dream has been regarded as a truth-telling oracle." He then adds with stiffly studied detachment, that "making allowances for exaggeration and prejudice, there is always a grain of truth in such widely disseminated views." At other times he was a good deal less cautious.

In his clinical practice, Jung encountered a number of precognitive cases. As he naturally dealt with these in terms of analytical psychology, definitions are in order. In her book *An Introduction to Jung's Psychology* (London, 1953), Dr. Frieda Fordham defines Jung's use of "collective" as the "psychic contents which are not common to one individual but to many." Thus, when these are unconscious, they are termed the "collective unconscious." Jung's "archetype" is defined as "a content of the collective unconscious which is the psychological counterpart of instinct," also "loosely used to designate a collective image or symbol."

Jung's concepts are illustrated by the case of a patient who had a suicidal prophetic dream. The man, about fifty years old, had been a casual acquaintance of Jung. He had an academic education and liked to tease Jung about his "game" of dream interpretation. With his usual playful approach, he once told of the following dream:

"He was alone in the mountains, and wanted to climb a very high, steep mountain which he could see towering in front of him. At first the ascent was laborious, but then it seemed to him that the higher he climbed the more he felt himself being drawn towards the summit. Faster and faster he climbed, and gradually a sort of ecstasy came over him. He felt he was actually soaring up on wings, and when he reached the top he seemed to weigh nothing at all, and stepped lightly off into empty space. Here he awoke."

The man, an ardent mountain climber, wanted to know what Jung thought of the dream. Jung waited; he discovered that this man loved to go climbing without a guide, was fascinated by the danger of it, and enjoyed daring escapades. Jung writes, "I asked myself what it could be that impelled him to seek out such dangerous situations, apparently with an almost morbid enjoyment."

The man, now more serious, added that he did not fear danger; he regarded a death in the mountains as very beautiful. To Jung, this remark conveyed an unacknowledged wish for suicide. The man further insisted that he would never "give up" his mountains; they were an escape from his family: "This sticking at home does not suit me."

Jung saw in this a "deeper reason for his passion." The man's marriage was a failure. There was nothing to keep him at home. Professionally, too, he was deeply dissatisfied. Jung says, "It occurred to me that his uncanny passion for the mountains must be an avenue of escape from an existence that had become intolerable to him. I therefore privately interpreted the dream as follows: Since he still clung on to life in spite of himself, the ascent of the mountain was at first laborious. But the more he surrendered himself to his passion, the more it lured him on and lent wings to his feet. Finally, it lured him completely out of himself: he lost all sense of bodily weight and climbed even higher than the mountain, out into empty space. Obviously, this meant death in the mountains."

After a pause in their conversation, the man asked Jung again what he thought of the dream. Jung told him frankly that he was seeking death in the mountains, and that, with such an attitude, he stood a remarkably good chance of finding it.

"But that is absurd," he replied, laughing. "On the contrary, I am seeking my health in the mountains."

Jung was unable to make his warning penetrate. Six months later, when descending from a dangerous peak, this man literally did step off into space. In fact, he fell on a companion standing on a ledge below him, and both men were killed.

In his paper on dream psychology, Jung compared dreams with the body's biological defense mechanisms: just as a fever counteracts infection, dreams compensate for a lack, or help to fill a need. Jung edged toward the idea that a deeply felt psychological need, expressed in a dream, might later be fulfilled by a corresponding event; a man might, as in the case of the mountaineer, consciously act out an event which his unconscious had earlier expressed a wish for in a dream. Jung suggested that the unconscious, expressed in a dream, might hold a wider view of possible future events than the waking conscious. Thus, a dream might "have the value of a positive, guiding idea or of an aim whose vital meaning would be greatly superior to that of the momentarily constellated conscious content."

But having acknowledged that a precognitive dream might open the door toward a future event in conscious, daylight existence, Jung quickly qualified this view. He was not a man to let such a daring thought stand unchallenged, even if he had expressed it himself. He quickly cautioned his readers to "distinguish between the *prospective* function of dreams and their *compensatory* function." The "prospective function" of a dream, he said, amounts to "an anticipation in the unconscious of future conscious achievements, something like a preliminary exercise or sketch, or a plan roughed out in advance." He then dealt with the concept of prophecy:

"The occurrence of prospective dreams cannot be denied. It would be wrong to call them prophetic, because at bottom they are no more prophetic than a medical diagnosis or a weather forecast. They are merely an anticipatory combination of probabilities which may coincide with the actual behavior of things but need not necessarily agree in every detail. Only in the latter case can we speak of 'prophecy.'

"That the prospective function of dreams is sometimes greatly superior to the combinations we can consciously foresee is not surprising, since a dream results from a fusion of subliminal elements and is thus a combination of all the perceptions, thoughts, and feelings which consciousness has not registered because of their feeble accentuation. In addition, dreams can rely on subliminal memory traces that are no longer able to influence consciousness effectively. With regard to prognosis, therefore, dreams are often in a much more favourable position than consciousness."

But hardly has Jung given the dream a prognostic superiority over our waking self than he urges caution once again:

"Although the prospective function is, in my view, an essential characteristic of dreams, one would do well not to overestimate this function, for one might easily be led to suppose that the dream is a kind of psychopomp [someone, as in Greek mythology, who conducts souls to the place of the dead], which, because of superior knowledge, infallibly guides life in the right direction. However much people underestimate the psychological significance of dreams, there is an equally great danger that anyone who is constantly preoccupied with dream analysis will overestimate the significance of the unconscious for real life. . . ."

In one central piece of research and writing, C. G. Jung

managed to put, as the English say, the cat among the pigeons. This was "Synchronicity: An Acausal Connecting Principle" in *The Interpretation of Nature and the Psyche* (New York, 1955), a long essay that ranges across psychology, philosophy, physics, parapsychology, and adjacent sciences. Its significance to prophetic experiences lies with the challenge which it offers psychology and physics in the time-space concept. Although Jung never suggests that a deeply felt human need will actually bring about certain events, he repeatedly emphasizes the correlation between emotion and event. As he puts it: "Synchronicity, therefore, means the simultaneous occurrence of a certain psychic state with one or more external events which appear as meaningful parallels to the momentary subjective state—and, in certain cases, vice versa." This is relevant to precognition, because Jung does not then let the word "simultaneous" stand in the way of an event happening in the future, as it is commonly perceived. "In all these cases," he states, "whether it is a question of spatial or of temporal ESP, we find a simultaneity of the normal or ordinary state with another state or experience which is not causally derivable from it, and whose objective existence can only be verified afterwards." He explores this idea further:

"The definition must be borne in mind particularly when it is a question of future events. They are evidently not *synchronous* but are *synchronistic*, since they are experienced as psychic images *in the present,* as though the objective event already existed. An unexpected content which is directly or indirectly connected with some objective external event coincides with the ordinary psychic state: this is what I call synchronicity, and I maintain that we are dealing with exactly the same category of events, whether their objectivity appears separated from consciousness in space or in time."

Jung cites Dr. Rhine's precognition experiments and continues: "How could an event remote in space and time produce a corresponding psychic image when the transmission of energy necessary for this is not even thinkable? However incomprehensible it may appear, we are finally compelled to assume that there is in the unconscious something like an *a priori* knowledge of the immediate existence of events which lacks any causal basis. At any rate, our conception of causality is incapable of explaining the facts."

Jung felt that precognitive phenomena are often accompanied by "archetypal" situations. In his 1958 paper on "A Psychological View of Conscience" (*Civilization in Transi-*

tion, Vol. 10, Collected Works), he relates time and space to his "synchronicity" concept. Specifically, Jung used the word "synchronicity" to "indicate the fact that, in cases of telepathy, precognition and similar inexplicable phenomena, one can very frequently observe an archetypal situation. This may be connected with the nature of the archetype, for the collective unconscious, unlike the individual unconscious, is one and the same everywhere, in all individuals, just as all biological functions and all instincts are the same in all members of the same species. Apart from the more subtle *synchronicity,* we can also observe in the instincts, for instance, in the migratory instincts, a distinct *synchronism.* And since the parapsychological phenomena associated with the unconscious psyche show a peculiar tendency to relativize the categories of time and space, the collective unconscious must have a spaceless and timeless quality. Consequently, there is some probability that an archetypal situation will be accompanied by synchronistic phenomena, as in the case of death, in whose vicinity such phenomena are relatively frequent."

Thus Jung seemed to feel that a precognitive dream of someone's death should fall into that basic, primitive, emotion-laden area of man's psyche which he calls "archetypal," and that all this takes place in man's collective unconscious (that depository of all we are and have ever been), which is both spaceless and timeless. Again, of course, we have the hypothesis that very basic factors must be at work if the present and the future are to be fused into a precognitive or—as Jung will admit in certain cases—an outright prophetic experience.

Jung regarded some premonitions as remnants of the child's world. In "The Significance of the Father in the Destiny of the Individual" *(Freud and Psychoanalysis,* Vol. 4, Collected Works), he stated in 1908 that as the mind matures, parental influences fade into the unconscious, but that out of this reservoir "the infantile situation still sends up dim, premonitory feelings, feelings of being secretly guided by other-worldly influences," just as "the power which forces the bird to migrate is not produced by the bird itself, but derives from its ancestors." A similar man-animal analogy occurs in Jung's 1958 monograph "Flying Saucers: A Modern Myth." *(Civilization in Transition,* Vol. 10, Collected Works). He says that there exists "the possibiility of a natural or absolute 'knowledge,' when the unconscious psyche coincides with objective facts. This is a problem that has been raised by the discoveries of parapsychology. 'Absolute knowledge' oc-

PROPHECY IN OUR TIME

curs not only in telepathy and precognition, but also in biology, for instance in the attunement of the virus of hydrophobia to the anatomy of dog and man," or the wasps' "apparent knowledge of where the motor ganglia are located in the caterpillar that is to nourish the wasps' progeny, the emissions of light by certain fishes and insects with almost 100-percent efficiency, the directional signal of carrier pigeons, the warning of earthquakes given by chickens and cats. . . ."

Jung's final word on the subject came in 1960, in a letter to Professor Hans Bender of the University of Freiburg im Breisgau, Germany. He stated that even Dr. Rhine's quantitative precognition experiments at Duke University were "conditioned by a psychological factor, namely the attraction of novelty." He reiterated his earlier views, but without circumlocution, adding that "the majority of synchronistic phenomena occur in archetypal situations, that is, in situations arousing the emotional patterns connected with risks, dangers, fateful circumstances, and the like. They manifest themselves in telepathy, second sight, precognition, and so on."

Disciples are often more daring than their masters. Not unlike the priests interpreting the more elusive utterings of the Delphic Oracle, some of Jung's students have formulated his ideas more clearly than old C. G. himself. Or, at least, they supplied fresh case data. Dr. C. T. Frey-Wehrlin, Secretary of the Clinic and Research Center for Jungian Psychology, Zurich, contributed a detailed case history in this connection entitled simply, "A Prophetic Dream," to the volume *Spectrum Psychologiae* (Zurich, 1965). The dream centered around the fate of a forty-four-year-old man who visited Dr. Frey-Wehrlin in 1962. The patient, who had failed in many areas of life, felt "psychosexually" overwhelmed by his sister, a woman three years older. He realized that, in fact, their relationship had been entirely correct; but his disturbed condition became serious enough to require his hospitalization in the fall of 1963.

The patient's sister then came to see Dr. Frey-Wehrlin. She had married late in life and felt about as strongly linked with her brother as he did to her. Her marriage, on the whole a good one, was severely taxed by the brother's illness. Relating a dream, she said: "My mother and my brother are breaking into my house, with a great deal of noise, at three o'clock in the morning, and demand to be sheltered. I find this quite annoying, but begin fixing the beds. My husband, rather subdued, remains in the background."

In this case, then, the sister feels that her brother is the—

presumably sexual—intruder, rather than the other way around. The analyst refers to "the symmetry of these events" as "partial mutual identification." He then cites a dream which the sister recalled as having had eight years earlier, in 1955:

"I am walking through a rather dark pine forest, down a wide and steep road, toward the edge of the woods. There, golden in the evening sun, stands a large and comfortable house. On its gabled front, sculpted in clear and sharp letters, I read: 'June 17, 1964.'"

The woman regarded this dream as prophetic. She wondered what the significance of this date, then no longer very remote, might possibly be.

In mid-June 1964, the woman who had this dream traveled in the Engadine region of Switzerland. The 17th was coming closer. Would it, she wondered, be the last day of her life? But when it arrived, it was just another vacation day. Together with a couple, she went on a hike. It was a hot day, and they came to a cool lake. At one point, the husband of her friend referred to the death of his sister; he had, on that occasion, turned off his telephone by mistake, and had heard the news only the next day.

Back at the hotel, the woman went to bed early. A female relative telephoned at 11 P.M., but decided not to have the woman awakened. The next morning, the woman received this news: Her brother, who had been transferred to a different hospital for treatment of physical illness, had left the premises. At the deserted edge of a lake he had taken an overdose of sleeping pills and then drowned himself. Death had occurred between noon and 3 P.M.

Dr. Frey-Wehrlin gives these additional details: The crucial dream had been recorded several months before the brother's death; the events and conversations of the hiking trip had been confirmed by the woman's friend. Although the analyst refrains from any comment, the "mutual identification" of brother and sister, reinforced by their emotional involvement with each other, makes this a prophetic case of true psychological significance.

Aside from such new case material, Jungians have sought to apply and organize some of the master's theories. In his paper "Psychosomatic Medicine from the Jungian Point of View," Dr. C. A. Meier points toward practical psychomedical application of the synchronicity concept. While too specialized for popular summary, this paper (*The Journal of Analytical Psychology*, Vol. 8, No. 2, 1963) represents a significant bridge between theory and practice. In this context, Mrs. Aniela Jaffé's paper, "C. G. Jung and Parapsychology," and her contribution to the comprehensive symposium *Science and ESP* (London, 1967) should be cited. Mrs. Jaffé, who was Jung's close collaborator during the years before his death, notes that "prophetic dreams and precognitions were no rarity" in his life, but "whenever they occurred he noted them with surprise—one is tempted to say, with the awe due the miraculous." She emphasizes with vigor that, whatever backing and filling one notes in Jung's earlier writings, his ideas after 1946 were characterized by the ultimate concept of a merging between psyche and matter (he used the word "psychoid" to define this process). She writes:

"Jung's investigations had led him to the conclusion that beyond the world of the psyche, with its causal manifestations in time and space, there must lie a 'transpsychic reality' where time and space are no longer of absolute but relative validity; what the psyche experiences as past, present and future merges 'there' into an unknowable unity of timelessness, and what appears to consciousness as near and far combines 'there' into a likewise unknowable spacelessness."

And that, for the time being, is the most authoritative summary of Jung's search for the reality of prophecy in our lives—his and ours.

10 Premonition on the Couch

Psychoanalysts keep records of their patients' dreams, and they are professionally conditioned to face esoteric truths about men and women. What is an analyst to do when a patient reports seeing a certain event in his dream, and when this event takes place later on—perhaps in the analyst's own life? Well, at least he can try to be honest with himself, with his colleagues, in his writings, and in his ruminations. When the vocabulary of parapsychology and psychoanalysis becomes intertwined, an experienced guide is needed. We can turn, for such guidance, to Dr. Emilio Servadio, in Rome, President of the Italian Society of Psychoanalysis. He has pointed out, for instance, the curious situation of dreams convincingly masquerading as "precognitive" or "telepathic." In doing so, he has moved a long way from such earlier analysts as Hitschmann and Zulliger, who were satisfied to document Freud's original concept of premonitory dreams as mere dramatizations of a suppressed wish, supported by retrospective falsification.

Servadio and other independent-minded psychoanalysts have recorded too many apparently telepathic and/or precognitive dreams to stand pat. They have given new meaning to Freud's idea that a dream's essence need not be apparent from its surface (its "manifest" content), but may be even more significantly found beneath this surface (in its "latent" content). Dr. Servadio believes that an apparently quite "normal" dream may well masquerade as being precognitive or telepathic (in other words, it pretends to be "paranormal"). Also, he finds that many a strictly "normal" dream may reveal truly "paranormal" elements, once you examine it carefully enough. Writing in the *International Journal of Parapsychology* (Vol. IV, No. 1, 1962), he notes that an apparently routine dream that is given an analytical explanation "may lead to the recognition of a telepathic—and perhaps also precognitive—communication, where, at first sight, and considering the manifest content" exclusively, "nobody would have been able to perceive it." Dr. Servadio looks forward to "ample and detailed confirmation" of this viewpoint, but warns that future research will demand "complete knowledge both of the mechanism of the normal dream and of the pertinent instruments of investigation made available by modern depth psychology." This, in his opinion, could lead to "a new comprehensive pluridimensional psychology."

In Dr. Servadio's own best-known case of precognition in the psychoanalytic situation, three elements stand out. The first is the presence of what the Italian analyst regards as "latent" material that might be called paranormal. The second is an interlacing of telepathic and precognitive aspects. And the third is the involvement of the psychoanalyst himself, the patient's attention-demanding pressures, and the emotional constellation in which the analyst finds himself.

Published in the *International Journal of Psychoanalysis* (January-February 1955), Dr. Servadio's report deals with a patient in his thirties, "suffering from an obsessional neurosis and labouring under the delayed influence of an emotionally 'dry' childhood." The dream that attracted the analyst's attention occurred on the night of August 27, 1953. The patient found himself, in his dream, near Dr. Servadio's house, not the real one but something "like a cottage in a suburb of a California city." The treatment, incidentally, was taking place in Rome, where Dr. Servadio has his practice.

The patient reported that in this dream the analyst's mind had "placed a bowl of Italian noodles near the garden gate." He "went for this dish," feeling hungry, cold, and miserable. While he made his way toward the bowl, a car drove up, and the patient said, "I knew that you and your wife were inside. I got alarmed and ran away."

The dream changed. The patient now saw himself inside the house, together with Mrs. Servadio and "three daughters." One of these the dreamer knew to be the analyst's daughter, then fourteen years old. The others were pretty blonde girls, one eight years old, the other three or four. The patient added: "I still felt miserable and neglected, although I seemed to know that your family was nice and had nothing particular against me."

Viewing the dream against the background of Dr. Servadio's own situation at that time, the two parts revealed telepathic and precognitive elements. The analyst had shortly before returned with his wife, Clara, from a visit abroad. The patient could not know that Mrs. Servadio had left Rome again; she was, in fact, at the time of his dream, near the sea, living in a little house with a garden. She was accompanied not only by her own daughter but by two little blonde nieces, one eight years old, the other three and a half.

Dr. Servadio himself felt rather lonely at this point, annoyed, he recalled, that "it was a maid-servant, and not my wife," who looked after his meals. On the evening of the 27th, the analyst had invited an American colleague, Dr. Ludwig Eidelberg, and his wife to dinner, being "especially eager for them to have some very special Italian noodles in a particular Roman restaurant, internationally known for this dish." Two members of the Italian Psychoanalytic Society were to join them at what any student of Rome's culinary landscape will recognize as Alfredo's Restaurant.

But in order to have time for the noodle feast, Dr. Servadio had to cancel an 8 o'clock appointment with the patient for the 28th. He could not reach him by telephone, and finally had to send his maid to cancel their appointment; this was the only time he ever had to send the maid on such an errand. The patient's dream had precognized the "exceptional occurrence" of the maid as messenger. Neither—and this is the crucial precognitive element—could the patient, at the time of his dream, know that Dr. Servadio would so dramatically "neglect" him as to cancel their appointment, in order to, as he put it, "offer a dish of noodles to others...."

Servadio categorizes the patient's dream knowledge of his wife's absence, her stay in a house by the sea, and the presence of the three little girls as telepathic, while the appearance of the maid and the bowl of noodles fall into the precognitive category. "It is possible, of course," Dr. Servadio writes, "that on the night of August 27 I may have thought vaguely of cancelling [the] session; but most certainly I had *not* thought of sending my maid to him with this announcement," but did so "only after having vainly tried to call him on the telephone."

The analyst notes that the dream would have been completely justified, from a psychodynamic viewpoint, if the patient had openly known all the facts to which the dream referred. His resentment over being fed like a dog while the analyst was driving about with his wife and had sent the maid with a miserable noodle dish was appropriate. But to build up a dream which "could thus make perfect and complete sense," Dr. Servadio notes, the patient's "unconscious apparently supplemented his conscious notions with extrasensorily perceived material."

However, when it comes to picking up precognitive and telepathic data, patients show a strong tendency—Dr. Servadio says, and several of his colleagues completely agree—toward "unmasking" what goes on inside the analyst's own mind to be "thrown, as it were, in the analyst's face." He adds: "Viewed from this angle, the dream is a challenge to the analyst's attempt to conceal, or to repress, something which might have appeared—or to a certain extent may have actually been—unfriendly and hostile to the patient." Dr. Servadio admits that he had, indeed, harbored somewhat hostile attitudes toward the patient, who, however, tended to exaggerate them. Servadio notes that it has by now become accepted—by psychoanalysts who observe precognitive and telepathic occurrences in their practice—that a "dovetailing" of the analyst's emotional pattern with that of the patient, "an unconscious dynamical configuration *à deux*," seems to be a strong precondition for parapsychological dreams or comments. In the language of the dream, as Dr. Servadio sums it up, the patient had made these points:

"Don't I know that you think more about your wife than

about myself? Don't I know that you offer nice food to strangers, and not to me? Don't I know that your wife gives her love and affection to young people, while *I* have no motherly woman who cares or has cared for me?

"Don't I know that you are going to neglect my needs, sending your maid to me and pretending that you 'give me something,' whereas in reality you disturb and prevent my feeding? Don't I know that all this goes parallel with similar feelings and reactions of yours, which are *your own* and should not interfere with my treatment?

"Well, yes: just as I felt my father's 'murderous' wishes when I was a child, so I can feel, and describe in detail, all this information, your hostility, your neglect of me, and the emotional drives which have been and are yours, that you have attempted to conceal from me. Yes: in spite of your efforts to 'keep me out' of all this, here you are: I do know!"

And, indeed, he knew a good part of all this—before it happened—and before it had even been planned.

Another therapist who has kept careful records of prophetic dreams is Dr. R. K. Greenbank, Associate Professor of Psychiatry at Temple University Medical Center. He relates, in a paper entitled "A Prophetic Dream" (in *Corrective Psychiatry and Journal of Social Therapy*, March 1966, Vol. 12, No. 2), the dream of a married schoolteacher in her mid-twenties who suffered "mild anxiety attacks" during her teaching experience. She reported her dream as follows:

"I was having dinner with three men, two of whom I saw distinctly and recognized. The third man's face was never visible, but I clearly remember his physique, height, and words. After dinner, we were all to spend the night in the house which belonged to this third person. I go to sleep, am awakened once to feel that my life is in danger, but go back to sleep. Then I reawakened with an intense feeling that the unknown man is going to commit suicide.

"In my dream," the patient continues, "I get out of bed, search the room, and find an incomplete suicide note. This man enters my room. I hide the note, he gives me a $20 bill and leaves. The scene then changes to the man's bedroom. He asks me for a rope, which I cannot supply. I knew he wanted to kill himself. Then I go to the door, stop and ask, 'Why are you doing this?' He answers, 'Because it hurts too much!'"

At this point, the patient recalls, she woke up. She immediately thought of a friend, identified as "Mr. M." She went back to sleep, but regarded the dream as important enough to recall it during her analysis with Dr. Greenbank.

A week later, the patient provided details on an actual suicide, confirmed by newspaper reports. She had been with her friend, who was identical in physique and manner to the "unknown" man in the dream. They had dined together, while two other men were in the room with them. The schoolteacher had bought some clothing for him earlier, at his request, and he had reimbursed her with a $20 bill. Nothing apparent in his behavior indicated a change in his usual disposition.

The next evening, to the surprise of his friends, this man committed suicide by jumping from the bedroom of his New York apartment. As Dr. Greenbank relates these events, the man was "pronounced dead at the scene at the precise hour of the morning in which the patient had awakened from her dream a week earlier, and on the same day of the week." The schoolteacher could not recall ever having a similar dream, in content and emotional impact. Like all of M.'s friends, she had been completely unaware of his suicide plans. Dr. Greenbank adds:

"The dream and its suicidal content were never verbally or consciously communicated to the victim. In fact, the dream was deliberately kept secret from any other person except for its description to the psychoanalyst. It did not occur to the patient to discuss this dream with anyone else, since she was following the rule of psychoanalysis that material discussed in the treatment situation should not be discussed with people outside the office."

Dr. Greenbank, in his comments on this case, shows himself to be fully aware of the counterarguments that rise as soon as a prophetic dream of this type is presented. He admits that simple coincidence is always possible, but regards the chances of the dream and the suicide's happening "within the same week, by chance alone" as rather slight. He then examines the possibility of "fraud for gain"; that the patient might have told a falsehood, not for any financial advantage, but to please the analyst, "especially where treatment was progressing well, as it was in this case." He says that "if all the details were known only from the patient, this gain could not be completely excluded." However, the dream was reported to the analyst before the suicide took place; date and details were then later confirmed from newspaper reports.

Next, Dr. Greenbank examines the often crucial element: the notorious unreliability of witnesses and testimony. He comments: "It may well be true that the dream as reported was not the same as the actual dream. This is something that we have no way of checking at the present time. But our inability to do this is not crucial. If there was distortion, then the dreamer's mind performed the distortion. Also, one cannot absolutely exclude distortion on the part of the psychoanalyst as he recorded the dream. However, his relative lack of strong emotional involvement and greater training would tend in the direction of reducing such inaccuracy."

Dr. Greenbank reported two other dreams that seemed to prophesy "psychosomatic" events at the American Psychoanalytic Association's meeting in New York on December 4, 1959. His account is reproduced below in full, as it integrates psychological impressions with detailed narration:

"A forty-two-year-old, intelligent housewife undertook psychiatric treatment for a neurosis characterized by depression and gastric symptoms. These were described as 'butterflies' and 'nervousness in the stomach.' She responded well to relatively brief psychoanalytically oriented psychotherapy, with symptomatic relief.

"The patient was a twin, born in a foreign country. At the age of six weeks, allegedly for financial reasons, her mother offered the choice of either twin to a childless, forty-four-year-old woman. The patient was adopted and brought to America. The rigid, possessive, and controlling foster mother taught the patient to be a 'very good girl.' She was taught to 'swallow' all her angry feelings and never to express anger, especially toward older people.

"Her development was otherwise apparently normal. After graduation from high school she worked briefly as a bank clerk. She then married an aeronautical engineer. Her twin, who had remained in Europe, died a week following the patient's marriage. Within the next few years, both of her foster parents died. This left the patient with neither a family of her own, nor one by adoption.

"The chart, reproduced below [on page 114], shows the sequence of events.

"Five months before the patient undertook psychotherapy, she was hospitalized for the treatment of a seriously bleeding peptic ulcer. Routine medical care relieved her symptoms.

"The ulcer was said to have been precipitated by the visit of her mother-in-law, who, like her foster mother, was a hostile and demanding woman; during this time, the patient felt realistically very angry. She felt quite unable to express this anger for fear of hurting her husband's feelings.

"One month prior to the first hospitalization, she had

Dream A. This was before her mother-in-law's visit. The patient was, and previously had been, without gastrointestinal symptoms.

" 'I was sitting on the toilet in the bathroom and all of a sudden the floor was covered with blood. It had welled up and flooded from my nose and mouth.' The patient, in the dream, was wearing a pink nightgown and sitting on the toilet as though she were sitting on a chair. She was alone. The vivid dream awakened her.

"The following morning: 'When I woke up, I thought the dream was nutty, so I told it to my husband, and he laughed, and I laughed, because it was so silly.'

"The patient remembers no other dreams involving blood or events of this nature. One month following the dream, the patient awoke in the morning with a pain in the abdomen. She felt nauseated and, on arising, she fainted. She went to the bathroom, wearing her only pink nightgown, closed the door, and sat upon the toilet. Her next memory was that she saw the floor coming up towards her. She had fainted. When she regained consciousness, she found the bathroom floor covered with blood which had welled out of her nose and mouth. In fainting, she had let out a cry which brought her husband and doctor to her. She was then hospitalized and treated medically. At the hospital, both patient and husband recalled the dream.

"The patient, while on a pleasant vacation [Dream B], dreamed 'she would have to enter a hospital for surgery.' Three days later, she became aware of an acute recurrence of an old Bartholin's cyst infection. This had been dormant for several years. On the occasion of the original infection, which had been treated at home, she was told, If this recurs, you will require surgery in a hospital. The pain of her infection was such that she had to return home and was operated upon successfully in the hospital. When she developed the infection, she said, 'Well, here is my dream come true; I wish it hadn't.' "

CHART

	WEEKS AFTER DREAM A
Dream A	0
Mother-in-Law Visit	3
Hospitalization for Ulcer	4
Start of Psychiatric Treatment	28
Dream B	50
Cyst Surgery	51

Dr. Greenbank observed that the patient had "little to be gained" from fooling the therapist, as it "in no way affected her treatment," and she was "consciously unaware of the psychiatrist's interest in this type of dream." The husband also remembered the original dream vividly. Seen analytically, Dr. Greenbank stated, "it is possible that the patient was unconsciously aware of gastrointestinal symptoms which would prophesy future bleeding. However, X rays showed scarring, which indicated that the patient must have had symptomatic ulcers previous to the one which bled." The psychiatrist noted that this woman patient showed "no awareness" of bleeding as a symptom of an ulcer and did not think of an ulcer at the time she vomited blood. She said, "It was pretty frightening, because I know that you don't bleed without something being seriously wrong, and although I had no idea of what it was, I feared for my life."

There is a certain ingrown quality about the patient-therapist type of prophetic experience; it seems cramped, somehow, and outside the open field of general human experience. There is, surely, a special rapport or hostility between analyst and analysand for which there is no true equivalent outside the analytic setting, probably not even in the parent-child situation. To the layman, an even more confining quality is associated with experiences that occur inside a therapeutic environment; it is a world unto its own while subject to all the pressures, including ethnic factors, that exist in the greater world around it.

Dr. Greenbank's account of precognition concerning a Japanese surgeon is, however, sufficiently remarkable and well documented to invite the attention of the informed layman who wants to understand some of the elusive intricacies that seem to affect prophetic experiences. In this case, a senior surgical resident was interviewed by an intern interested in psychiatry. The resident's roommate let on that his companion, a Japanese surgeon, was depressed and behaving strangely; he had, for instance, kept "a pile of tiny bits of paper, several inches high, on his dresser."

The psychiatrically oriented intern concluded that the Japanese surgeon was suffering from an acute paranoid schizophrenic reaction. He feared that he might harm others, but did not think of suicide as a possiblility. Other medical authorities felt that he was simply suffering from "homesickness." Psychiatric consultation was impractical.

The night after the interview, the surgical resident asked to be left alone. He said, "I am writing a letter." Written in

Japanese, this letter said, "I am a disgrace to my profession; I have heard repeated profane and derogatory comments about me over the doctors' paging system; I, therefore, have no honorable choice open but to die." He then committed suicide by slashing both femoral arteries (the arteries of the thigh) with a surgical knife. He bled to death in his bed.

Dr. Greenbank noted that "while no one consciously thought of suicide, the awareness of his plans apparently made an impression at a deeper level on at least two of the people concerned." The roommate reported a horrible dream which awakened him from sleep, the sort of thing that just did not happen to him: "I dreamed of a chicken with his head cut off flopping around the room; it was spurting blood all over. I was terrified."

The intern who had worried about the Japanese resident continued to be concerned about him all through the night. He was awakened at 4 A.M. by an emergency phone call from the hospital ward. He was not consciously thinking of the resident when he passed a large, bright-red Coca-Cola machine in the hall and thought, "What if I should find the resident in a pool of blood." He had not yet come to the door of the resident's room. As he did pass it, he noted that it was slightly open and the light was on. His thoughts were consciously, "Gosh, he must have stayed up all night worrying." He went back to say hello. He opened the door and found the bed covered with blood and the Japanese resident dead. Greenbank observes that "two doctors were aware, unconsciously, of the exact method that was to be used in the suicide (bleeding to death), but neither had conscious thoughts even of the possibility of suicide."

A second suicide case reveals similar aspects. It includes a permanent record, a painting, revealing an individual's fantasies particularly relevant to the case. As in other instances, the borderline between telepathy and precognition is thin. Still, Dr. Greenbank, intimately familiar with its details, categorizes it as "prophetic."

The situation itself is dramatic. It involved a young woman college student who began psychotherapy following serious depression. Her mother was a paranoid schizophrenic; her father had committed suicide when the patient was two years old; a young uncle had hanged himself in a house across the street when the girl was in her teens. The eighteen months of therapy had been, Dr. Greenbank recalls, "stormy." In the midst of it, the girl saw a woman throw herself under a subway train; this made the student "feel better"—it apparently showed her that suicide was a concrete way out of her dilemma.

The girl had left her psychotic mother, but had encountered a "mass of emotional trauma." Visits to the therapist had to be cut down. In the midst of all this, an armed man, described by Greenbank as "of another race," forced his way into the girl's apartment and nearly choked her to death in a rape attempt, but was frightened off. Her mother was hospitalized with a recurrence of her psychosis, and the family blamed the girl, in a traditionally rigid way: "If you had stayed home, this would not have happened." The girl also began having economic and social problems. Her main emotional support, her successful college work, was threatened by the chaos around her.

The next time this girl came to the therapeutic session, she carried a razor in her pocket. Because she was obviously disturbed, Dr. Greenbank offered her an additional hour if she would wait while the next patient was being interviewed. She accepted this suggestion, but during the hour locked herself in the office toilet and slashed her wrist. She lost about a pint of blood from superficial wounds. When she was found, the therapist treated her cuts and went ahead with a "satisfactory" therapy hour.

When the girl came home, she had a telephone call from a young female art student, who asked, "What happened at seven tonight? I had the strangest feeling and drew a picture of it." The young artist had been sitting in her living room, reading a magazine, when she felt impelled to draw the picture of an upraised, tense, transparent human hand against a multicolored background of blotches of vivid color, laced with irregular thin lines. The wrist of the hand was cut. Brilliant red blood was flowing freely from the cut. A number of tiny human figures were drawn as climbing up on the hand.

The artist commented that "the hand represents a human being wanting to commit suicide." The little figures, she said, were "mocking human beings, for taking life so seriously, instead of accepting it." She said the thin lines represent "life as a puzzle or broken as glass."

The artist was seen by Dr. Greenbank as "clinically normal," and "with no particular knowledge of psychiatry." The two young women had had no communication "of an ordinary kind," as Greenbank phrases it, for two weeks before the drawing. Neither the patient, her therapist, nor the artist could have known beforehand that the patient would have an appointment at that particular day or hour. The appointments were irregular, scheduled only a week in advance. As for the specific picture of the suicide attempt—the girl patient's threats and fantasies had always dealt with jumping in front of a train, or taking an overdose of barbiturates.

Dr. Greenbank, in reviewing the case of the Japanese surgeon's suicide in conjunction with the attempt of the girl student, concludes that the first case "is understandable if it is assumed that there is nonverbal and unconscious communication of emotional feelings between individuals," and he adds that "this is reasonably accepted."

He finds that "it is difficult to account for the phenomena on the basis of coincidence alone, especially in Case Two, since the artist had not drawn violence before or after the single water color described." Greenbank says that "the most striking point is the knowledge of the exact moment the suicidal action took place, as well as the method." He writes that "the reliability of the information in both cases is felt to be good," and he finds it difficult to see much in the way of "secondary gain" for the people involved.

Dr. Greenbank believes "the fact that the events were reported within a very short time of their occurrence should help minimize the effects of memory distortion." One cannot help feeling that telepathic elements, at least in these two cases, are potentially very strong. Once it is accepted that precognition can be explained by telepathic communication of intent—then it can be assumed that the intern could have "tuned in," as it were, on the specific plans of the Japanese resident surgeon to cut his arteries, and the young artist could have tuned in at 7 o'clock on the student's intention of cutting her wrists and killing herself by loss of blood.

But the categorization of prophetic statements can be only theoretically clear-cut. The intrusion of clairvoyance on telepathy or of telepathy on precognition are too frequent to permit dogmatic boundary lines to be drawn between these fields. Life is just not neat; rather, it tends to be chaotic, whimsical, and certainly defiant of academic disciplines.

Dr. Greenbank, noting the additional data that has become available since the days of the early or middle-period Freudians, believes that "there is much more known today concerning the explanation of prophetic dreams than there was in the past." He states that accumulated evidence has "increased our scientific sophistication and objectiveness" and "greatly reduced the number of such events that are unexplained." As case material of a precognitive nature mounts up, analysts have begun to use it to deepen their understanding of unconscious mind processes.

11 Beyond Freud

The raw material of psychonanalysis is the abnormal. The confines of their profession force analysts to spend the better part of their days with patients or colleagues, and their main task is to cure emotional instability. Thus, the premonitory or telepathic experiences they encounter usually occur within the patient-analyst relationship. As we have seen, Freud, while struggling for acceptance of his therapeutic ideas and methods, tended to regard reports of psychic phenomena as just another category of neurotic symptoms. Jung, because of his own experiences, took a more tolerant view.

But while the patient-analyst setting restricts observation of apparently prophetic knowledge, it provides a specific means by which such experiences can be documented. Conscientious analysts keep careful, dated records of their patients' reports. Thus, when a precognitive claim becomes reality, they are able to check the actual event against the details and date of the premonitory dream. At times, as Hitschmann noted, they can debunk a patient's prophetic grandeur; at other times, their records help to document the sequence of events.

There is striking agreement among parapsychologically-oriented psychoanalysts on three basic factors concerning psychic phenomena in the analytic situation:

(1) The patient seems to experience a precognitive or telepathic event, most often a dream, at a time when he feels neglected or rejected by the analyst. It seems as if patients sometimes make special efforts to draw attention to themselves and away from others—the analyst's family, other patients, etc.—through the device of startling psychic incidents.

(2) If it weren't for the time reversal, the dream material presented by the patient would often be undistinguished and, in its own setting, orthodox. The material in most such cases

fits the analytical situation, its progress and constellation, quite well—except for the disconcerting fact that the dream comes first and the event on which it seems "based" follows later.

(3) The psychodynamics behind a procognitive dream are, in a number of reported cases, quite classical. Freudian analysts find that Oedipal situations are often strongly involved in precognitive dreams. Jung has reported that a breakthrough of the archetype is usually present in a premonitory experience. To the degree that both terminologies point toward an emotion-laden unconscious pattern of events, they agree on the psychodynamics of precognitive dreaming.

For every dream reported to an analyst, there are doubtless thousands outside the analytic setting on the part of the same patient that remain unremembered, unreported, and unrecorded. When a patient knows that his or her analyst is interested in such phenomena, there seems to be a tendency to please him by making, as it were, an offering of a psychic experience. It is a little like bringing an apple to the teacher.

Dr. Jan Ehrenwald of New York has gone one step further than the above hypothesis. He has developed the concepts of "telepathic leakage" and "doctrinal compliance." These suggest, among other things, that a patient may become aware of his analyst's interests by means of telepathy; also, the patient may comply with the analyst's particular "doctrinal" orientation (Freudian, Jungian, Adlerian, etc.) by experiencing or selecting events that fit "Oedipal," "archetypal," or other molds.

Freud and his immediate successors did not have a wide variety of parapsychological case material at hand. But during the 1940's and 1950's a fascinating number of case histories in this area were collected by analysts, geographically as separated as Rome, Italy, and Denver, Colorado. In fact, one of the most adventurous pioneers in this field is Dr. Jule Eisenbud of Denver, author of *The World of Ted Serios* (New York, 1967), which deals with the seemingly paranormal ability of Mr. Serios to project pictorial images from his mind onto photographic film. During several decades of analytical work, first in New York and later in Colorado, Eisenbud collected data on a number of significant cases. His first major paper on precognitive dreams, "Behavioral Correspondences to Normally Unpredictable Future Events," appeared, in two parts, in *The Psychoanalytic Quarterly* (Vol. XXIII, 1954).

At the outset of this paper, Dr. Eisenbud noted that para-

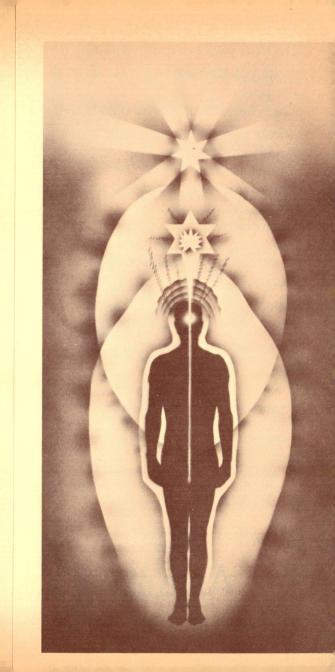

UNRAVELING THE MYSTERY OF MAN ⇨

Astara

800 West Arrow Highway
Upland, Calif. 91786

PLACE
STAMP
HERE

psychology had provoked deep distrust among scientists because of "its extraordinary claim that something on the order of genuine foreknowledge—more or less accurate prophecy or 'prevision'—of the normally unknown future is possible." Precognition, he said, is so "unacceptable to most members of Western culture" that even the Church, though tolerant of miracles, has taken "a negative stand" on prophecy. He noted, too, that Freud's well-known curiosity, fairness, and tolerance had not kept him from "complete, unconditional rejection" of foreknowledge. After some backing and filling, Eisenbud writes, Freud in 1925 returned to his original assumption that "such things as genuinely prophetic dreams cannot be."

Eisenbud recalls Hitschmann's and Zulliger's efforts to follow Freud's lead and show that, instead of "genuine premonition in dream or waking state," they encountered "an unconscious wish deriving from the past." He mentions that these analysts attributed "sometimes extraordinary correspondence with future events" in every case to "chance, unconscious self-deception or self-fulfillment, with strong motives of narcissism and magical omnipotence of thought." It isn't that Eisenbud does not allow for such "normal devices" as these in producing pseudo-prophetic experiences; but he wants to leave room for open-mindedness toward the genuine event when it does occur.

Dr. Eisenbud is well aware of the limitations in recording or proving precognition, because "the very spontaneity and unexpectedness" of the experience makes control of methods, personnel, and chance factors virtually impossible. The perfect case, he feels, can hardly be said to exist, as "there is always some inherent and unresolvable ambiguity in the case to which objection can be taken." After allowing for all this, Eisenbud presents two cases from his collection. The first one took place while he was still practicing in New York, and he reports it as follows:

"A patient dreamed that he was having an argument with his mother-in-law, who was rather sharp in her attempts to dissuade him from going swimming. Then he found himself in bathing trunks and robe in the lobby of a hotel which was either the Pennsylvania or the Wellington. An elevator took him up to the top floor, where he was let out in what appeared to be a service corridor. He felt anxious about being stranded there."

Dr. Eisenbud notes that the patient reported this dream at about 10 A.M., but was unable to fix the time of its occurrence during the previous night. He had awakened, he claimed, at about 7:30, his usual time. Now, at least one hour after the latest time at which this dream could have taken place, an odd crisis occurred at the Hotel Pennsylvania, now the Statler-Hilton, at Seventh Avenue and 33rd Street in Manhattan. Workmen were revarnishing the inside of an elevator when a drum of cleaning fluid blew up on the level of the top service floor, where there were no guest rooms.

No one was hurt by the explosion, but the blast caused a water-main break on one of the lower floors, which filled the hotel lobby with five inches of water. *The New York Times* reported the incident (April 28, 1944) with this detail: "One group of hotel guests seemed to find the flood particularly amusing. One of this group went around shaking hands with hotel employees and saying 'Cornell '44'. The group was the Cornell swimming team." There was a caption under an accompanying picture which read: "After waters receded in the Hotel Pennsylvania: cleaning up the lobby which was flooded by a bursting water main." The picture showed the clock in the hotel lobby at 11:05 A.M.

Dr. Eisenbud observes: the dreamer had, in fact, placed himself either in the Hotel Pennsylvania or the Wellington; although the hotel did not have a swimming pool, its lobby a few hours later certainly resembled a pool; a university swimming team used this situation to have some fun; the top floor of the hotel, where the dreamer had found himself in a state of unaccountable anxiety, was the scene of the accident that had triggered the event. (The dreamer had no specific association with the Hotel Pennslyvania.)

Dr. Eisenbud notes that the dreamer was a man of marked scientific curiosity; although almost entirely self-tutored, he had made a discovery in physical chemistry from which he derived a good livelihood. He had come to the therapeutic session the night before with ambitious plans for a vital breakthrough in X-ray technique. He left in a rather tense state because the therapist could not reassure him about the feasibility of this project. It was on the following night that he had the swimming-pool dream.

Dr. Eisenbud's analytic approach to such dreams treats their contents, although they unfold in the future, as though they were snippets of past experiences, remnants, or memories. He is, from a psychoanalytic viewpoint, unconcerned with the reverse chronology. He deals with the hotel explosion as if it were "a typical day's residue" and proceeds to interpret its latent content. He found therein the dreamer's childhood and contemporary family relations interwoven with resentment of the analyst.* Quite aside from these elements, Dr. Eisenbud reminds us, precognitive dreams refer almost always to "a current problem in the analyst's own experience, a problem to which the analyst is reacting in terms of his own unconscious anxieties."

What were Dr. Eisenbud's own anxieties as mirrored in the patient's dream? What was the patient trying to tell his therapist? In this case, on the very night of the patient's dream and only a few hours before it, Dr. Eisenbud had tried to coax a hypnotic subject into "precognition." He did this first by regressing the subject, under hypnosis, into his childhood, and then taking him forward into the present, hoping to lead "to a forward displacement in time." Naturally, he recalls, "I had worked myself up to a keen pitch and was considerably on edge. I had no idea how to go about getting my subject to 'jump the time barrier,' and was not particularly optimistic about the outcome of the experiment."

Having first moved the hynotic subject backward in time, to get something like a "running jump" on the future, Dr. Eisenbud gave him a specific task. He suggested that he was holding in his hands *The New York Times* of two days hence, looking at the headlines. What did he see? What did the headline say? The hypnotized subject became restless, and, finally, to please the hypnotist, made up a rather routine headline. Eisenbud concluded the experiment with a feeling of disappointment. When, a day later, the first patient dreamed precognitively of what was soon confirmed in a *New York Times* story, Eisenbud felt that "my analytic patient had, so to speak, 'hijacked' the task given my experimental subject and had, for reasons of his own, carried it off quite brilliantly."

In his own way, then, that patient had given the analyst what he had wanted: "You want headlines two days hence? Here they are . . . Now give me the reassurance I want; tell me to go ahead with *my* revolutionary way of 'seeing.'" But was this really precognition? There is, of course, the "easier" explanation that nothing more unusual than telepathy might have been at work! At this Dr. Eisenbud throws up his hands: this would call for a compound hypothesis involving ordinary telepathy, plus the pure assumption that the patient

---

* As a child, the dreamer reverted to similar situations with the equivalent of the bursting water main, bed wetting.

was quite mistaken as to the time and setting of his dream—an alternative that would be favored only by those who would "rather be hung for a comparative lamb, telepathy, than (to switch metaphors) for the big bad wolf of paranormal 'foreknowledge' of the future."

Another precognitive dream also dramatizes the possible element of rivalry, of a patient's desire to outrank someone else in the analyst's attention. In this case, a woman patient dreamed that she saw her mother in a new automobile, as a car immediately behind her caught fire: "I am frantically alarmed that it may explode and that my mother will get hurt unless she gets out of the way."

Shortly after leaving the analyst's office, the woman came upon a crowd being held back by police. Bits and pieces of a taxi were strewn over the road. She was told that the car had exploded; its gas tank had caught fire. When she came to see the analyst the next time, she said triumphantly, "Well, this time I'm really psychic." In actual fact, Dr. Eisenbud found out from the fire department, the taxi had not exploded, but firemen, in order to prevent the fire from reaching the gas tank, had completely demolished the car.

Aside from the outward elements of the dream, the analyst remembered that a few days earlier he had discussed a *telepathic* dream with another woman. In this discussion, he had been particularly outgoing, talking about his past, and about incidents in his current life, that had been perceived telepathically by this woman and woven into her dream. Eisenbud writes, "Perhaps I had given so much and so warmly because I felt that this patient had produced for me one of the most beautiful psi-conditioned [parapsychological] dreams I had ever seen." The precognitive dreamer had outdone her rival by trumping her "simple telepathy."*

Dr. Eisenbud believes that attitudes toward "the inexplicable phenomenon of 'precognition' will vary from individual to individual, practically from mood to mood." He observes that views of time, "like attitudes toward authority or toward oneself, are not entirely static." However, concludes this particular paper, "The deeply disturbing idea that there might after all be something to 'precognition' has to be repeatedly confronted, and the many-faceted resistance

---

* But there were in her dream production itself clues both to the childhood basis of her rivalry as well as to the infantile "anal" significance of the "gas explosion" she used as a fantasied weapon.

to such an idea has to be repeatedly identified and worked through...."

Dr. Eisenbud contributed further thoughts on this problem in an article entitled "Time and the Oedipus" (*The Psychoanalytic Quarterly*, Vol. XXV, 1956). Taking issue with the view that prophecy is a mere "relic of infantile magical thinking," he asked what precognition could do for psychoanalysis. He chose to "adopt the artifice" of presenting his material as if "the factuality of paranormal foreknowledge of the future were incontrovertible and completely taken for granted by everyone," and proceeded to "see what this assumption in particular instances can do for us."

The first such instance he cited in this context was that of a young woman patient who had "heard," perhaps on the radio in a dream, that the Philadelphia plane carrying her roommate to the latter's fiancé in the Midwest had crashed, killing her. As a matter of fact, the roommate did leave on such a plane the next day, but it did not crash. A plane leaving Philadelphia later the same day did crash and many people were killed. Dr. Eisenbud adds: "The crash occurred several hours after my patient had reported her dream to me."

Why did this girl go out of her way of normal chronology, to express her feelings in terms of the future? Eisenbud writes: "We may take it for granted that it is not just a matter of hastily patching together, out of whatever scraps of reality that happen to be around, something that will do for lack of better as the appropriate vehicle for the latent thoughts, with time elements a matter of complete indifference." On the contrary, he says, the immediate past could have provided the girl "with numerous props of equivalent symbolic potential, if the job be simply to provide one residue which satisfies the two conditions of the dreamer's death wish against her roommate as well as her sexual vindictiveness; and second, that if an item from the future is selected this is not done casually but against considerable resistance and on pain of breaking one of the sacrosanct unconscious rules on which society and its peculiar view of reality rests; the rule, namely, that the secret of man's ability to scry the future never be betrayed."

Subsequent analysis provided the clues that prompted Dr. Eisenbud to entitle this essay "Time and the Oedipus." In the fourth month of this patient's analysis he was able to define her Oedipal attachment to her father, born forty years earlier than she: fixed, irreversible time put father forever out of her reach. "Of all conflicts," Eisenbud notes, "the one which bears most unmistakably the special seemingly irreversible and inescapable stamp of destiny is that which we have come to know as the Oedipus. Classically, too —as witness the ancient story from which this conflict theme derives its name—the Oedipus in its various guises has been associated with the phenomenon of prophecy (e.g., Cassandra in the Agamemnon legend). The element of prophesied doom and of heroic struggle against fate which characterizes this theme in myth and folklore, as well as in the serious works of modern literature which spring from this seemingly inexhaustible reservoir, is too well known to need repeating here. But this is the reality side of the coin. In much myth, folklore, and fairy story, crystallized out of mankind's secret fantasies, the corresponding wish to undo and escape from the bonds of fate and bring about a reversal of its decree by magic or hoped-for miracle, has also been prominent." In this patient's case, writes Eisenbud, "Only in her prophetic dreams, it would seem, was she able to capture the illusion of accomplishing the impossible and to overcome, if only momentarily, the crushing handicap of having been born 'too late.'"

In the last of Dr. Eisenbud's cases that we shall cite, he notes that the literature of parapsychology is full of accounts of train wrecks, airship crashes, fires, and other catastrophes foretold in dreams and in other ways. But most of these records, he observes, fail to indicate some background psychological drama whose finale, as it were, "called for just such a stage effect as the phenomenon of 'precognition' itself." He finds that many precognitive cases are "so exceedingly trivial that one can only speculate on the number of such occurrences that pass by us totally unnoticed."

In one superficially trivial case, a woman in her forties who had long given up the search for the "right" man and who had settled into a "finicky and rather weepingly complaining middle age," dreamed that she found herself in bed with a business associate from whom she had recently received a letter. In the dream, the patient and the man kept their clothes on, and she was aware that he would not "proceed sexually" because he was married.

The dream scene changed and she found herself with the same man in a kitchen where a woman ("she might have been my mother or his") brought out from storage a brown cake loaf with nuts in it. The woman recalled: "She apologized that the cake was very old, implying months or years, and probably wasn't any good; but then, this cake was supposed to be very good when old because there were nuts in it. She got a knife and cut a piece for me. I tasted it and found it very good. Then I noticed the time. I saw a smallish clock with a dark face and the hands pointing to seven o'clock. I verbalized something like, 'It's seven o'clock, I must get up now.'" At this point the patient awoke and saw that it was exactly seven o'clock, fifteen to thirty minutes later than her usual waking time.

Dr. Eisenbud speculates on the latent meanings of the dream, including the mother's permission, in handing her the cake, to gratify her "very old" wishes, presumably her sexual yearnings for her father. But then, the fantasy ends, "Cinderella must tear herself from her dream and get back to her wretched reality, where time once more stands inexorably athwart any possibility of the fulfillment of her wishes."

Several days after the dream, the woman visited a friend who lived with a married brother in a "relationship of sublimated incestuousness that had often caused talk." The brother's wife, to top it off, looked so much like the patient's friend that the two were always taken for sisters. During the visit, which was spent in the kitchen, the woman patient found herself in a highly euphoric mood, something, she said, she had never experienced in her life before. When teatime came, the patient's friend brought out a loaf of banana bread with nuts, saying, "Would anybody like some? It's terribly old. I've had it in the refrigerator, oh, I don't know how long; but then it's supposed to be good when it is old."

Dr. Eisenbud is quick to add that "here is exactly the sort of borderline coincidence that one would ordinarily have little hesitation in passing off as a chance event," but he finds it highly significant that, as in the previous case, the dreamer's "fantasied triumph over time is her private fairy story in which an early decree of destiny is reversed and the forbidden love object is allowed to remain."

At this point, himself Cinderella-like, the analyst notes that he must "face the fact again that the idea of paranormal precognition of the future is generally considered scientifically preposterous." However, he concludes that a human "need to project into the future in defiance of the natural order of things" should be acknowledged and that we should take seriously "the possibility that what are generally termed precognitive phenomena may actually occur." He adds: "Without this our attempted illumination of a certain kind of time experience, as a function of the unresolved Oedipus loses its whole point, which hinges entirely on the assumption that the relationship between the dreams presented here and their after-coming 'residues' was not a chance one."

Professor Hans Bender, director of the Institute for Border Areas of Psychology and Mental Hygiene, reported in the *International Journal of Neuropsychiatry* (Vol. 2, No. 5, 1966) on the case of a German motion-picture actress whose dreams appeared to have forecast specific scenes and situations that later occurred in her films. Professor Bender's Institute collected over 1,000 dreams of this actress, identified as "Mrs. M.," who began to record them in 1954. Twelve of these dreams showed striking correlation with a film, *Night Fell on Gotenhafen*, which dealt with shipwrecked refugees, as well as with a comedy, *Triplets on Board*, filmed on the same set as the Gotenhafen movie.

Among the dreams that suggested precognition was one, recorded on September 15, 1957. In it, the actress observed: "I am swimming together with several girls—I don't know whom—and with several babies. The baby of S. is born—a sweet little girl with beautiful eyes. She is swimming, too, under water and especially long. We are playing 'meeting under water,' and I am afraid because she stays down so long."

Two years later, the actress had to play a role that was filmed on the night of September 14, 1959. She noted in her diary: "Today, my first day of filming. 6:30 P.M. in a Heligoland skiff in the open sea. We sit in a lifeboat for a long time. Rough sea. Then from the float into the water. The scene 'Where is my baby?' is shot twice." Dr. Bender noted that it was the theater director, whose wife was expecting a baby in 1957, who engaged the actress for her part in the film. Analyzing all twelve dreams, Professor Bender offers the hypothesis of "a motivational link between the actual meaning of the presumably precognitive dreams at the time of dreaming and the life situations which later on seem to fulfill them."

Dr. Jan Ehrenwald, whose concepts of "telepathic leakage" and "doctrinal compliance" I mentioned before, has reported "an apparently precognitive dream of a patient undergoing psychoanalysis for an anxiety hysteria" in *The Psychoanalytic Review* (January 1951). He reported in a paper entitled "Precognition in Dreams?" that this patient, a department-store floor manager, had experienced anxiety attacks in subways and buses, while crossing streets, in restaurants, and at the soda fountain of the department store. The analysis had shown that these fears were "a defense mechanism directed against unconscious homosexual impulses" which surfaced in these situations.

Apparently the patient responded well to the treatment, once he understood his unconscious impulses. On November 5, 1947, in the fourth month of therapy, he dreamed that he was in the store when "a guy who apparently worked for us" acted as if "he was after something, ready to hold up the place." He recalled the subsequent dream events as follows:

"He had a large flip-open knife, opening, closing it, suggesting he is a dangerous fellow. I got scared, called for Mr. X and Mr. Y to catch the man. I myself retreated into the telephone box to call the police to get him.

"All of a sudden the whole situation seemed to have dissolved. The guy was sitting there; I was talking to him. It was a much more friendly conversation. He took out the knife, flipped it open. It was not large any more—just half an inch or maybe one inch long. I thought how foolish it was to be afraid of the knife. It was not nearly as dangerous. It was very small."

The psychoanalytical significance of the dream was fairly obvious. Ehrenwald noted that "the phallic symbolism of the knife" needed no further elaboration. What happened afterward, however, suggested that events took place which, had they occurred before the dream, might have been perfectly routine—but as they occurred they reenacted the dream events in reverse.

Two days after the dream, on November 7, the patient was a little late for his session. A man had sat next to him on the bus, had taken out a knife, and although it was only a small pen knife, as in the second half of the dream, the patient "felt quite uneasy, ready to get panicky any time." But the man only took an apple from his pocket and, using the knife, started to eat it.

The patient was amazed by the similarities between dream and actual event: "The knife was like taken out of the dream. But please don't think that I am suffering from hallucinations. Never has a similar thing happened to me before."

On the 17th, the patient reported a second real incident involving a knife. He was rather alarmed by this apparent coincidence. This is Ehrenwald's account of the patient's statement:

"Yesterday morning I was on the floor of the store when some character walked in. He looked like a real tramp, with a battered hat, dishevelled shirt, with holes in his shoes. He looked fierce, like a maniac. I knew him from before. He had come to our place about three or four times before. I always watched him whether he was not out for stealing. But as a rule he bought something: stationery, pencils, or soap.

"This time he walked straight to the cutlery counter. I was just two counters away and saw that he picked up a large kitchen knife, four to five inches long, and said something to the girl at the counter, though I could not hear what he was saying. At that he turned round towards me, looked at me, and with a savage gesture brandished the knife towards his throat.

"I got very uncomfortable. In fact, I ran downstairs to the basement. After a while I pulled myself together and went back to the girl at the cutlery counter. 'What happened to your boy friend?' I asked jokingly. 'Did he buy the knife?' The girl answered in the affirmative, adding, still somewhat taken aback, 'He said, "when that guy bothers me I'll cut his throat open." Then he paid and walked out with the paring knife.'"

Dr. Ehrenwald wanted to get any superstitious notions out of the patient's mind. He said that the two waking incidents involving the knife might have been due to his increased awareness of objects of this sort. But the analyst then asked himself and his psychoanalytic colleagues: does that explanation really account for this sequence of events? Looking at the various elements in the waking incidents, Ehrenwald finds that they fit together, "in the same way as two complementary plates whose imprints are superimposed on one another to make up a two-colored print." In the dream, the knife was first big and then small; in the real-life events, it was the other way around. And anyway, Ehrenwald notes, "Comparing the contents of the dream with two separate happenings, listed in the reversed order and occurring ten days apart, runs counter to our rational way of thinking."

However, Dr. Ehrenwald, as we have seen earlier, does not disregard the "intrinsically improbably"—he is quite willing to set aside "some of our familiar notions of the unalterable law of temporal order, or the rigid and irreversible sequence of past, present, and future." He finds that the really meaningful events and moods in the dream and the subsequent events are virtually identical: the different size of the knife; the air of menace at one point, and the sudden relaxation of tension at another.

Ehrenwald feels that it may be "just as legitimate to inquire into the chain of events succeeding the dream of a particular dreamer as it is to probe into his experiences preceding the dream." The psychoanalyst cannot go in for statistical experiments; but he cannot, either, Ehrenwald says, in all conscience pass up evidence suggesting that a precognitive dream has actually occurred any more than he can pass up any other clinical development.

Comparing the dream and the following events, Ehrenwald found a number of distinguishable features common to both; while probability cannot be estimated, the odds against such features occurring by chance are, in his view, enormous. How often do people eat apples in buses, using small pocket knives? How often do they go brandishing larger knives in department stores? Next: did the patient lie? Did the analyst record the events accurately? Ehrenwald examines all these possibilities and concludes that "the striking correspondence between dream and waking event was not, after all, due to chance alone." Did the patient perhaps practice some form of suggestive telepathy on the man in the bus and the tramp at the cutlery counter? "A telepathic interpretation," Ehrenwald writes, "can hardly account for the materialization of his dream with all its paraphernalia, including the appearance of the big and the small knife, measured to order, as it were."

As the reader knows by now, and as Dr. Ehrenwald observes at this point, "a strict borderline between contemporaneous and post- or precognitive telepathy is impossible to draw." At this point, the relationship between patient and analyst must be taken into consideration. The man who dreamed of these knives had been making good progress in reducing his anxieties. Insight into his problem was increasing. After the therapeutic implications of the dream became clear to the patient, he made rapid progress; it was on this bus ride that the knife-and-apple incident took place. (C. G. Jung would have loved all this, although it happened in a Freudian analysis: here was "synchronicity," alive and kicking!)

While this was going on, Dr. Ehrenwald was correcting galley proofs on an article on telepathy. It made him puzzle over precognition; just about then a friend told him a well-documented precognitive dream. He writes: "My attitude toward precognition, still undecided at that time, thus received a definite bias in its favor. Three days later my patient produced the dream described here." Did the patient, then, respond to the "emotionally charged wishes and expectations" of the analyst? Was he, pleased with the therapy, providing an "apple for the teacher" in an area of inquiry absorbing the analyst's interest? Ehrenwald writes: "One could say that the dream occurred at the exact intersection of two lines of force that can be plotted within two overlapping emotional fields: the one pertaining to my patient, the other to myself."

Dr. Ehrenwald concluded that "the precognitive aspect of a dream" seems to "play a major part on a deeper level of mental functioning, and added: "It may well be that observations of this kind (provided they stand the test of scientific scrutiny) will permit a glance into the workshop of nature in which the future is in the making, even though they cannot break through the barriers which separate us from the immediate awareness of the *Future* writ large."

He developed these ideas at the conference on "The Study of Precognition: Evidence and Methods," in New York in December 1959. On that occasion, Ehrenwald presented his exploratory thoughts in a paper entitled "A Psychiatrist Looks at Precognition—and Discovers a 'Syndrome.'" He defined "syndrome" simply as "that which occurs together." But what, exactly, "occurs together" when precognition leaps onto the stage of everyday life? In Dr. Ehrenwald's view, such rare but "dynamically well-defined circumstances" represent "anomalies" in the traditional categories of time, space, and causality. "Clinically speaking," Dr. Ehrenwald pointed out, "an experience of this order can be described as a syndrome." He regards it as rather arbitrary to single out a special aspect, such as precognition, from "the context of a more complex human experience." Ehrenwald feels that our personal, scientific, or cultural bias prompts us to pick out one or another category of experience. He suggests that a good deal more is involved than an event that seems to be out of joint with "natural" law. Dr. Ehrenwald compares such unusual events with those that happen "on the microphysical scale" in quantum physics.

I believe that he is easing us into the shock of discovery that the seemingly unusual, such as a prophetic experience, operates according to rules that have wider application than we either know or can imagine. Is precognition, or any other parapsychological event simply the expression of different laws than prevail in our "macrophysical" world?

Ehrenwald urges us to set aside "classical" cause-and-effect concepts, the "causal deterministic laws of mental functioning." He has an affinity for the intellectual ferment that is going on among theoretical physicists. Never mind, he says, being in awe of prophetic or otherwise unorthodox happenings in our lives; our tendency to be rigid is simply reinforced by the anxiety and disbelief with which we observe "the occasonal breakthrough of organically or culturally repressed (or as yet underdeveloped) anomalous patterns of experience." To him, a premonitory dream is not something that pops into our lives out of nowhere, defying what we regard as our normal way of existence; rather, he sees it as an integral part of a "non-Euclidian, micro-psychological, nondeterministic" area of life, existing within the inclusive world which William James has called the "Pluralistic Universe." Put more simply, Ehrenwald views precognition as merely one segment of a world beyond our present concepts and senses, observable as we glimpse it during those improbable moments of "fleeting contact and interpenetration" between two areas. And that moment of contact, that "syndrome," is a window on a mode of existence which differs drastically from "the pattern familiar to western man of our days...."

It is at this point that the psychologist, and the psychoanalyst in particular, finds himself in a trialogue with the philosopher and the physicist, all of them concerned with seeking to explore and comprehend a world to which our relatively primitive concepts of time and space have little application, and that our limited knowledge cannot encompass but only glimpse in passing.

12 From New Jersey to the Grand Canyon

The American Society for Psychical Research in New York has collected close to two thousand cases of "spontaneous phenomena," which include specifically detailed precognitive and telepathic experiences. While its researchers are interested in the psychological dynamics of these cases, their first concern is with documentation. They screen the letters reporting personal experiences carefully. They seek to obtain statements of witnesses, confirmation from other sources, such as newspapers, and general independent documentation as well. With this, they also inquire into the personalities of individuals involved and their families, and they try to find out just how "prone" they are to parapsychological experiences.

A typical example is the following case.

In November 1956, Mrs. G. Zabriskie of Bergenfield, New Jersey, dreamed that her husband had been painfully injured in an accident. As she recalled the dream, "There seemed to be a jumbled mess around him that was not too clear," and she "could not determine just what type of accident" had occurred. One thing stood out: "I saw a small boat nearby, very plainly, which seemed to have no significance to the scene or with his being injured." When told the dream next morning, Mr. Zabriskie said, joking, "What am I supposed to do about it?" His wife replied, "I cannot forget it. Just be careful."

One evening, about a week and a half later, Mrs. Zabriskie began to worry because her husband, who always took a bus from New York City across the George Washington Bridge, had not returned by 6:15, his usual arrival time. When he had not come back by 7:10, his wife telephoned the Bergenfield police and asked them whether there had been an accident on the Hill Bus Line. They told her that there had, indeed, been an accident, but that she should not worry: only one passenger, a woman, had been seriously hurt, although quite a few other passengers had been taken to the Englewood Hospital. Mrs. Zabriskie was told to telephone the state police in Hackensack, as they had just returned from the accident, which had taken place on Route 4, leading from the George Washington Bridge into New Jersey. The state police also reassured Mrs. Zabriskie. She then decided to telephone the hospital. But first she went to the door once again. At that moment, her husband was coming up the walk toward the house. She describes the subsequent scene as follows:

"He had a badly cut lip, swollen out the size of an egg. Our doctor attended his lip and said he was in a state of shock. He had four teeth loosened. . . . We were indeed thankful he wasn't badly injured, but still it was bad enough.

"My husband said, 'What made you call and ask the police if there was an accident?' I told him I just felt it.

"Later, after things were under control, I asked him just where on the highway the accident occurred. He said it was directly opposite the showroom where they have motor boats on display. This was the part of the dream the significance of which I could not understand. It did not have any connection with the accident other than that this place is directly across the highway from where the accident occurred."

The Society's researchers subsequently learned a number of facts from Mrs. Zabriskie. The original dream had been a particularly vivid one. She occasionally had told her husband of other dreams when they seemed particularly realistic. He had not been in an accident during the year prior to the dream. She had not recalled the dream when she telephoned the Bergenfield police, and not even when he arrived at home. Only after the doctor had left, and her husband had managed to overcome his shock, did she ask him about the scene of the accident and he said that it was directly opposite the motor-boat place. It was then, Mrs. Zabriskie recalled, that "my dream came to me like a flash" and she asked, "The motor-boat place?" Her husband said, "Yes." And she asked him, "Do you remember that dream I had about your being in an accident and I saw a small boat nearby, although it did not seem to have any significance to the picture?" The husband did recall it, and he later sent the Society this statement:

"Yes, I remember very well that my wife told me about the dream she had early in November, 1956, this being a week and a half prior to the accident of the Hill Bus that I was on November 14, 1956. The accident was caused by a sudden stop of the car ahead, and there were many passengers injured. The location of the accident most certainly was within view of the motor-boat salesroom, it being directly across the way."

The local newspaper, *The Bergen Evening Record,* carried the following report in its issue of November 15, 1956:

"A quick stop by a car on busy Route 4 at 6:30 last night caused a collision of two buses which sent five persons to Englewood Hospital with minor injuries. . . . All the injured were in the Hill bus and were on their way home from New York. The collision tied up traffic on the highway for a time."

Psychologists of various schools would have a field day with case material of this type. Freudians might project death-wish patterns upon it; Jungians would probably fit it into the pattern of the "synchronicity" concept of a meaningful coincidence. Interpersonal dynamics may well play a role in a prophetic dream of this kind. But one question will surely remain unanswered for a while: How did the motor boat get into Mrs. Zabriskie's dream?

And even in those telepathic dreams where death plays a significant role, it may concern individuals among whom there seems to exist no significant personal relationship. Among the American Society's files is a case from Louisiana that illustrates this point. The comment in the Society's *Journal* notes that "although centered around a death experience, it deals with it obliquely."

The case was reported by Mrs. Roy J. Segall of Metairie, Louisiana, who noted that on June 4, 1954, she, her husband, and their little girl left New Orleans to drive to New York to visit her parents. In the car also was a friend, whom, for the story, she called Mrs. Blair; she had just come along for the trip and to visit an aunt. They arrived in New York on the 7th, and on the night of the 11th, Mrs. Segall dreamed that they were driving through Alabama, "when suddenly I was hit by a flash." The thought that "We had forgotten Mrs. Blair!" suddenly occurred to her, in this dream. Still in the dream, she told her husband about it, "but he said that it was too late to go back and I just broke my head trying to understand how we could have possibly forgotten her and how she would ever get home with all her luggage—over forty pounds—and having to go back to work."

In the morning, Mrs. Segall told the dream to her husband, her parents, and, in the afternoon, to Mrs. Blair, who "laughed very much and said we better not forget her, and the whole thing slipped out of my mind."

On the following Wednesday, the Segalls were invited to visit Mrs. Blair's aunt, with whom she was staying while in New York. Mrs. Blair's brother and sister-in-law, whom the Segalls had previously met in New Orleans, were also there; it was an enjoyable evening. The sister-in-law, whom we shall call Alice for purposes of this narrative, complained of a headache when the Segalls were leaving.

On the following Monday night, Mrs. Segall dreamed her earlier dream all over again: "We were driving home and again I was struck by a flash and realized that we had forgotten Mrs. Blair. It was so violent, so annoying that I woke up and told the incident to my husband. It was 5:30 in the morning. I could not go to sleep any more and the dream just would not get out of my mind when at 8 o'clock the telephone rang. Mrs. Blair was on the phone and I hastily told her my dream again and she replied in a tearful voice: "You will have to forget me. My sister-in-law died last night! I'll stay here until Sunday."

Additional details include the following: Mrs. Segall dreams often, but these had been particularly upsetting dreams. She tells a dream "almost always when I remember it." The sister-in-law was forty years old at the time of her death, which was quite unexpected and apparently caused by a cerebral hemorrhage. Mr. Segall, in 1960, corroborated the details as follows:

"As far as I can remember, my wife told me of her first dream shortly before June 12, 1954, the seventy-fifth birthday of my father-in-law. She told me that in her dream we had left New York and left Mrs. Blair behind. I remember her telling this dream to Mrs. Blair on June 12, P.M. It seemed odd when a few days later my wife told me of the recurrence of the same dream—that we were driving along, having left New York, and turning toward the rear seat of the car she discovered we had left Mrs. Blair behind. She seemed rather upset. One hour later, Mrs. Blair called, telling us that we would have to leave her behind as her sister-in-law, whom we had met a few days before, had died."

And Mrs. Blair herself recalled the incident this way: "Mrs. Segall called me one morning and told me she dreamed that I would not go back with them. We laughed about it and I told her not to forget to take me back. A few days later my sister-in-law died very unexpectedly, so I called Mrs. Segall and when she answered the phone she said, 'I just wanted to call you because I dreamed again you are not coming home with us.' I told her what happened and that I had to stay with my brother; her dream really came true."

The American Society researchers added a cautious psychological postscript to these accounts, noting that Mrs. Segall had "correctly precognized the fact that her friend would not accompany her on the return trip but was unable to get the true reason." Why, the researchers ask, did her dream take on its particular air of guilt? Why did it limit itself, as it were, to an empty back seat of the car? They speculated that Mrs. Segall, even in her prophetic dream, could not discern its true reason, possibly "because the sister-in-law was not a close friend or relation." Her "dreaming mind then assumed that in some way she and her family were to blame. Is this possibly a characteristic reaction of the dreamer, and if so, do veridical facts tend to be embedded within a framework that allows such characteristic personality dynamics to be expressed? It would seem that to better understand why some things are perceived extrasensorially and others are not, we must learn more about the underlying drives and needs of the percipient."

The files of the American Society for Psychical Research contain one dream that is almost painfully concrete in its details on suffering and death. It contains elements in a daughter's precognition of her father's death that could not have been "in somebody's mind" before they occurred.

The case was reported to the Society by Mrs. Antoinette Terlingo of Clifton Heights, Pennsylvania, in a letter dated February 25, 1957, who recalled a dream that took place in December 1953. Mrs. Terlingo dreamed of seeing her father in a box or coffin with a white towel around his neck. Only the upper part of his body, his head and shoulders, were visible: "Dad was dead in this dream, and a woman dressed in doctor's 'whites' addressed us and was saying it was better to have him embalmed now. My mother entered the dream, and she and I agreed to have him embalmed and dressed before coming home."

Mrs. Terlingo woke up screaming and sobbing. Her husband Jerry tried to calm her, as she narrated the dream to him. But to herself she kept saying, "It's true; Daddy is dead; Daddy is dead." Mr. Terlingo convinced her that it had been only a dream; they would have heard, by then, if anything had really happened to her father, who had been ill for seven years at the Veterans Administration center in Martinsburg, West Virginia. Nevertheless, Mrs. Terlingo spent the next few days sick with fear. Three days after the dream, she received a letter from her father, saying he was "feeling fine, a little tired, but okay." Several days later Christmas presents arrived, sent by her father for every member of the family.

By then, Mrs. Terlingo was angry with herself, arguing against "silly dreams," thinking they "will drive you crazy if you believe them." Shortly afterward, on December 13, they were notified that the father had had a stroke and was gravely ill. The Terlingos drove to West Virginia, where they found the father in an oxygen tent. He had a white Turkish towel around his neck.

Mrs. Terlingo wrote afterward that she had told her dream "to my mother and anyone who would listen," and that, standing at the oxygen tent, her mother exclaimed, "Oh, Nanette, look!" She had also been struck by the presence of the white Turkish towel. The father died the next day, and Mrs. Terlingo stated: "The family had understood that Daddy had a male doctor. Well, he had, until a few months before, when his new doctor was a woman. This handsome lady talked to Mother, my two sisters, and me and she was introduced as his doctor. Another piece fitted into the dream. It was uncanny."

Nanette Terlingo's account continued:

"When we had regained our composure, Jerry was caring for Gerald [their son] while Mother, my sisters, and I started to make arrangements to have his body prepared for travel. We were advised to have him dressed at the hospital. Being a V.A. Center, all these preparations were available there. I did not know there was a law you must embalm or a corpse cannot be brought over the state line. There, again, another piece fitted in the dream.

"The task of choosing his casket and clothes came next. Daddy was a veteran of World War I. Mother decided that a military coffin was desirable for father's body to rest in. Well, that was the final piece in the puzzle. That was why I only saw a bust of my father in my dream—because the coffin was only viewing his bust. The other half was draped with the United States flag. I have never dreamed of my father since that night. . . . As you can see, I haven't forgotten the dream; I never shall."

The Terlingo case was handled in a meticulous fashion. It began with a series of questions from the Society addressed to Antoinette Terlingo. "Was there," the Society asked, "anything about this dream to distinguish it from your 'ordinary' dreams—that is, was it more vivid, more realistic, etc?" Nanette answered, "This dream was very vivid, very real; in fact, when I awoke and calmed down a bit, I still thought the dream was a reality."

The Society then wanted to know whether she had, as far as she could recall, "awakened from a dream screaming and sobbing," before or since. The answer was, "No." Next, the Society inquired whether the father's condition was a chronic one, and did Mrs. Terlingo have any particular reason to fear that "he would die at the time you had the dream?" Nanette Terlingo answered: "You are right in assuming my father's condition was chronic. He had been sick for five years (hospitalized). I had no reason to fear his death at the time of the dream, although I felt he would die soon, because of the dream."

Continuing its inquiry, the American Society for Psychical Research asked, "Had you ever visited your father at the V.A. Center in Martinsburg? If so, how long before the date of the dream was your last visit?" Mrs. Terlingo said: "I hadn't seen my father for six months. In fact, it was the 13th of June 1953; he visited me at home."

The next question was, "Did your father ever mention the fact that he had a woman doctor in his letters to you or to other members of the family?" "No," the reply said, "he never said he had a woman doctor to me or anyone else."

The Society required clarification on one specific point: "In the dream, the woman doctor told you about having your father embalmed. In the actual life situation, was it the woman doctor who told you he would have to be embalmed because of the state law, or was it someone else?" She replied, "It was the woman doctor who explained to us where to go, whom to see, and what to do for the funeral arrangements and embalming. She directed us to a clerk in another part of the building. There everything was taken care of. The clerk told us about the state law."

The Society had two more questions. "Prior to the time of the dream, had you ever seen anyone in a military coffin, with only the bust exposed?" No, Mrs. Terlingo had never "seen coffins with the flag draped over them." The second question was, "Have you had other psychic experiences, or was this one a unique event in your life?" She replied, "I have had premonitions and feelings of things that turned out to be true. But this experience was the first and only one."

The husband, Jerry Terlingo, sent the researchers a statement which read: "This is to verify that all my wife told you concerning the events of the dream are true, and they happened as she told them to me and other members of our family. She can still relate them after three and a half years just as clearly as though she dreamed it last night."

The mother, Angelina Amato, added the following information:

"I would like to verify her dream as she has told you. So far as the towel around my husband's neck [is concerned], as they placed the oxygen tent over him, he remarked about being cold, so the doctor brought a towel and put it around his neck.

"I addressed her as 'nurse' and she said, 'No, I'm his doctor!' I asked her how that was and she said she was transferred from another ward and assigned the ward my husband was in just recently. My husband was confined to Martinsburg Hospital for five years, and in all that time that I visited him I always managed to have a talk with his doctor as to how he was progressing, and his doctor was always male.

". . . The morning of his death this woman doctor directed us where to go for burial arrangements. I was introduced to this clerk and she said the body had to be embalmed before leaving the state, as it was the law. The clerk took us to a room where we could pick out his clothes and casket. She showed us all types, and we saw this half-casket. The clerk said this type was used in the event a flag [was] draped over the casket. My husband always told me if ever he should die before me, he wanted a military burial. So, thinking of his wishes, I thought the half-casket was a good idea—but *never, never* thinking or even giving a thought to my daughter's dream. But, as things worked out, everything was taking pattern as to her dream.

"After all arrangements were made and everything settled, we drove home, and talking things over, we realized the dream and how uncanny it all was . . . her dreaming these things two weeks before the death! He was all right at that time, because she had received a letter from him that very week, and he said he was just fine. Everything she has told you is the truth and just as she really dreamed."

The Terlingo case was related in the *Journal* of the American Society for Psychical Research (January 1962), in a paper by Laura A. Dale, Rhea White, and Gardner Murphy. Mrs. Dale is editor of the *Journal,* Miss White is Director of Information and a well-known psychical researcher, and Dr. Murphy is one of the nation's foremost psychologists, former Director of Research of the Menninger Foundation, Topeka, Kansas, as well as the president and chairman of the Research Committee of the ASPR.

Evaluating the Terlingo case, the authors note that "there are no inconsistencies between the accounts of mother and daughter as regards the dream experience or the events involved in its fulfillment, but there is one between different statements made by the percipient as regards the length of her father's stay in the V.A. hospital. In her original account she states that it was seven years, but in answer to Question Three, she states that it was five years. In the mother's statement the length of time is given as five years."

The Society's researchers were impressed with this particular case, because it not only anticipated the father's death, but the prophetic dream contained "several unexpected details concerning the final attentions given her father, details which, even given the knowledge of her father's death, she would still not have been able to predict, as they concerned circumstances not known to her consciously." They add that "for one thing, he had a *female* doctor; whereas, to the best of the percipient's knowledge, his doctor was a man. In other words, the dream at this point broke through the percipient's customary train of association, although she was not aware of this until later. She had also not known previously that the body would have to be embalmed before leaving the hospital, nor that in the arrangement of a military coffin the lower half of the body is not visible."

The Terlingo case is one of very few in which such detailed verification has been possible. The Society's questions illustrate the technique it uses in documenting cases of this type. These methods apply not only to precognitive cases, in the waking state, in dreams, or in some in-between state, but to the whole category of spontaneous phenomena.

These methods of collecting and evaluating cases go back to the ancestor of the American Society, the renowned Society for Psychical Research, founded in London in 1882. Four years later, the British Society published an enormous pioneer work, a collection of spontaneous cases edited by Edmund Gurney under the title *Phantasms of the Living*. Another survey, published in 1890 and called a *Census of Hallucinations*, contained similar cases. The *Proceedings* and the *Journal* of the British and American societies have published thousands of cases, including many of a prophetic nature. Much material on this subject is also to be found in the *Journal of Parapsychology* and the *International Journal of Parapsychology*.

The author of this book attended an international Conference on Spontaneous Phenomena at Cambridge, England, in the summer of 1955, as a representative of the Parapsychology Foundation of New York. The meeting had been called jointly by the British and American psychical research societies and was attended by representatives from the European continent as well. This conference decided on the establishment of world-wide criteria for research and evaluation. It called for "the discovery, careful sifting, authentication, and intensive study of a large number of cases, for the development of hypotheses underlying them, and for the testing of hypotheses by experiment and other methods."

Follow-up meetings sought to divide world cases among the various societies, with continental research in the hands of George Zorab, The Hague, as chairman of the International Committee on Spontaneous Paranormal Phenomena. A number of authorities, notably Dr. Emilio Servadio, later president of the Italian Psychoanalytic Association, suggested that the psychodynamics underlying spontaneous phenomena should be explored wherever possible.

The American Society was greatly helped by a series of articles, on psi case-collecting, by Dr. Murphy in the Sunday newspaper supplement *This Week*. As a result of these pieces, which appeared in February and March of 1957, the ASPR received about 1,200 letters from persons who wrote that they had had telepathic, precognitive, clairvoyant, and similar experiences. The Society applied the criteria of eliminating cases that were "hopelessly vague or fragmentary, or were accounts of personal experiences containing no apparent reference to the paranormal, or contained direct evidence of mental abnormality which made it appear improbable that correspondence would be of value." They placed great emphasis on independent corroboration.

One good example of this documentation technique surrounded a case that came to the Society from Alabama. It concerned Mrs. Velma C. Vann, her son, and the child of her daughter, Mrs. R. B. Storrs, all of Birmingham. The incident began with a dream by the grandmother in November 1952. She dreamed that she had picked up her grandson Bobby from the bed in his room and taken him to sit on her lap in a rocking chair. She describes the following in her dream then:

"I kissed his forehead, and he was burning with fever. He seemed to be very limp and he did not know me. While I was sitting there rocking Bobby, I was crying because he seemed almost dead."

Mrs. Vann further describes that, in the dream, her son Bud came to the door and leaned against the frame with his hand to his head, saying that he had fallen from a telephone pole. Mrs. Vann had been worried about his job, ever since he had become a lineman for the Southern Bell Telephone Company. In the dream, he said, "I fell and I feel a little sick at my stomach," and when he moved the hand from his forehead, blood came streaming from a wound above his eye.

Mrs. Vann recalled that she screamed in the dream and that her son said, "Now I think I am going to be all right." But she woke up with a feeling of terror that lasted well into her waking state. She wrote of that morning:

"I didn't sleep any more and I got up very early the next morning and went home. The dream I had was reenacted completely. I went directly to my daughter's house hoping the whole thing had been only a dream but I did go into Bobby's room and picked him up. I kissed his forehead and he was burning with fever and did not know me. While my daughter dressed so we could take Bobby to the doctor, I asked about Bud and she told me he was all right."

Incredibly: "In the meantime, Bud had fallen from a pole

while he was at work and had been brought home. His wife was terrified when she saw him. [As] she knew we had returned home, she ran across the backyard screaming for me, and my son followed her. When they came into the house, I saw that the second part of my dream had come true."

Now, Mrs. Vann's account was not quite clear as to where she had been while she had this terrifying dream, and just what she meant by returning "home." However, the account of her daughter, Mrs. Storrs, clarifies these points; she wrote in 1954 that her parents, two years earlier, had been on a short vacation and that little Bobby had fallen ill, with an extremely high temperature, shortly after they left. She continues:

"Early the next morning, I was surprised to see my mother and father driving in the driveway. Mother rushed in and said, 'I had a terrible dream. I dreamed I kissed Bobby and he was burning with fever, and when I turned around, Bud was standing there with a big hole in his head, pouring blood.' I told her that Bobby was terribly sick, but that my brother Bud had gone to work as usual that morning and was just fine. In less than an hour my brother, a lineman for Southern Bell Telephone Company, had been brought home by his foreman with a big hole cut above his left eye and bleeding profusely."

The additional facts were that Mrs. Vann's son, Bud, and his wife had come to live with Mrs. Vann for a month after their daughter was born in October, at which time Bud had taken the lineman's job. Mrs. Storrs, Mrs. Vann's daughter, lived in an apartment behind the Vann home. Before the dream, the Vanns had left on a five-day vacation. They spent the first night of their vacation, the night of the precognitive dream, seventy-six miles away, at the home of Mr. Vann's parents, who did not have a telephone. According to the ASPR account, Mrs. Storrs reported that her mother had never before cut short a vacation due to a dream or a hunch, and when Mrs. Vann had last seen Bobby, before leaving on the trip, the boy had appeared in good health.

Bobby first became ill late in the afternoon of the day the Vanns left. He began vomiting, his temperature reached 105°, and it turned out that he was suffering from severe tonsillitis. The Society's investigators asked the child's mother whether, when the child was ill, she wished that her own mother was with her; she replied, "Not at first, but later in the night his temperature ran higher and higher and I could not break it with any of the methods I had ever heard of, I began to panic. Because then I did not know it was tonsillitis; as a young mother with only one child, I feared the worst thing I could imagine. I was quite desperate, and neither my husband nor I went to bed at all that night. I prayed a lot and it was quite possible that I thought of my mother, but I cannot be sure. I do know that whenever Bobby had been sick before, I had relied heavily on my mother's experience with children and on her assurances that nothing seriously was wrong with them."

Mrs. Vann did not have an easy time convincing other members of her family that her dream had been "the real thing." Her daughter recalls that her father had objected very much to their returning to Birmingham just because of a dream, and so had the grandfather, with whom the Vanns were staying. In fact, Mrs. Vann had to threaten that she would take the car and drive home herself, and that Mr. Vann could take the bus back. Mrs. Storr wrote:

"My father's relatives with whom they were staying thought the whole thing pretty ridiculous. My grandmother thought someone had offended my mother, but since she had been in the family for twenty-some odd years and had never behaved in such a way, they soon realized that she really felt that something was wrong, and my father brought her home. She said the silence in the car all the way home was pretty uncomfortable. If the feeling had not been so strong, I am sure she would not have caused and persisted in creating such an awkward situation."

In cases such as these, the researchers try to define what has actually happened prophetically in pretty sophisticated terms. For instance, the questions asked of Mrs. Vann and Mrs. Storr are obviously designed to find out whether "only" telepathy was involved—did the mother respond to a telepathic plea from her daughter—or whether the events indicate pure precognition. In the case of Bobby's illness, telepathy could account for Mrs. Vann's worry over the child's health on the night before her return to Birmingham. But only a prophetic image could encompass particularly the precise nature of Buddy's injury above his eye. The researchers are aware of the fact that overanxious people have frequent visions of disaster and, life being what it is, some of them do come true by sheer coincidence. This woman was not in this category.

The ASPR, among its carefully selected cases, has published one reported by Mrs. Paul H. McCahen of Inglewood, California. She described it as her only psychic experience, and it took place in the waking stage. It contains none of the crisis drama common to most of these cases, whether they can be verified or not. Its very setting, in the great outdoors of the American West, gives it a quality that differs radically from the atmosphere of the uncanny that surrounds much of this material.

Mr. and Mrs. McCahen visited the Grand Canyon in September 1956. On the first evening of their visit, in the twilight, on September 4, Mrs. McCahen saw a woman walking up to one of the cabins. A man and a boy accompanied her, carrying her luggage. Mrs. McCahen turned to her husband and said, "There is Mrs. Nash, a lady I served jury duty with a year ago. Her husband has one arm. But I will see her in the morning, as she is probably tired.

"The next day I saw her sitting on the veranda, and I went to talk to her. Our husbands met each other and we had a pleasant chat until I mentioned I had seen her the evening before, but didn't speak then. Mr. and Mrs. Nash both looked astonished and said they had just gotten there with a busload of tourists. He doesn't drive far, because of his arm."

Mrs. McCahen had met Mrs. Nash only once before, and Mr. McCahen had never seen them before. It had been a year since Mrs. McCahen had seen her, and Mrs. McCahen had no idea that the Nashes were going to be at the Grand Canyon at that time. Paul McCahen confirmed the incident: "My wife pointed out a lady to be Mrs. Nash about ten or fifteen feet away from us the evening before. The next day about noon my wife met Mrs. Nash and told her she had seen her the evening before. Mrs. Nash said that was impossible because they had arrived only that morning."

What Mrs. McCahen had experienced closely resembles a traditional psychic phenomenon which, in name and specific pattern, is usually restricted to Norway; and, even there, it has become quite rare. Its name is *Vardøgr*—even in modern Norwegian something of an archaic word with linguistic roots in ancient devil worship. Norse migrants brought the phenomenon to Scotland, but it is rarely recorded at present. Wiers Jensen, writing in the *Norwegian Journal of Psychical Research,* stated that the *Vardøgr* reports are virtually all alike. They run along these lines: Steps are heard on a staircase; there are sounds of an outside door being unlocked; somebody is taking off his overshoes, putting his stick against the wall—but when the inside door is opened, there is no one there. The sounds were those of the *Vardøgr,* the "hu-

PROPHECY IN OUR TIME

man double," the forerunner, so to speak, of the actual visitor, who may arrive five to ten minutes later. One may call these doorstep noises the "sounds of intention." Cases like these seem to be reported at about the time at which a husband leaves his office; they are, possibly, anticipating his arrival at a comfortable home after stomping through a bitter Norwegian winter.

In the summer of 1965, the writer of this book visited Thorstein Wereide, the Grand Old Man of psychical research in Norway, at his Oslo home. Then eighty-five years old, Professor Wereide, emeritus in physics of the University of Oslo, believes that the *Vardøgr* is unique to Norway, because the people of its countryside and mountains have for centuries been more isolated than people of other European countries. Until quite recently, and I quote him here, "communication between individuals has been difficult, and hence nature seems to have made use of 'supernatural' means to compensate for this isolation." Professor Wereide feels that the phenomenon, a sort of "physical prophecy," has been taken by Norwegian city dwellers from the countryside in which they lived a generation or two ago and that they have "brought with them the faculty of *Vardøgr* observation, even though city conditions make this phenomenon less necessary than in the countryside."

Professor Wereide's interpretation of the *Vardøgr* phenomenon fits well into the widely held hypothesis that telepathic and prophetic phenomena fill psychological needs, jump gaps in time or space, and establish a line of communication that does not otherwise exist. It can easily be argued that the eager husband and wife, in the midst of a Norwegian winter, establish a psychic rapport that expresses itself by auditory means, with sounds similar to those associated with "poltergeist" phenomena. Yet, the *Vardøgr* of Mr. and Mrs. Nash, on the evening of September 4, 1956, outside a mountain cabin in the Grand Canyon, eludes all such explanations. Still, there are many other parallels in psychical research; we can even give them a quite respectable parapsychological name: "precognitive apparitions."

Mrs. McCahen would be hard put to it, to search for her "underlying drives and needs" as a "percipient," as the ASPR researchers would put it. Did she, in the mountain dusk, feel lonely? Did she want companions for herself and her husband? Had she developed a rapport with Mrs. Nash of which she was not even consciously aware—and did, in a brief moment, her psyche reach out toward these friends, by then already on their way, and bring them up the mountain half a day ahead, as "probably tired," luggage-carrying, prophetic apparitions?

Systematic collection and evaluation of precognitive experiences is a very recent development. It is fair to assume that many thousands of such cases remain unreported, or even unrecognized, by those who experience them. And the established social and cultural patterns of Western civilization usually discourage people from admitting even to themselves that they are capable of "seeing the future"—much less telling others about it.

13 Can You Change Destiny?

A man living in East Orange, New Jersey, got up early one morning, because he and his wife were thinking of beating the traffic on the Jersey Turnpike; they were planning to drive to the mountains. At 5 A.M. he received a telephone call from his sister in Detroit. She had dreamed that he was on a trip and that his car had overturned, pinning him underneath. The dream was so vividly frightening that she put through the long-distance call in spite of the early hour. The Jersey man decided not to take the trip.

If his sister had not had the dream, if she had disregarded it, if in spite of her urgent feelings she had failed to place the call, if the call had been delayed, if the New Jersey man had gone on his trip—would he have had a potentially fatal accident? No one can tell, of course. There are just too many "ifs." But questions such as these are weightily discussed by philosophers and theologians; they intrude on basic religious concepts, such as "God's will," and on fatalism —"If the bullet's got my name on it, it'll get me!"—but also on the very concrete question: Can prophecy prevent disaster?

Fairly remote from the disputes of philosophers, one intensely practical woman has tried to answer these questions. She is the white-haired, grandmotherly wife of Dr. J. B. Rhine, Dr. Louisa E. Rhine, whose common sense cuts through high-flown arguments with refreshing simplicity. Mrs. Rhine's office at the Institute for Parapsychology in Durham, North Carolina, accommodates numerous filing cabinets that contain some 14,000 reports of spontaneous phenomena. She, more than anyone else, has the raw material on which answers to questions about prophetic warnings can be based.

Mrs. Rhine, after some twenty years of intensive studies of thousands of precognitive cases, feels that "they are like any other warnings." In her book, *Hidden Channels of the Mind* (New York, 1961), from which the New Jersey case was taken, she writes that "if proper preventive measures are taken, they succeed." But often a prophetic impression is vague, and it is not clear what countermeasures should be taken. In any event, such measures may be inadequate or outside the power of an individual—in the case of an earthquake, for instance. Mrs. Rhine says :"The theoretical aspect of events foreseen and avoided is very complicated. Even if one considers only cases which seem definitely precognitive, one cannot say for sure that an event would otherwise have occurred but was prevented by human will."

The thousands of precognitive cases that have been collected in Durham, most of them dreams, are categorized and analyzed by Mrs. Rhine, mainly to see whether or not they suggest new patterns for experimental work. She has categorized spontaneous phenomena, which also include telepathy (person-to-person); clairvoyance (object or event perceived directly); "intuitive" and "hallucinatory" impressions, which occur when a person is awake; "unrealistic dreaming" (fantasy images); and "realistic dreaming" (which is as clear as real life).

In the intuitive category can be vague feelings, such as disquiet or even deep anxiety, but no specific images. One woman wrote to Mrs. Rhine that on the night of October 31, 1947, she "became suddenly worried" about her sister, who lived in the same town. She walked the floor, restlessly, until three in the morning. She tried to telephone her sister the next day, picking up the receiver twice but not completing the call. She wrote: "An hour went by, and then the telephone rang. My sister had been instantly killed in her car. A gravel truck struck her three blocks from her home. I almost went mad thinking that I could have prevented the accident if I had only talked to her instead of hanging up the receiver."

No one, of course, could either reassure this woman or

tell her that her sister's fate was "foreordained." In some cases, Mrs. Rhine notes, people simply have a certainty of danger, but are not sure what form it will take or even whom tragedy will strike. One woman describes that she had "a sense of tragedy hovering between our new home and my brother-in-law's roof, just as though a depressive sadness hung between." She thought that this feeling must somehow apply to her daughter—a natural motherly concern, to be sure—and one night she again had the familiar feeling of "something being wrong, tingling fingertips, chills, hair raising, and a sense of inner panic." She wept, her husband gave her three aspirins and put her to bed; there she cried herself to sleep. The telephone rang, and they were told that her brother-in-law's daughter, the same age as her own, had been struck by a car and killed.

In their false targets but emotional accuracy, these precognitive experiences suggest that a prophetic image may be trying to break through but is blocked by certain factors—such as a mother's anxiety about her own daughter, rather than about another's. In a paper on "Subjective Forms of Spontaneous Psi Experiences" (*Journal of Parapsychology*, Vol. 17, No. 2, 1953), Mrs. Rhine cites this case, narrated to her by a musician:

"A little less than a year ago, I was beginning to plan my two annual pupil recitals. Sometime during the early spring I experienced a vague uneasiness about the health of one of my brothers. Both brothers had had very serious operations the year before, and had recovered. However, my uneasiness was all concerning the one who lived about 500 miles from me. There had been no word from him or his wife, except that he was teaching.

"Nevertheless, there was uneasiness. I did not want to ask directly how he was, because family mail was opened by either of them, and any little note I might send his wife might reach him first and cause him to worry. As time passed, the uneasiness became a clearer fact, and also it became connected with the two recitals, which were to take place April 25 and May 2. Something told me I would not attend the first recital. I even planned in my mind, for I said nothing to anyone else, to ask a friend to take over. Each time the singer who was to assist came to practice, the impression was intensified, until, on the night before the recital, as I sat down to play her accompaniment, a thought came almost like a voice. 'There is not much use in this practice. You are not going to play for her. Mrs. S. will play.' However, I went on because I did not want to make her nervous.

"Just as she was leaving, the message came that my brother had passed away at 7:00, just a moment before I started to play. I did not attend the recital and Mrs. S. presided and accompanied."

This incident shows a merging of precognition and telepathy. Mrs. Rhine has noted that, in experiences of this kind, distinctions between the present and the future are often blurred, and the past and the future are sometimes perceived as if they were in the present, so that "the extrasensory perception of these various situations seems simply to encompass all, as if in a timeless, spaceless purview."

To return to an earlier question: can disaster be prevented? Here is a case in which the disaster itself took place, but a prophetic hunch really saved a life. It is the case of a newly married woman, who insisted to her husband, Billy, that she "just had to go home." He fussed a little, but quickly gave in, ordered the one and only taxi in the small town to take her to the usual morning train that would get her to her parents. The young bride recalled the incident in these words:

"I remember how joyful I was and how I danced about the house waiting for the taxi. Billy and the driver teased me, but I was too happy to care. Just as he bought the tickets, cold fear gripped me. I started to cry. 'Give him back the tickets,' I said. 'Please, Billy, we can't go on this train.' Billy went into one of his rages, but the ticketman reached out and took the tickets: 'Do as she says. Always do as she says.' We got into the taxi and all the way to the hotel they asked me why. I did not know.

"At dinner there was a commotion. The taximan was coming toward me, pushing people to one side and upsetting chairs. He cried, 'How did you know not to go on that train? It was wrecked in the next town. The car you always ride in turned over, and everyone was killed.'"

As Mrs. Rhine puts it, in the terminology of scholarly evaluation, "Cases like the above seem to indicate awareness of some situation related to or suggested by the stimulus event, but that event itself remains unknown." And, of course, the event had not yet taken place.

Future events do not simply cast their shadows backward —they seem to use any and all channels to gain entry into the conscious mind. One of these is what one might call a sympathetic pain. Take this case, also that of a newly married woman. Her husband was working away from home.

Before going to sleep one night, she had a numb feeling in one arm and a leg. She recalls: "For no reason, I suddenly thought of something happening to my husband. I wasn't at all excited, which is unexplainable, as I am and always have been nervous and excitable. The next day at noon, my husband was brought home with a badly mashed and broken arm. I still wasn't excited, as I felt I had been told hours before, though actually the accident occurred several hours after my feeling."

Other precognitive experiences may correspond only partially to the actual event. One man described a dream he had had when his family was living in Cologne, Germany. As reported by Mrs. Rhine, they had been to a delightful party and were in anything but a morbid mood when they returned home. Yet his dream that night was filled with foreboding; he saw men carrying a small casket, covered by a black cloth, down an enormous staircase. At the same time —in the dream—a voice said to him quite distinctly, "This is a sign that a member of your family will soon die."

The dream took place on a Tuesday night. On the following Saturday, his sixteen-year-old son had to undergo an operation because of a sudden attack of appendicitis. The father recalls that, during hospitalization, "On Sunday night he fell, owing to some unfortunate circumstances, through the window into the street. Some passerby carried him, dying, back into the hospital."

As we have already seen, precognition can concern itself with such vital matters as life and death, or it may stray into the utterly trivial. The prophetic link may momentarily pull together the closest family members, or mere acquaintances. It may clearly be full of significance, or seemingly without any meaning whatsoever. Nothing would be easier than simply to pick the most hair-raising, intimate, ever-so-significant examples from the files of prophetic images. But to illustrate, let me select a case that is symbolic, prophetic, possibly fraught with psychological significance, but weirdly trivial:

"When I was young we lived in a heavily wooded part of northern Maine. We lived there until I was seventeen and at that time there was a lot of big game there, such as deer, moose, and bear. We got part of our food by hunting and fishing. When I was sixteen, one night I dreamed that I killed people with my rifle. Next day I went hunting and killed as many caribou as I had killed persons the night before in my dreams. After that, every time I dreamed of shooting people, I would go hunting and I was sure of getting big game. One night I dreamed that I shot two little girls. They were dressed alike and they looked alike. Apparently they were twins. The next day I went hunting and shot two little doe deer. They looked exactly alike and no doubt were twins. Those dreams never failed to come true."

One precognitive dream was reported by the wife of a soldier who had been away from home for two years. One night, the wife dreamed that their little boy was tossing in his bed, hot and feverish and with his arm in a cast. In the dream, the boy's mother "felt faint from the smell of ether." The very next day, the little boy broke his wrist. The mother reported, "The only thing that was different was the ether smell, for they had given him gas when they set it."

Curiously, then, what really stood out in the mother's mind was not the prophetic nature of the dream, but the fact that her anticipated smell of ether had not been borne out by the event. In the laboratory situation, which I shall discuss in the next chapter, extrasensory perception creates little errors and displacements. In spontaneous cases, emotional or other predilections may get in the way of, hold back, distort, color, or falsely dramatize events. I have described some of the work of the well-known Dutch clairvoyant, Gerard Croiset. He has had many "hits" to his credit. Yet to me one of his "misses" is among the most dramatic illustrations of the elusive quality of ESP. He was looking, clairvoyantly, and not involving the chairs this time, for an English tourist, who had been reported missing on the North Sea coast. Croiset, at one wooded section, received the strong impression that it was there that the Englishman had "hanged himself." As it turned out, a poacher had trapped and strangled a deer at this spot. This surely must mean that Croiset received a strong strangling-or-hanging impression, though he interpreted it in terms of what he was looking for.

Such a relatively neat explanation does not fit each type of prophecy. In fact, every case seems to represent a constellation all its own, and though certain patterns soon become familiar, variations make definite conclusions impossible. Here is one case in which, as Mrs. Rhine puts it, "the picture is exact, but tangential to the meaning" of the actual event:

"The first night we lived in the new house, my mother had a dream. She said she saw a funeral down the street a way. The house where she saw it was quite small and occupied by Italians. The hall in it was so narrow that it was necessary to bring the casket out through the window. But there was not much sense to that dream, and what could it mean, if anything.

"But early in March, sure enough, a funeral procession came by our house. We heard afterwards that the coffin was passed out through the window of the little house. On the other side of the street, waiting for the hearse and carriages to pass, was a uniformed Western Union boy. He hurried over to our house as soon as he could get by and gave mother a telegram. Her favorite cousin had been killed in an accident."

As noted, then, prophecy concerns itself with death and matters of consequence as well as with the trivia of everyday life. Mrs. Rhine's files contain many cases that are so striking in their horror that she has deliberately chosen not to publish many in these categories. Some people who experience telepathic or prophetic phenomena become badly frightened by them. At times they are concerned about their mental balance. In other instances the event leaves a traumatic impression, a wound within the soul that refuses to heal. This is one reason why most people would rather not undergo such experiences, or hear about them, or tell them to others.

One woman had an electrifying experience along these lines when she was a nine-year-old girl in Nova Scotia, Canada. Later, as an adult, she recalled her prophetic dream as follows: "A coffin stood in a corner of our living room. As I approached it I saw the face therein was that of my beloved grandmother. I awoke, stricken with grief. I slept no more that night. I could not bring myself to tell anyone of the dream that haunted me so—not even my grandmother. After several days my spirits arose again and the dream was almost forgotten." She recalls the following events:

"Within a fortnight my grandfather died suddenly of a heart attack. On the day of the funeral I was taken into the room of my dream. There was the coffin as I had seen it. The only difference lay in the cold, still face—the face of my grandfather and not, as in my dream, of my grandmother. My grief was now mingled with a strange, gripping alarm, almost terror. Still, I spoke of the dream to no one. In my child's mind I feared mentioning the dream would in some way add to the sorrow of an already stricken family.

"Years afterward, my mother told me that on the day my grandfather died, he had said to her in the morning, 'Last night I dreamed that everybody in town was dead—I was the only person alive.' She told me that he looked at her keenly as if to ask whether she understood what he was thinking. Then he went out, waving his hand in his usual light-hearted manner. Within an hour he was dead. It was then I told my mother of the dream I had had almost twenty years before. For years it had had the grip of an icy hand, and as I write, the retelling of it opens old griefs as if they were yesterday's wounds."

Mrs. Rhine comments on this case in her book, urging that such experiences are better told than held back: "In twenty years a perfectly healthy 'wound' should have so healed that retelling would no longer raise the old emotions so vividly. No doubt the reason it still did so was because the question raised had gone unanswered all those years. If the girl had been able to discuss her dream normally with her parents, much of the disturbing mystery of it would have disappeared, the strain would have been relieved, and the episode taken for what it was: a perfectly healthy precognitive experience remarkable mainly for having occurred to a young child."

But those, of course, are the words of a researcher who has studied thousands upon thousands of prophetic dreams, foretelling dull or glamorous, routine or terrifying experiences. The lightning-like impact of a precognitive experience borne out by events is a bone-chilling experience for the average person. If time itself is unstable, just how distorted is our overall view of the world in which we live? If events happen out of sequence, if they are recorded by a human mind days, months, or years before their occurrence, just what do such terms as past, present, and future really mean?

They may, in fact, be meaningless. They may be no more than the man-made devices that calendars and clocks are. It shouldn't be too surprising to contemplate that our own, routine, sense-oriented concepts of time and space may well not encompass the actuality behind these concepts—virtually yesterday in man's history, the shape of the earth and the force of gravity were misunderstood, and dogmatically defined.

But when the future does come crashing back into the present, its repercussions can range from puzzlement to shock. Here, for instance, is a woman baking a cake. She is very much awake, mixing dough, adding spices. A mental picture forces itself on her: her husband has been in an automobile accident; his head is bleeding; his body is twisted from the waist down, so that it lies on the right side, flat on his back from the waist up, his arms arched over his head. Right there, in her kitchen, in broad daylight, this woman just "knows" that her husband has been in a car accident and that he is unconscious, although she does not "see" a car.

The impression is so strong, so overpowering that then and there the woman starts crying. But shortly she remembers that what she is experiencing is probably just her imagination; maybe the oven heat is too much for her. There must be some simple, everyday explanation.

There was an explanation, simple and tragic. Seven days later, when her husband was standing by a parked car, he was sideswiped by a speeding vehicle, which threw him, bleeding, twisted, and unconscious to the ground.

In contemporary Western society, one does not go around telling experiences of this sort easily. As Mrs. Rhine sagely observes, the fact that extrasensory impressions may occur to "perfectly sane and healthy persons is still an almost entirely unrecognized fact."

There is another overwhelmingly strong factor that restrains many people from admitting prophetic incidents to others, or even to themselves, and that is the often highly intimate nature of these phenomena. Where profound emotional factors play a role, it is self-evident that sexual aspects are certain to be prominent. An unusually candid case was communicated to Mrs. Rhine by a mature woman; she reported an event that took place when she was in college. The report, which was anonymous, stated that she then once telephoned home to tell her mother that, instead of coming to see her parents over the weekend, she would stay and finish an experiment on Saturday afternoon.

"Then," she wrote, "Saturday evening on my way back to the dorm a man I shall call Bill asked me if I would go with him on a picnic the fraternity he belonged to was having the next day. It was at a lake some fifty miles away. I had dated Bill occasionally before, and said I would go.

"I thought no more of the matter until about ten o'clock the next morning, when Mother phoned me. She was upset, I could tell, and asked me please not to leave the dorm that day but to stay there in my own room, saying she would explain when I came home the following weekend. I comforted her by saying I would, and promptly upon hanging up the phone began gathering things I would need for the picnic, including my bathing suit. But I was a little worried over the phone call, as my mother is not an excitable woman and it was not like her to worry about me.

"Bill arrived in his car about then, and we drove to the lake. We were the only couple to go in swimming that day, and when we came out we did not go immediately to the bathhouses to get into our dry clothes, as it was a warm day and the bathhouses were on the far end of the park, a drive of about three miles. Along toward sunset, though, we drove to the bathhouses and changed. The drive back led through two stretches of forest where there were no picnickers and it was here that it happened. To make a long story short—I can think of no way to soften the word—I was raped. It is to be remembered that Bill was not a roughhouse type. He came from a well-to-do family, was president of his fraternity, and was well liked on the campus. I was too shocked and ashamed to mention it to anyone and to this day no one knows, though it got around the small campus that Bill and I had had a fuss and weren't dating any more.

"The following weekend I went home, and as soon as we were alone Mother asked me if I had stayed in the dorm Sunday. Recalling her phone call, I assured her that I had, not wanting to remember the happening of that day. I asked her why she had made the request and she laughed and said she just wanted to be sure I had studied, but after some persuasion she told me the truth. She had had a dream Saturday night in which she saw me at the lake with a boy who met Bill's description very well, and she told me about the rest of the dream, which was practically word for word what happened on the way back from the bathhouse. Mother said she knew it was silly, but that the dream was so vivid that it had upset her. I successfully concealed my shock and comforted her as best I could, assuring her that no such thing had happened.

"I am very happily married now and have a son of my own, so from necessity I want my name to remain secret. I do hope that this may be of some use to you, as it is not easy for me to remember this incident."

Now, here is a case of exceptionally high emotional content, in which the precognitive dreamer never even knew that, shocking as it was, her dream had come true. Conversational material and a limited amount of recorded information suggest that the number of precognitive dream or waking cases involving the whole range of sexual and other emotional experiences is a good deal higher than published material indicates.

14 Precognition in the Laboratory

A white three-story house, just across the street from the campus of Duke University in Durham, North Carolina, since 1966 has served as the headquarters of the Foundation for Research on the Nature of Man, of which the Institute of Parapsychology is a part. Both are directed by Dr. J. B. Rhine, whose name is virtually synonymous with the scientific study of parapsychology. The rugged, white-haired Dr. Rhine expanded his research plans when he retired from Duke University late in 1965. To him, precognition remains a major area of challenge, within the wide scope of what he calls "the fundamental question of the relation of man's subjective self to the physical self of which he is also a part." It is one thing to record, classify, and seek to authenticate individual cases of prophecy; it is quite another to develop laboratory experiments which actually capture the elusive forces that seem to be at work in phenomena defying time and space as we know them.

Dr. Rhine, assisted by members of his staff, affiliated with Duke's renowned Parapsychology Laboratory for nearly four decades, was led to investigate precognition as the result of a search for something quite different: evidence for man's immortality, then known as "post-mortem survival," or survival of the human personality after death. Professor William McDougall began parapsychological research in the Department of Psychology of Duke University in 1927. Eventually, major sections of the inquiries on mediumistic data showed that the "spirit entities," which seemed to be communicating through mediums, might well be dramatic creations of the mediums' own subconscious minds, utilizing information picked up by extrasensory means.

In the Psychology Department, under McDougall, Dr. Rhine was the leading staff member interested in this research. He was free to test any hypothesis whatsoever. Dr. Rhine recalls, "We were already aware of the strong possibility that the medium herself might possess abilities capable of acquiring information extrasensorially from living, mundane sources. We examined all possible extrasensory channels, and that included not only telepathy and clairvoyance, but precognition as well."

The Duke group consisted of J. B. Rhine and his students. He published a history-making monograph called *Extrasensory Perception* in 1934, but this volume did not contain so much as a hint of the precognition research which by then had already begun to show high promise. "We were experimenting all over the lot," Rhine recalls, "and precognition research emerged as part of a backhanded—to put it exactly, counterhypothetical—approach to the problem of spirit communication." He describes the situation at that point as follows:

"Nobody cared about precognition. The world of science was not ready for it; it did not wish to have its hypothetical applecarts overturned. At the same time, those who finance research in post-mortem survival could see that the case for ESP provided an explanation for phenomena that they thought related to spirit entities. We didn't get much encouragement from either side, to put it mildly. And we realized quickly that the mood of the times, the scientific culture all around us, were cool or even hostile to the things we began to discover."

The prophecy breakthrough came in December 1933. The famous ESP card tests had already borne clairvoyant fruit. But the researchers were looking for ways to refine their methods and explore more deeply the perceptive faculties that seemed to be involved. The cards were, as always, of five images: of a cross, a circle, wavy lines, a square, and a star. Up to that time, persons tested were asked to identify, or guess, the ESP cards in their existing order in the deck.

A key figure in the experiments leading up to the breakthrough was Hubert E. Pearce, then a theology student at the Duke University School of Religion, and today a Methodist minister in Arkansas. Pearce had attended one of Dr. Rhine's lectures, and spoken to him afterward of his family's long-standing interest in psychic ability, and had reluctantly agreed to take part in experimentation. Pearce, during the initial informal tests, averaged ten out of twenty-five cards—made up of the five images—or twice the number chance suggests. Dr. Rhine and his assistant, Dr. J. G. Pratt, tested

Pearce until the summer of 1933, when Pearce was away on ministerial work. On his return, Dr. Rhine suggested that they try distance experiments and set up the arrangement that Pratt recalls in his book *Parapsychology: An Insider's View of ESP* (New York, 1964); he had a place in the psychology laboratory then located in the Physics Building on the West Campus of Duke University, while Pearce had "a study cubicle in the library stacks on the side of the library away from the Physics Building." He recalls: "Each day when we planned to work, Hubert would come by my room shortly before the time agreed upon for the test. We compared our watches and set them together, even allowing for the difference between the second hands. Then I watched Hubert walk across the campus and disappear into the library." Pratt describes the procedure as follows:

"I selected a pack of ESP cards, shuffling it thoroughly, cut it, and placed it face down on the near right-hand corner of a card table at which I had taken my seat. At the time agreed upon for starting the test, I picked up the top card from the pack and, without looking at it, placed it face down on a book in the center of the table. After one minute I removed that card and placed it, still face down and still unknown to myself, at the far left-hand corner of the table and immediately placed the next card from the pack on the book.

"Proceeding in this way, I placed the twenty-five cards, one after the other, on the book in the center of the table. When all the cards had taken their turn on the book, I made a record of the twenty-five cards in the order in which they had been used."

This was the basic procedure for the distance experiments. Distance between Pearce and Pratt was increased when a second series of experiments was made while Pratt sat in the building of the medical school and Pearce stayed in the library. The distance during the first series was a hundred yards; the second took place at a distance of about 250 yards. Pearce's scores were significantly above chance, but there were many variations above and below the chance level. The experimenters concluded that greater or lesser distance did not make any real difference. Considered as a whole, the Duke researchers report that the seventy-four runs in the experiment, which became known as the Pearce-Pratt series, faced chance of odds in terms of statistical probability of 1 in 10,000,000,000,000,000,000,000,000 (*Journal of Parapsychology*, September 1954).

But these were experiments in clairvoyance at a distance,

PROPHECY IN OUR TIME 161

not in precognition. Having found that distance did not affect Pearce's scores, the experimenters decided to defy time, to bring a statistically measurable element of prophecy into the laboratory. As Dr. Rhine recalls, "We were encouraged in our safari into these unexplored areas by the many spontaneous experiences of precognitive ESP among the records of mankind. We were young and daring, but we did have sage antecedents, notably Professor Charles Richet of France and H. F. Saltmarsh of England, who had compiled vast collections of apparently prophetic experiences, including many premonitory dreams and occasional previsionary experiences in the waking state. They served to point up the problem and the need for further study. Taken by themselves, they could offer no definitive proof of prophecy. What were needed were planned experiments, yielding results that could be subjected to statistical analysis."

But the road of quantitative research is treacherous, winding, and strewn with rocks. Rhine and Pratt asked Pearce to write down his vision of the deck of cards as it would be *after* it had been shuffled—and the scores were, again and again, just as good as if he had been applying his extrasensory gifts to the present rather than the future. But the experimenters were worried. Were they overlooking something? After all, here they were defying the alleged natural laws of cause and effect—this man saw the effect before it had been caused!

The trouble was partly that they had been too successful in another type of experiment, psychokinesis, or PK. This test is usually done with dice. The experimenter "wills" the dice to fall in a certain way. His intent is recorded, as in playing dice. The evidence suggested that a mind-over-matter element at times defies the laws of chance.

The Duke experimenters asked themselves, "Is Pearce, in writing down his guesses, perhaps influencing the shuffle in a psychokinetic way? Does this account for the significant results?" Dr. Rhine recalls, with some amusement, that the experimenters "were for a time engaged in a colossal shuffling spree." They shuffled one deck of cards thousands of times with the "intent" of making it match another deck, or a list of the twenty-five ESP cards. They began to worry about a possible "psychic shuffle"—were their minds influencing the shuffling process itself? They could not rule it out. They had to find a way around it.

When in doubt, use machines. Being nonhuman, machines must be considered immune to extrasensory stimuli—until the day the psychic computer begins to rear its parapsychological head. Two mechanical methods were used. One was an electric card-shuffling device; the other threw six dice mechanically, and their total was used to determine the order of the cards. Having thus eliminated the "psychic shuffle," the card-guessing results came out, nevertheless, again significantly in favor of precognition.

Yet, the possible influence of mind over cards or dice (psychokinesis) could not be fully ruled out, so a still more ingenious way of bypassing the psychokinetic influence was worked out. The experimenters turned to meteorology. They wound up by basing the number of mechanical shuffles and the point of cutting the deck on maximum and minimum temperature readings on a given day, fixed from two to ten days ahead. According to Dr. Rhine, "The procedure left no alternative to the precognition hypothesis—unless one were to consider the possibility that the weather itself was being influenced by those participating in the experiment. . . ."

As anyone can see, laboratory work of this type must at times be exciting, truly in the nature of a scientific adventure; it can also be a gigantic bore, frustrating, irritating, and almost "too far out"—except for the dedicated experimenters themselves. After all, the Duke group was pitting one impossible hypothesis, "psychokinesis," against another one, "precognition"—worrying about whether or not one was intruding on the other, as they tried always to strengthen and refine their research methods.

Later they found confirmation of a kind in the experiments undertaken in England by Dr. S. G. Soal, then a Lecturer in Mathematics at the University of London, and Mrs. K. M. Goldney, researcher of the Society for Psychical Research. Dr. Soal had engaged for years in card tests with individuals. His efforts, painstakingly narrated in *Modern Experiments in Telepathy* (New Haven, 1954), centered around an unusual subject, one Mr. Basil Shackleton. This man, a studio photographer who later migrated to South Africa, had crossed Dr. Soal's path after years of fruitless experimentation. As far back as 1936, they had engaged in telepathy experiments. But he did not manifest telepathic abilities; as far as anyone could judge from a long series of experiments, his guesses were quite random.

Soal was disheartened. Here was a man who had come to him with quite a show of confidence in his own abilities— and a positive belief in the reality of ESP and in one's own ability seems to be a positive psychological factor in laboratory testing—but the results were nil. In the late 1930's a colleague of Soal's, Whately Carington, discovered something he called a "displacement effect"; according to this, a subject might with some regularity hit a target card *adjacent* to the one that he was supposed to be guessing. With this in mind, Dr. Soal took another good look at his records; Shackleton had, over and over again, guessed the card that was just before or just after the one that had been fixed as his target. What was going on?

It wasn't prophecy. It was some sort of vision, if you like, because the cards were right there, lined up, when Shackleton made his hits. He wasn't guessing at something that had not yet occurred, even when he was listing the card beyond his supposed target. Then Soal and Goldney, in the middle of the London blitz attacks, developed yet a new technique. They substituted cards picturing animals, including zebras and giraffes, for the standard ESP cards. They consulted a random number list to establish the cards' positions. When the experimenter showed the sender the number for a given trial, the sender lifted the appropriate card and looked at it. Shortly after Shackleton was given a signal, he recorded the name of the animal he was guessing as the one the sender was looking at. In this way, the experimenters avoided a fixed order of cards over which Shackleton might scatter his guesses. There was no card on the table, waiting its turn to be looked at. There was only the list of random numbers.

Now Shackleton became a prophet. He continued to avoid the card that Soal and Goldney might be looking at. But he no longer listed the preceding card, either. He went right on and named the card that was going to be selected next, over and over again.

This was as puzzling, or worse, as what had happened with Pearce in Durham. What was Shackleton doing? Was he reading the sender's mind ahead of time, when the sender didn't even know what he would see next? Was he clairvoyantly reading the random number list, and then identifying the proper animal card even before it had been selected or looked at?

Soal and Goldney were just as pleased, confused, and worried by Shackleton as Rhine and Pratt had been by Pearce. And they, too, proceeded to make things still tougher for their prophetic experimental subject. How could they get around his possible "precognition telepathy" or roaming clairvoyance? They abandoned the number list which, after all, had been prepared ahead of time. Instead, they used a bag of colored chips from which they picked a chip only at the very moment of the actual individual card test. A given color was chosen to signify a specific card position. At each choice of chip and card, Shackleton faced a brand-new situation. Even with telepathy and clairvoyance, there was no pre-existing clue that he might tap.

Sure enough, Shackleton did it again! Chips, lists of numbers—it made no difference to his prophetic ability to name just the right animal. He *averaged* about seven hits per twenty-five trials (five would have been chance) on the card just ahead of the actual target card.

It is difficult to define the significance of this success. One has to make oneself aware, with an effort at high imagination, that Shackleton *could not* have grasped any contemporary thoughts when he made his choice. This was not one of these "easy" spontaneous cases in which a sensitive wife, say, is aware, even at a distance of many miles, that her husband is distraught behind the wheel of his car and therefore more than usually prone to have an accident—and so, she actually visualizes the accident that is only psychologically in the making.

No, Shackleton did not even have anything that elusive, but nevertheless contemporary, on which to fasten his psychic ability. Soal and Goldney varied their experiment. They speeded it up. The prophetic element became even more marked: now Shackleton was guessing two cards ahead of the actual target. Now, he could not even have clairvoyantly selected the *next* chip to be chosen. One more hypothesis remained: that Shackleton, in what amounted to reverse impact, was influencing the experimenter's selection of the chip.

One other alternative, of course, was that they were all cheating. It was the crudest hypothesis of all, and it was voiced some years later in the magazine *Science,* in an article by George R. Price. This kind of convoluted notion cannot be definitely denied. Another severe critic is Dr. C. E. M. Hansel, who has found fault with much of parapsychological research method in his book *ESP: A Scientific Evaluation* (New York, 1966). In the end, twenty-one persons were watching Shackleton's prophetic performance; the details of these experiments and their methods were printed in the *Proceedings* of the Society for Psychical Research, London, in December 1943, and later in Dr. Soal's book. Dr. Rhine, to this day, will allow that picking chips out of a bag might be explained by possible "reverse telepathy"—from Shackleton to Soal—but that "when this work is considered against the background of the other evidence for a prophetic capacity, the precognition hypothesis seems the more reasonable one for Soal's work in this case."

On October 12, 1965, Rhine gave a lecture at London's Guildhall, sponsored by the British Association for the Advancement of Science, during which he presented his conclusions on the precognition work in very restrained terms. He said:

"The precognition test has in recent years become more or less just another routine type of psi test, its use incidental to other research objectives. It has certain advantages: for example, sensory leakage would be impossible, and so, too, would be any deception on the part of a subject. With the two-experimenter procedure also used in the checking of record sheets, the experimental reliability of this method is about as good as anything could be in the psychological sciences. Precognition testing, too, has already been handled with success by machine methods."

Today, as director of the Foundation for Research on the Nature of Man, J. B. Rhine is deeply concerned with the wide implication of prophetic experiences in terms of the nature of man. Precognition, to him, is just one of a variety of experiences that call for a drastic re-evaluation of scientific concepts. Still, he feels keenly that "research on the precognitive ability has not yet brought it under control; work in this area has been relatively limited, and it is too early to develop a definitive explanation."

Very well, then, if the explanation here cannot be definite, it can be tentative because the evidence is strong. If man *can* be prophetic, where does this faculty lead; what, specifically, is its challenge? A septuagenarian ex-marine who chops wood for recreation and plays the mouth organ for relaxation, Rhine believes that precognition is the parapsychological avant garde; that its significance needs to be recognized by science as well as by theology.

Rhine has said that precognition contributes to the "very incomplete map of nature." He regards "the bewilderment commonly experienced in confrontation with the evidence for precognition as due not merely to the strangeness of this effect, but fully as much to the limited knowledge psychology and neurology have contributed on the question of what the essential nature of human personality really is." Rhine does not hold with the pseudo-self-assurance that masks much of the uneasiness prevalent in science today, because, as he says, "we are no less ignorant of the nature of consciousness itself than we are about precognition."

According to Rhine, psychology stands particularly in need of revolution. He states quite bluntly that "the field and leadership in psychology has never been quite clear as to what the basic object of its study really is." Psychology will have to acknowledge, Rhine urges, "the independent reality of something beyond the physical brain system on which psychological research has largely centered." He feels that there must be "a shift from a cerebrocentric to a psychocentric view of man."

New thought in modern physics is in many exploratory ways sympathetic to parapsychology and its phenomena. In Rhine's opinion, the establishment of precognition may well help physics to recognize that parapsychological phenomena are, in a very specific sense, "energetic," and that "energy is not the exclusive province of physics." He puts it this way:

"We know now, at least in parapsychology, that space-time as generally known does not comprehend the whole of the universe; that this spatio-temporal structure of the physical universe is a consequence of the experience, sensory and inferential, of the changing physical order. Man, of course, projects the framework of his experience into the physical world from which stimuli come to his sense organs—and he projects it, inferentially, to all those occurrences that change in ways lawfully characteristic of space-time experience."

In Rhine's view, "physics is today, for the first time in science, a subject delimited in the order of nature, and man therefore belongs to a bigger universe than he has known hitherto." The very complexity of these thoughts—which call for a rereading even by someone well steeped in the field of inquiry—is an indication of their novelty and significance beyond accepted criteria. What Rhine is saying, in effect, is that man tends to judge everything, including his own more elusive faculties, by a system of outmoded ideas. Man, even man the scientist, has difficulty viewing himself from a vantage point outside the comfortable symbolisms of clock and geography, where one thing follows another and events lose impact the further away they are.

When Rhine places man in a "bigger" universe, he adds that it does no matter "how much bigger" it might be, because "magnitude outside the space-time universe is not a comparable matter," and words such as bigger or smaller, higher or lower, are "without meaning" in this context.

But the acceptance of such insights must await a maturing

within science, and new developments in culture and thought. Rhine looks forward to a time when "the spotlight of scientific interest will turn upon parapsychology in a way and degree more proportionate to its significance to mankind." As has happened before, science is responding to trends within its community as a whole. Interest in prophetic phenomena, widespread as it is today, may well prompt modern science to put itself into new focus, even in the age of the supercomputer.

15 Prophecy and Youth

The Duke experimenters continued to refine their methods throughout the 1940's and 1950's. One dramatic test involved transatlantic precognition over the span of one year. The idea for such an experiment arose in March 1956, when Miss Rose Hynes, then a Duke sophomore, was tested for ESP at Dr. Rhine's laboratory. On her first ESP card test of five runs, 125 of the standard cards, she correctly named 37 cards; 25 would have been chance. She was tested until the end of the semester, and the results continued to be encouraging.

Dr. Margaret Anderson, then on the laboratory staff and later a Pittsburgh educator, found that Miss Hynes shared an interest in precognition with her. As Dr. Anderson reported in the *Journal of Parapsychology* (June 1959), the two young women spent the summer planning an experiment that would explore whether or not "a person can bridge a time interval of one year in a precognition test."

As Miss Hynes was going to Paris to spend her junior college year, she took a large supply of standard ESP record sheets with her. The experiment ran for nine months, ending in May 1957. Rose Hynes made monthly guesses of precognition runs, completing two sheets each month, which she sent to Dr. Anderson in Durham. The total came to ninety runs.

Miss Hynes was well aware that she was supposed to guess ESP symbols which would later be "randomly determined and entered on her record sheets in the card columns corresponding to the columns with her guesses." To compare long-range with short-range results, she was told the results of her first five runs of guesses right away, but the other five monthly runs were not to be checked until twelve months later. In other words, the final results would not be known until June 1958.

Each record sheet containing five runs through a deck of twenty-five cards, 125 calls altogether, were mailed to Duke University. As soon as the sheets arrived, Miss Rhea White, then a member of the laboratory staff, decided which runs should be checked immediately and which were to be checked a year later. Dr. Anderson reports:

"In order to assure that this separation could not be subjectively influenced by herself, Miss White used a complicated but strictly prescribed method," selecting an entry from a random number table to "get a sequence of numbers for dividing the runs into those to be checked immediately and those to be checked after one year." An order of events is "random" when it displays no trends or regularities that would allow any inference regarding one event from one or more of the others in a series.

Anderson and White checked the record sheets independently, and "the run scores were then relayed to the subject along with encouragement and comments." When they had finished the whole experiment, in May 1957, a third staff member independently checked the forty-five immediate-check runs.

They began the one-year check-up at the first of each month, beginning in October 1957 and on through June 1958. Meanwhile, Miss Hynes had returned to Duke University, now as a college senior. The short-range guesses (the five-day precognition attempt between Paris and Durham) were statistically not significant. However, the one-year-ahead guesses *were* significantly above chance.

Hiss Hynes, in other words, had beaten the odds in guessing one year ahead, but not five days ahead. If one added up the total number of hits, which was 496, for the two experimental undertakings, "a positive deviation of 46 [hits] above chance expectancy" was recorded. Taking the five-day guesses alone, only 230 hits were recorded, a deviation of only 5 above the chance level; however, the one-year-ahead guesses came to 41 above chance level. Dr. Anderson noted that Rose Hynes apparently was able to bridge a time interval of one year in a precognition test, perhaps because she felt "more challenged by the long-range than by the short-range test." She added that this would mean that "she knew precognitively which runs would be checked a year later."

The experiment ended on a romantic note. Miss Hynes had made her guesses during a variety of moods. While, at times "she was sustained by a deep philosophical interest in precognition," at other times she had difficulties adjusting herself to the social and scholastic environment in France. This was reflected in relatively poor results, particularly at the beginning of the tests.

However, Dr. Anderson noted that as Rose Hynes "became acclimated to her new situation, her scoring began to improve." She also observed, with appropriate scholarly detachment: "In December she wrote of her interest in a young Frenchman, and subsequent letters indicated her excitement and happiness in this developing romance. One cannot say that this factor explains the larger deviation on the last part of the experiment, but it seems a reasonable possibility. If this interpretation is correct, the findings suggest that the psychological state of the subject is an important factor in a precognition experiment as well as in other psi tests."

The role of psychological factors in ESP success is the special province of Dr. Gertrude R. Schmeidler, Psychology department, College of the City of New York. She is well known for applying the label "sheep" to experimental subjects who have a positive attitude toward extrasensory perception, and "goats" to those who are critical of it. One of her more dramatic precognition tests, of which there have been many, divided people into "dynamic-hasty" and "naturalistic-passive" types. These categories were established by Dr. R. H. Knapp and Dr. J. T. Garbutt, authors of the Time Metaphor Test. According to their metaphor categories, dynamic-hasty people see Time as a "dashing waterfall" or a "fast-moving shuttle," whereas the naturalistic-passive group thinks of it as "a vast expanse of sky" or "a quiet, motionless sea."

To Knapp and Garbutt, the dynamic-hasty people are those who like to get things done; they are highly competitive and "in need of achievement." The naturalistic-passive metaphors suggest an "oriental or mystical time sense," a sense of time that is "surrounding and encompassing in a passive sense." Dr. Schmeidler was curious to find out how the two Knapp-Garbutt metaphor types would correlate with results in a precognition test. She used seventy-five City College undergraduates and built the Time Metaphor Test into an overall precognition experiment.

This is how it worked. The students were asked to make three sets of calls for precognition, using five colored ESP cards. There were fifty calls per set. A computer selected the targets and scored the hits, so this aspect of the experiment was, as it were, "untouched by human hands." At first, the students were alarmed at being asked to be prophetic, to have to name targets "which had not yet been selected," and they reacted with a combination of incredulity and protest. Dr. Schmeidler reassured them by comparing their guesses to "bets on an honest wheel of fortune" at a fair. The giving of the Time Metaphor Test to each student was sandwiched in between two separate sets of precognition calls.

One set of calls, labeled "Subject Sees," they were told, was later to be copied out and mailed to them, along with a copy of the targets and a letter which discussed their hits and misses. Another set, called "Experimenter Sees," was to be examined by the experimenter, but target and hit patterns were not shown to the subjects. A third set did not have its targets printed out by the computer.

The results were studied by the experimenter from various points of view. One element stood out: the dynamic-hasty types of subjects scored notably higher in the "Subject Sees" category than in the others. They apparently wanted to know how well they did in their ESP scores, and their scoring "mechanism" made them guess better. Perhaps the notion that the experiment was like betting on a wheel of fortune made it better suited to the dynamic-hasty types, but put the others off. Dr. Schmeidler wondered, afterward, whether the naturalistic-passive types might not have come up with better results if they had been told that "precognitive impressions indicated a contact between the ongoing present and the future, a unity of the universe, a being at one with the stream of events."

Another segment of Dr. Schmeidler's precognition tests employing a computer—all of these were reported in the *Journal of Parapsychology* (February and June 1964)— was concerned with the possible correlation between a person's creative capacity and his precognition performance. Put simply, the experiment was designed to answer this question: "Is a particularly imaginative person also a particularly prophetically gifted one?"

Creativity was measured by true-or-false tests developed by Dr. F. Barron, author of *Creativity and Psychological*

Health (Princeton, 1963). Subjects were also given a more open creativity test developed by Dr. J. P. Guilford. They were asked, for instance, to describe as many different uses as they could think of for a brick and for a wire coat hanger. The creativity tests were completed before the precognition results of the standard card tests were known. The Time Metaphor Test was included as well.

To most outsiders looking at the combination of factors involved in these tests, too many ingredients would appear to have been thrown into the experimental pot to concoct a definite dish. One factor stood out, though, when the various elements were untangled. Those who had scored high on creativity had actually scored below the chance level on the "Subject Sees" category—as if, Dr. Schmeidler noted, those with personalities yielding "higher creativity scores may have resented the restrictions" of the test procedure. They were, after all, "asked to choose a target which an unthinking, unfeeling machine would later select at random," and they could thus have had less interest in the eventual targets.

It used to be said of the Chicago stockyards that they used every part of the hog "except the squeal." Dr. Schmeidler is similarly frugal with her experimental subjects. The seventy-five undergraduates involved in the Time Metaphor and creativity tests were subjected to yet another inquiry: how is a "feeling of success" related to precognition results?

While the precognition tests were going on, subjects were told: "There's one more thing. When people are making these calls, they sometimes have a special hunch that one of them is right: it might be clearer, more vivid, somehow different. If you have any feelings of confidence about a particular call, put a check next to it on the record sheet. And if there are any differences in the way ideas come to you, write that down next to the response, if there's room. If you need more space, use this other sheet of paper. It should make it more interesting to score the responses later, and see if there was a difference between the ones you were right on and the others."

The experimenter found that those subjects who had only vague feelings about their calls were wrong just about as often as they were right. But those who said categorically that they felt they had scored "high" or "low" were "right much more often than they were wrong." Also, subjects who stated in *general* terms whether they had a feeling of success or failure were not accurate. But those who estimated their success as *specifically* high showed significant accuracy.

Relationships between teachers and pupils are in many ways as psychologically basic as those between mothers and children, particularly if younger children are involved. This tendency, shown in a number of teacher-pupil tests of extrasensory perception, prompted Dr. Rhine to conclude that as far as the term "repeatable demonstration" can be applied to any psychological experiment, ESP tests, "especially those conducted in recent years in the schools, have been found to show orderly repeatability if the same conditions are reproduced."

Unique experiments in children's ESP were undertaken from 1957 to 1959 at the Hawthorne Elementary School of Wheaton, Illinois. They centered around a particularly popular and outgoing teacher, Mrs. Elsie Gregory. The Duke Laboratory definitely noted that experiments carried out among her sixth-graders at Wheaton proved especially outstanding.

Margaret Anderson, an educator herself, had hypothesized that if a teacher could hold her pupils' interest in regular grade school material over ten months of the school year, she might be able to keep them interested in ESP tests with equal success.

Dr. Anderson reported in the *Journal of Parapsychology* (September 1959) that Mrs. Gregory, an excellent teacher, was interested in parapsychology and so genuinely enjoyed working with children that "her classes over the years had all enthusiastically responded to her." Anderson and Gregory had gradually worked out an experiment covering two stages, each to take place within one school year. Mrs. Gregory taught the fifth grade and gave music classes for the fifth and sixth grades.

The first tests, in 1957, were clairvoyance experiments with the fifth-grade pupils. When these same pupils, now a grade higher, asked whether the ESP tests might be continued, "the experiment for the second year was planned as an extended test of precognition." Dr. Anderson felt that the shift to precognition would be a novelty and a "challenge to the children," while promising new insights into precognition, "the most puzzling of psi phenomena."

Thirty-two fifth-graders took part in the first-year clairvoyance test, which resulted in 4,479 hits, or 119 above chance. The youngsters, according to Dr. Anderson, "demonstrated clairvoyance, at better than the five-percent level of significance." (Incidentally, during one experiment, when soft music was played in the background, scores fell off, and the pupils, although they had at first asked for it, then wrote that they did not want the music any more.)

The new precognition tests that followed were carried out with twenty-seven of the original thirty-two youngsters who had gone on to the sixth grade, plus five new pupils. They met with Mrs. Gregory for a music-appreciation hour four times a week during the 1958–59 school year. The youngsters went through the precognition tests from November to April. They had received the concept that ESP ability exists quite casually, and "the introduction of precognition was accepted by them in the same unquestioning way." The tests were designed around a musical theme, to provoke the children's imagination, and, as Dr. Anderson wrote, to "take their minds off the illogicality or irrationality of precognition."

The program was set up as a "musical flight into space." The pupils were called the Orchestra of Tomorrow. The standard ESP symbols were used, but by calling the table of random numbers the "earth-time code" and adding other colorful space-age terms, the experiments got the youngsters to endorse the plan excitedly. Regardless of a good deal of attention-getting window dressing, the testing techniques were tight. Results were checked against original copies and carbons, so that tabulations were checked and counterchecked for each student. The final results showed 3,808 hits, or 148 more than one would expect by chance.

Sixty-nine percent of the students in the precognition experiment showed a "positive deviation" from chance for the twelve testing sessions. Thirty-one percent showed "negative deviations," or fewer hits than chance could call for. In general, the nineteen boys and thirteen girls scored equally well. One girl gave an astonishing precognition performance during the first session. Where one would expect five hits by chance, she made fourteen.

All through the experiments, but particularly during the precognition phase, an atmosphere of enthusiasm was maintained. Dr. Anderson felt strongly that although she had been dealing with material that would eventually become just another statistical record, the psychological climate of the test had been crucially responsible for its success. She concluded that a researcher who ignores the atmosphere in which a test takes place runs a "grave risk of excluding the very phenomena he is trying to capture."

A number of precognition tests with children have been made, or initiated, by Dr. John A. Freeman of the Institute of Parapsychology (of the Foundation for Research on the

Nature of Man). Among other things, he has sought to find out whether or not, and if so, how and why girls and boys differ in their ESP scoring. The results seem to vary a good deal, and this has puzzled experimenters. At one point, the girls in a group gave better results than the boys when they were tested by a man; in the same group, the results were reversed when a female experimenter supervised the test. Dr. Freeman responded with enthusiasm when a public-school teacher with a class of mentally retarded children, after visiting the Duke Parapsychology Laboratory, asked to give an ESP test to her class.

Reporting on this experiment in the *Journal of Parapsychology* (September 1963) Dr. Freeman noted that previous experiences suggested that "the sex of the experimenter might be one factor contributing to the breakdown in scoring between girls and boys, depending upon the age group being tested," and he suspected that the woman teacher might "get better results with boys than with girls." The test employed an ingeniously designed mimeographed booklet devised by Dr. Freeman, made up of a whole network of drawings of animals, children and fruit, and permitting the kind of quantified scoring and analysis developed by the Durham experimenters.

Freeman's precognition experiment is geared to the interests of children. A story about a little girl or a little boy playing with animals, eating breakfast, etc., goes along with the booklet. The children checked off the activities they preferred. In this particular case, thirteen boys and four girls were in the class, and booklets numbered from one to seventeen were randomly distributed among them. Targets were determined about a week later on the basis of digits taken from a random number table. After two series of tests had been completed, the teacher was asked, somewhat to her embarrassment, to make a list of the children according to her feeling toward them. As it turned out, the four girls wound up at the bottom of her list (which may be one reason why the identity of the school and its location were, diplomatically, left anonymous in the experimenter's report). The results of the experiment, translated into the usual twenty-five-trial pattern, showed that in the first series the girls scored way below chance, while the boys scored above chance; in the second series, results were not as obvious, but a difference between the sexes could be noted again, and, according to Dr. Freeman, they were "not likely to be due to chance alone." He found it "difficult to say whether the difference in scoring between boys and girls was due to the fact that the teacher was a woman or because she preferred the boys." Possibly, he said, it was a combination of the two.

At another time, when testing a group of boy and girl high-school students, Dr. Freeman tried to link some of their personality characteristics to their performances in a precognition test. He sought to gain a picture of their attitudes by employing a Word Reaction Test. The students were to check with "L" for Like or "D" for Dislike a list of words including such emotion-laden ones as Worm, Candy, Vomit, Eagle, Magnolia, Prison, and Cupid; there were twenty-five words, in all.

Freeman gave this test, along with the standard ESP card one, to members of a science club at its monthly meeting. He first talked about research standards in parapsychology. The experiments then followed a question period. Reporting on the test, Dr. Freeman wrote in "A Precognition Test with a High-School Science Club" (*Journal of Parapsychology*, September 1964) that he had briefly discussed precognition, but "this apparently did not present a problem to them, since they raised no questions about it." Dr. Freeman did not tell them that, until then, the only group precognition test that had been published was the Anderson-Gregory test with sixth-grade children, summarized earlier in this chapter. The ESP targets were selected by another laboratory member who threw a ten-sided die twelve times; random numbers determined which blank spaces were to be used as targets.

Of the forty students, twenty-two were girls and eighteen boys. Each was classified as a "Liker" or "Disliker" according to his or her response to the word test. A number of results were tabulated. Among them: out of a total of seventeen, the "Likers" precognized thirteen "L" responses, while the "Dislikers" picked only four. Conversely, among twenty-three "Dislike" targets, the "Likers" hit only six, while the "Dislikers" scored seventeen. Freeman noted that "the reaction which is in accord with the dominant outlook of the individual, be he Liker or Disliker, is linked with a positive deviation, while its reverse suggests psi-missing [below mean chance expectation]. Saying it another way, although this is not the way Dr. Freeman put it: "Dislikers" like to precognize what they dislike.

These and other precognition experiments suggest that a number of psychological factors may be at work influencing results. The most striking general conclusion is that precognition appears to exist as clearly as telepathy or clairvoyance.

Experimenters in many instances prefer precognition tests, as there are fewer opportunities of some slip-up—a test subject could, at least in theory, sneak a peek at a card being displayed while he makes his guess; but how do you peek at the future?

16 Prophecy Involving Animals

On the afternoon of August 17, 1959, thousands of terns, gulls, and other water fowl, which had settled for some months on Montana's Lake Hegben, lifted themselves off the water and flew away. When the sun set, the lake's surface was virtually without a ripple. Within hours, several earthquakes were ravaging mountainous western Montana. The Hegben Dam cracked under the strain of the earth's movements. The flooding killed residents and nearby Yellowstone tourists alike, but the birds, of course, were safe.

What had warned the birds on Lake Hegben? Any number of hypotheses are possible, ranging from "pure" prophecy, actual knowledge of the earthquake danger, to a delicate early sensing of the movements below the earth's crust. Reports to the Interior Department's Fish and Wildlife Service and to the Agriculture Department's Division of Wildlife Management revealed that rangers had found no animal carcasses, either, in the zone affected by the earthquake. Dr. John W. Aldrich of the Department of the Interior recalled at the time that geese and peacocks are known to have an acute sense of hearing—or perhaps another sensory or extrasensory capacity—which enables them to detect sounds at great distances. Dr. Aldrich noted that birds are acutely aware of changes in atmospheric pressures which signal new weather conditions, and that the sensory apparatus which functions to serve migratory fowl may also help them to detect approaching dangers, including forest fires, at an early stage.

Research into possible extrasensory powers of animals is still relatively limited. Reports are numerous of pets that manage to return to their masters, covering long distances through unknown terrain. The Institute for Parapsychology at

Durham has made such cases the subject of several studies in "psi trailing." In these instances, precognition does not play a clear role; the obvious overlapping between seemingly prophetic impressions and telepathic or clairvoyant images is an acknowledged research problem. The Lake Hegben mass flight of birds strongly suggests that they "foresaw" the earthquake danger in some way, but the means and categorization of this foreknowledge completely elude speculation. Dr. J. B. Rhine wrote in 1951 (*Journal of Parapsychology,* Vol. XV, No. 4) that among case reports of "unusual behavior in animals there are a fair number of cases in which the reaction is taken to be premonitory."

Robert Morris, in a paper on "Precognition in Laboratory Rats" presented at the 1967 Winter meeting of the Foundation for Research on the Nature of Man, noted that spontaneous cases reported to the Foundation's Institute for Parapsychology contain a number suggesting extrasensory powers that "often some sort of emotional bond between man and animal provides the impetus for the manifestation of psi on the animal's part."

Mr. Morris told of an incident reported by a visitor to the Foundation headquarters whose young brother had left the family home for a long stay out of town. Neither he nor his family knew how long the trip would last. A few days after the boy had left, his pet dog became disconsolate, eating very little and spending much of his time "lying outside the boy's bedroom." As time went on, eventually the dog seemed to get used to the boy's absence and act quite normally. One day, however, it became very excited. It ran up to the boy's door and started pawing on it; then raced down the stairs, out the door, and up the road to the main highway, where it looked both ways and then scampered back to the house. It did this, with gusto, several times that day. About an hour after this excited behavior, the boy returned—to the surprise of everyone except the dog.

Mr. Morris deduced from this and similar cases that animal precognition may yield "a readily observable emotional response." The animal psi study group of Duke University consequently sought to devise an experiment that would bring measurable emotion into a laboratory setting involving animals. As maze experiments with rats provided the only readily available setting, the researchers studied case reports to find a suitable pattern. A frequently reported case was that of a hunting dog that eagerly runs to his master whenever he shoulders his gun—except on the day when the dog, old and feeble, is to be put out of his misery with this same gun. Morris noted that "on such occasions the dogs often are found hiding somewhere, cowering under the house whining and whimpering, and reluctant to come out."

This prompted Morris to recall that at the end of his experiments, rats taken from their cages to be killed "tend to be more aggressive and recalcitrant" than usual. But how could an experiment isolate sensory or telepathic links between the rat-about-to-die and a reluctant experimenter who "dislikes very much the task of killing rats and thus may be less at ease in handling them" on the eve of their execution? And how does one measure a rat's emotional state? And if the experimenter's nervousness simply transfers to the rat, is that a psychic phenomenon?

Several means of testing whether or not a rat was keyed-up, could sense its death, were examined. One method that pointed toward significant results employed an "open field," an eight-foot-by-eight-foot box whose floor was marked off into small squares. The rat was placed in a corner of the box and, among other observations, "a record was kept of the number of squares the animal crossed." Morris stated: "Taking our cue from the cowering dog under the house, we figured that a rat who is about to die would show more restricted activity in the open field, spending most of his time in the corner in which he was put, compared with a rat who was not about to die." He added:

"The actual procedure was to take a group of rats that were scheduled to be killed and to run each of them individually in the open field for two minutes. Immediately after running, each was taken to a co-worker who either destroyed it or returned it to its own colony, according to a random plan unknown to the open-field scorer. Thus the open-field scorer did not know which animals were to live and which were to die, and the co-worker did not know how each animal had performed in the open field. After the series was completed, a record of each animal's performance was compiled and compared with the record of which ones lived or died."

The pilot experiment, involving only sixteen animals, was described by Mr. Morris as enlightening: In the short two-minute period of observation, half of the animals that lived were active enough to leave their original square, whereas none of the animals that died showed such activity." Although this is but the first step toward statistically based laboratory research of animal precognition, it is cited here because, as Morris states, it points a way toward an assessment of "animals' emotional responses to situations which either do not yet exist, or which do exist but of which the animal could have had no sensory awareness."

Precognition *about* animals has particularly fascinated those who dreamed the results of horse races. Mr. A. S. Jarman, an English writer known for his sprightly prose and occasional fierce debunking of fraud or naïveté, has recorded a vivid and practical premonitory dream. Jarman reported in *Tomorrow* (Winter 1959) that toward the end of World War II, he began to keep records of his dreams. On the night of November 9, 1947, he dreamed of standing on a flat moorland, between a sea shore and a green road of grass, a racetrack, that "almost fled way into infinity." The track was faced by "a great crowd of people, all gazing intently down the track." Slowly, first mere dots on the horizon, horses came into sight; but as they approached, all but one wheeled to their left and galloped toward the sea. The single remaining horse dashed through the standing spectators, without touching them. Mr. Jarman continues:

"Everyone turned to watch its progress and then I saw a great grandstand full of people who also were waving in wild enthusiasm. Facing the stands was an enormous long white board supported on posts, and on this appeared, one after another, the figures 2-0-2-0. The horse and horseman had disappeared but they had evidently won the race and it was a popular victory. I felt a sense of elation and shared in the excited talk among the racegoers."

In the morning, Mr. Jarman telephoned the director of a building firm, Mr. Michael B. Campbell, and during their conversation reported on the dream. The two men wondered whether the figures 2-0-2-0 could be statistical, relating to a horse, but decided that it was improbable. They consulted the London *Daily Telegraph*'s racing program, to see whether the figures might indicate the placings of the horses for that day. Jarman also considered the possibility that the dreamed figures might refer to the age or weight of a horse; but this would have made the horse either very old or outrageously heavy, and, Jarman notes, "we abandoned the quest and I decided that it was one of those many dreams which are meaningless." However, that evening, on the way home, he bought a copy of the *Evening News*, which contained the results of the 3:45 P.M. race at Leicester. Jarman says, "It had been won by a horse with the improbable name of Twenty-Twenty, of which, of course, I had never heard." He adds: "It was a flat race and named the Stoughton Plate, the jockey being Gordon Richards. Twenty-Twenty was a bay gelding by Rosewell out of Thirteen, and this was only the second race it had won in its career. Why the sea appeared in my dream I do not know; Leicester is as far from the coast as is possible in England. During our inspection of the racing program in the morning, we had not given attention to the horses' names but only to figures. (I admit that had I seen the name among the runners, I should have risked a handsome stake in spite of my disapproval of betting.) I have since had no similar dream and perhaps it happens only once in a lifetime."

The Jarman account was confirmed in a letter, written by Mr. Campbell, Director of Campbell & Co., Richmond, Surrey, stating that he had discussed the dream on the morning of November 10 with Jarman, and the possible meaning of the "2-0-2-0" image, but "had not considered the names of the runners."

Another horse-racing case, reported by a woman to the Society for Psychical Research, London, was published in its *Proceedings* (Vol. 53, Part 191, 1960), as a "Report (1959) on Enquiry into Spontaneous Cases." The incident, recorded as case No. E. 71, was related as follows:

"It started on Monday night, December 17th. I was awakened from a deep sleep with a name repeating itself like a broken gramophone record. Cabalist-ie-Cabalist-ie-Cabalist-ie. I woke to full consciousness repeating this name, and so I spelt it to myself to impress it on my memory.

"The following morning, the first thing I did was to write it down and then asked my husband if he knew of a horse called Cabalistie. He said no. Neither of us takes an interest in betting.

"On Christmas Day at a party held by a friend, I distinctly saw in the fire a formation resembling a racehorse, complete with jockey and stirrups, with his neck outstretched, running. I showed it to my friends, and they all could see it, and my husband said, 'There is a big race on tomorrow, Boxing Day, at Kempton Park.'

"I jolted my memory. I said, 'See if a Cabalistie is running.' He looked and said no.

"I took the paper from him and the first name I saw in the first race was Cabalist, an outsider with no jockey, 10 to 1. Needless to say, we and our friends backed this tip and won at 25 to 1. I have the betting slip from the bookmaker to prove this, and also my friends' at the party who took part in the bet."

The Society's report also included the precognitive dream of an Irish jockey (Case E. 423), who had dreamt, on the night before he was supposed, in reality, to ride a horse named Phoenicia on the Manchester Race Course that he "did not ride the horse, which won, all right." In his dream, his father, back in Ireland at Ross Races, saw "from the evening paper that Phoenicia had won without me in the saddle." The next day, as he was dressing to prepare for the race, the jockey was handed a telegram sent by the horse's owner, saying that another jockey would take his place. Phoenicia won the race. When the jockey returned to Ireland, the owner told him that the jockey's father had walked up to the owner, and angrily denounced him for not letting the son ride Phoenicia. (This encounter had also been precognized to a degree in the dream, but the jockey's fear that his father's complaint would lead to still more difficulties with the owner did not materialize; in fact, the owner apologized to the jockey.)

Earlier British surveys contain similar cases. Professor Haslam, cited in the Society's *Proceedings* (Vol. 14, Part 251), was thinking of a forthcoming horse race while he was half-asleep at one point. He saw a jockey in scarlet pass before him, pulling his horse in hard, and winning the race. While he thought to himself, "Scarlet is a common color," the vision of the jockey passed before his eyes once more. He told several friends of this dreamlike impression. Haslam attended the race; he went to the saddling paddock to look for a jockey dressed in scarlet. He did find such a man, and he put some money on the horse. The jockey actually did pull the horse in hard—and he won the race. Cited in *Foreknowledge* by H. F. Saltmarsh (London, 1938), the incident was described as a case with "good independent confirmation."

Saltmarsh mentions as the "most impressive" of these "winner" cases ones reported by Mr. John H. Williams, published earlier in the *Journal* of the Society for Psychical Research. Mr. Williams, over eighty years old, was a Quaker and strongly opposed to betting. On May 31, 1933, he woke up at 8:55 A.M., having just dreamed that he had listened to a radio account of the Derby which was to be run at 2 o'clock that afternoon. In his dream, Williams had heard the names of the first four horses, among them Hyperion and King Solomon. He could not remember the other two. When he went out, later that morning, Williams told a neighbor whom he met on a bus about the dream. He also mentioned it to a business acquaintance. Although opposed to betting and uninterested in horse racing, curiosity prompted Mr. Williams to listen to the radio report of the Derby. He heard then the identical names and expressions that had occurred in the dream. Mr. Saltmarsh adds that "the two gentlemen to whom he had told his dream that morning, had given ample confirmation of the account."

Saltmarsh, rather plaintively, notes that "it seems most inappropriate" that such a striking precognition experience should come to someone "so strongly opposed to racing and betting." Ah, but Saltmarsh, what about the underlying reverse emotions, which Williams so determined to suppress? Any cocktail-party psychologist might conclude that the very "suppression" of his baser instincts might prompt the Quaker to experience a horse-racing prophecy. . . .

Dame Edith Lyttelton, President of the Society for Psychical Research (London) in 1933 and 1934, received many letters citing precognition experiences as the result of a series of BBC radio broadcasts. She published a selection of these cases under the title *Some Cases of Prediction* (London, 1937). Among them was a letter from Phyllis Richards of 3/32 Lindon Gardens, London W. 2, dated February 25, 1934, which described her crossing from Belfast to Liverpool on the night of Thursday, March 23, 1933, to attend one of England's most prominent races, the Grand National. On the boat, Mrs. Richards dreamed that "a horse beginning with K and ending with Jack had won the race, although he was not the first horse past the winning post."

Before going to the race, Mrs. Richards, at lunch with friends, mentioned the dream and was told, at first, that it might concern a horse called Pelorus Jack. However, she insisted that the name should start with "K." She found that Kellsboro Jack was running and decided that this was the horse. She had misgivings about the prediction, as "it was pouring with rain" in her dream, while the day of the race was "heavenly." The race was, in fact, won by Kellsboro Jack, which was not the first horse to go through the post; a horse ahead of him had thrown its rider.

The dream was corroborated by Major A. Kent Lemon in a letter to the Society dated March 15; he said that it was "quite correct that Mrs. Richards attended the Grand National race meeting with us last year and that when we met at the course she said that she had dreamt that Kellsboro

Jack had won. I believe she and my wife backed the horse and made some money." *The Times* of March 25 reported that Kellsboro Jack "won a gallant race by three lengths. . . ."

Earlier, a noted Polish psychic researcher, Dr. Julian Ochorowicz, had reported that a blindfolded medium, identified only as Mrs. S., had been able to anticipate changes in racing line-ups and actual race results with striking accuracy. He wrote in his book *Zjawiska Mediumiczne* ("Mediumistic Phenomena"; Warsaw, 1913) that, accompanied by a cousin, he visited the sensitive on May 31. Wearing blindfolds, Mrs. S. "read" the whole program of several forthcoming races from the magazine *Jezdziec i Mysliwy*, ("Horseman and Hunter"), precognizing changes "that were going to take place the next day," while rattling off the names of some thirty horses.

For the first race, Mrs. S. forecast that a horse named Kartuz would come in first and another, named Alina, would arrive second; in the actual race, run the next day, the order was reversed. For the second race, with seven horses running, she prophesied that Sylfida would come in first. This turned out to be correct, although she predicted that "Bonboniere would be second," whereas that horse placed third and Rubin ran second. In the third race, out of four horses, the medium correctly placed Sesam in first place, but named Lissa as second, whereas second place was won by a horse named Hector.

The fourth race, out of six horses the medium correctly named the two that came in first and second, Emtral and Galatea. She was wrong in naming the first two winners in the fifth race, when she said that Remus and Tumry would win; two other horses, Konfetka and Aspazja, won the race. On the other hand, Mrs. S. named the winner of the sixth race, Aquilla, correctly. Ochorowicz summed up the score by saying that "she guessed the four first horses correctly in six races, and once the reverse." Later, on October 8, her score was less than satisfactory; Ochorowicz noted that "she read part of a racing program correctly," presumably with the eyes covered, and "foretold one race correctly, four races partly correct, and two wrong."

Actress Jan Sterling, quoted by Jess Stearn in *This Week* (March 27, 1966), once took her three-year-old son Adam to a racetrack near Denver. When the first race was called, Jan explained the listing of the horses to Adam, who listened gravely and said, "Bet six and four, Mommy." Well, six came in first and four was second. In the next race, only ten horses were running, but little Adam insisted, "Eleven, Mommy." A few moments later, an eleventh entry was announced, to run as No. 10A. The report does not say whether Jan Sterling bet on the eleventh horse herself, but a bystander, impressed by Adam's accuracy in the first race, obviously had; he shouted, "Your son just won a month's pay for me!"

17 Toward the Year 2000

Scientific prophecy, in the forecasting of social and economic events, has been formalized in the United States through the "Commission on the Year 2000" of the American Academy of Arts and Sciences, under the chairmanship of Dr. Daniel Bell, professor of sociology at Columbia University in New York. The proceedings and findings of the Commission were published in the Academy's journal, *Daedalus* (Summer 1967). Dr. Bell sees four sources of change in society that are subject to prediction: technology, which opens up means of mastering nature and transforming resources, time, and space; the changes in the diffusion of goods and privileges in society; changes in the structure of U.S. society; and the relationship of the United States to the rest of the world.

Among the technological forecasts examined by the Commission are changes growing out of new biomedical engineering, the computer, and weather modifications. In medicine, organ transplants, genetic modification, and control of disease promise a substantial increase in longevity. In the economy, the Commission foresees a wider spread of all goods and services. The Commission points out that in many instances it is anticipating or listing alternatives, rather than making single and specific predictions. Bell emphasizes that "what matters most about the year 2000 are not the gadgets that might, on the serious side, introduce prothesis in the human body or, on the lighter side, use silicones to lift wrinkles, but the kinds of social arrangements that can deal adequately with the problems we shall confront." He adds:

"The only prediction about the future that one can make

with certainty is that public authorities will face more problems than they have at any previous time in history. This arises from some simple facts: Social issues are more and more intricately related to one another because the impact of any major change is felt quickly through the national and even the international system. Individuals and groups, more conscious of these problems as problems, demand action instead of quietly accepting their fate. Because more and more decisions will be made in the political arena than in the market, there will be more open community conflict. The political arena is an open cockpit where decision points are more visible than they are in the impersonal market; different groups will clash more directly as they contend for advantage or seek to resist change in society."

The most specific forecasts submitted to the Commission came from Dr. Herman Kahn, director of the Hudson Institute, and from the Institute's research director, Anthony J. Wiener. They see long-term trends in the direction of what they call "increasingly sensate cultures." Their definition of "sensate" includes "empirical, this-worldly, humanistic, pragmatic, utilitarian, contractual, epicurean, and hedonistic." They anticipate strengthened elites of a bourgeois, bureaucratic, "meritocratic," democratic, and possibly nationalistic type. Further, they see trends toward greater accumulation of scientific and technical knowledge; institutionalization of change, especially in research, development, innovation, and diffusion; world-wide industrialization and modernization; increasing affluence and leisure; faster population growth; a decreasing importance of primary occupations; rapid urbanization and the growth of megalopolises; wider literacy and education; increased capability for mass destruction; a mounting tempo of change; and, finally, an increasing universality of all these trends.

Specifically, Kahn and Wiener predict the following one hundred technical innovations before the year 2000:

1. Multiple applications of lasers and masers for sensing, measuring, communicating, cutting, heating, welding, power transmission, illumination, destructive (defensive), and other purposes
2. Extremely high-strength or high-temperature structural materials
3. New or improved super-performance fabrics (papers, fibers, and plastics)
4. New or improved materials for equipment and ap-

pliances (plastics, glasses, alloys, ceramics, intermetallics, and cermets)
5. New airborne vehicles (ground-effect machines, VTOL and STOL, superhelicopters, giant supersonic jets)
6. Extensive commercial application of shaped charges
7. More reliable and longer-range weather forecasting
8. Intensive or extensive expansion of tropical agriculture and forestry
9. New sources of power for fixed installations (for example, magneto-hydrodynamic, thermionic, and thermo-electric, radioactive)
10. New sources of power for ground transportation (storage-battery, fuel-cell propulsion or support by electromagnetic fields, jet engine, turbine)
11. Extensive and intensive world-wide use of high-altitude cameras for mapping, prospecting, census, land use, and geological investigations
12. New methods of water transportation (large submarines, flexible and special-purpose "container ships," more extensive use of large automated single-purpose bulk cargo ships)
13. Major reduction in hereditary and congenital defects
14. Extensive use of cyborg techniques (mechanical aids or substitutes for human organs, sense, limbs)
15. New techniques for preserving or improving the environment
16. Relatively effective appetite and weight control
17. New techniques in adult education
18. New improved plants and animals
19. Human "hibernation" for short periods (hours or days) for medical purposes
20. Inexpensive "one of a kind" design and procurement through use of computerized analysis and automated production
21. Controlled super-effective relaxation and sleep
22. More sophisticated architectural engineering (geodesic domes, thin shells, pressurized skins, esoteric materials)
23. New or improved uses of the oceans (mining, extraction of minerals, controlled "farming," source of energy)
24. Three-dimensional photography, illustrations, movies, and television

PROPHECY IN OUR TIME

25. Automated or more mechanized housekeeping and home maintenance
26. Widespread use of nuclear reactors for power
27. Use of nuclear explosives for excavation and mining, generation of power, creation of high-temperature/ high-pressure environments, or for a source of neutrons or other radiation
28. General use of automation and cybernation in management and production
29. Extensive and intensive centralization (or automatic interconnection) of current and past personal and business information in high-speed data processors
30. Other new and possibly pervasive techniques for surveillance, monitoring, and control of individuals and organizations
31. Some control of weather or climate
32. Other (permanent or temporary) changes or experiments with the over-all environment (for example, the "permanent" increase in C-14 and temporary creation of other radioactivity by nuclear explosions, the increasing generation of CO_2 in the atmosphere, projects Starfire, West Ford, Storm Fury, and so forth)
33. New and more reliable "educational" and propaganda techniques for affecting human behavior—public and private
34. Practical use of direct electronic communication with and stimulation of the brain
35. Human hibernation for relatively extensive periods (months to years)
36. Cheap and widely available or excessively destructive central war weapons and weapons systems
37. New and relatively effective counterinsurgency techniques (and perhaps also insurgency techniques)
38. New kinds of very cheap, convenient, and reliable birth-control techniques
39. New, more varied, and more reliable drugs for control of fatigue, relaxation, alertness, mood, personality, perceptions, and fantasies
40. Capability to choose the sex of unborn children
41. Improved capability to "change" sex
42. Other genetic control or influence over the "basic constitution" of an individual
43. New techniques in the education of children
44. General and substantial increase in life expectancy,

postponement of aging, and limited rejuvenation
45. Generally acceptable and competitive synthetic foods and beverages (carbohydrates, fats, proteins, enzymes, vitamins, coffee, tea, cocoa, liquor)
46. "High quality" medical care for underdeveloped areas (for example, use of referral hospitals, broad-spectrum antibiotics, artificial blood plasma)
47. Design and extensive use of responsive and super-controlled environment for private and public use (for pleasurable, educational, and vocational purposes)
48. "Nonharmful" methods of "overindulging"
49. Simple techniques for extensive and "permanent" cosmetological changes (features, "figures," perhaps complexion, skin color, even physique)
50. More extensive use of transplantation of human organs
51. Permanent manned satellite and lunar installations—interplanetary travel
52. Application of space life systems or similar techniques to terrestrial installations
53. Permanent inhabited undersea installations and perhaps even colonies
54. Automated grocery and department stores
55. Extensive use of robots and machines "slaved" to humans
56. New uses of underground tunnels for private and public transportation
57. Automated universal (real time) credit, audit, and banking systems
58. Chemical methods for improved memory and learning
59. Greater use of underground buildings
60. New and improved materials and equipment for buildings and interiors (variable transmission glass, heating and cooling by thermoelectric effect, electroluminescent and phosphorescent lighting)
61. Widespread use of cryogenics
62. Improved chemical control of some mental illness and some aspects of senility
63. Mechanical and chemical methods for improving human analytical ability more or less directly
64. Inexpensive and rapid techniques for making tunnels and underground cavities in earth or rock

PROPHECY IN OUR TIME

65. Major improvements in earth moving and construction equipment generally
66. New techniques for keeping physically fit or acquiring physical skills
67. Commercial extraction of oil from shale
68. Recoverable boosters for economic space launching
69. Individual flying platforms
70. Simple inexpensive video recording and playing
71. Inexpensive high-capacity, world-wide, regional, and local (home and business) communication (using satellites, lasers, light pipes, and so forth)
72. Practical home and business use of "wired" video communication for both telephone and television (possibly including retrieval of taped material from libraries or other sources) and rapid transmission and reception of facsimiles (possibly including news, library material, commercial announcements, instantaneous mail delivery, other printouts)
73. Practical large-scale desalinization
74. Pervasive business use of computers for the storage, processing, and retrieval of information
75. Shared-time (public and interconnected) computers generally available to home and business on a metered basis
76. Other widespread use of computers for intellectual and professional assistance (translation, teaching, literary research, medical diagnosis, traffic control, crime detection, computation, design, analysis, and, to some degree, as a general intellectual collaborator)
77. General availability of inexpensive transuranic and other esoteric elements
78. Space defense systems
79. Inexpensive and reasonably effective ground-based ballistic missile defense
80. Very low-cost buildings for home and business use
81. Personal "pagers" (perhaps even two-way pocket phones) and other personal electronic equipment for communication, computing, and data-processing
82. Direct broadcasts from satellites to home receivers
83. Inexpensive (less than $20), long-lasting, very small, battery-operated television receivers
84. Home computers to "run" the household and communicate with outside world

85. Maintenance-free, long-life electronic and other equipment
86. Home education via video and computerized and programmed learning
87. Programmed dreams
88. Inexpensive (less than 1 cent a page) rapid, high-quality black and white reproduction; followed by colored, highly detailed photography reproduction
89. Widespread use of improved fluid amplifiers
90. Conference television (both closed-circuit and public communication systems)
91. Flexible penology without necessarily using prisons (by use of modern methods of surveillance, monitoring, and control)
92. Common use of individual power source for lights, appliances, and machines
93. Inexpensive world-wide transportation of humans and cargo
94. Inexpensive road-free (and facility-free) transportation
95. New methods for teaching languages rapidly
96. Extensive genetic control for plants and animals
97. New biological and chemical methods to identify, trace, incapacitate, or annoy people for police and military uses
98. New and possibly very simple methods for lethal biological and chemical warfare
99. Artificial moons and other methods of lighting large areas at night
100. Extensive use of "biological processes" in the extraction and processing of minerals

Speaking generally, Dr. Kahn foresees a stabilization of the nation-state system; no major depression; a bourgeois Soviet Union; Japan in economic ascendancy; a weak China; and a wealthy United States in a state of "wholesome decadence," where leisure-drenched individuals will search for meaning and purpose in their idle lives.

Of course, Kahn forecasts with an eye to the past. Speaking of Japan, he looks back on that nation's effort, since the middle of the nineteenth century, to catch up with the West. He sees the twenty-first century as a Japanese century, and asks: "But what will the Japanese do when they pass the West? I can't imagine a Japanese without a goal. Can they find one in organizing the political economy of Asia along new lines? Or, in the absence of a new fashion, will they turn to an old—imperialism?"

For the United States, Kahn foresees a gross national product of $3.5 trillion in the year 2000, with a disposable income per household of $25,000 per year. He expects that one-fourth of the nation will live in "Boswash," the urban complex reaching from Boston to Washington, one-eighth in the "Chipitts," or Chicago-to-Pittsburgh area, and one-sixteenth in the "Sansan" area, from Santa Barbara to San Diego. Kahn expects Americans and other earthlings to pose with increasing earnestness the eternal question, "What's it all about?"

In the field of economic forecasting, some trends seem irreversible. For years, the promotion leaflets of the *Kiplinger Newsletter,* published in Washington, have carried the slogan: "Boom and Inflation Ahead!"—varying it only to *"More Boom and Inflation Ahead!"* A good number of Wall Street forecasters can also point to accurate prognoses, but their job is becoming more difficult every year. The growing complexity of the economy and added politico-military elements multiply the elements they have to include in their calculations. On May 25, 1966, *New York Times* financial writer M. J. Rossant observed that " there is no rest for weary economic forecasters," as they are "forced to make constant revisions in their projects." Matters had become more complex still, a year later, when the National Bureau of Economic Research announced an overhaul of its "statistical intelligence system." The Bureau stated on March 20, 1967, that it was increasing its list of key business-cycle indicators to a total of eighty-eight, in order to provide "improved materials for early warning of business recessions and recoveries."

The Bureau's announcement came a week after it had noted that forecasts of the U.S. gross national product generally miscalculate by an average of ten billion dollars. At the same time, Rossant noted in the *Times* that economic forecasters of the U.S. Government in 1966 and 1967 "were far off target, serving to complicate economic problems rather than cure them." This article referred to a White House decision to restore the seven-percent investment tax credit, which had been withdrawn earlier to counteract inflationary trends. Restoration was decided on when forecasters warned of a severe slowing down of the economy. Mr. Rossant allowed that "there are a few visionaries who have been much more skilled than Washington's crystal-ball gazers." He added: "Yet the state of the art is still too primitive to assure good results. Despite a wealth of statistical information and the application of computer technology, forecasters are still groping in the dark with their projections, often missing turning points altogether."

One of Wall Street's most experienced forecasters, William F. Butler, Vice President and Director of Economic Research at the Chase Manhattan Bank, admits that projections are "the Achilles' heel of the 'new economics,'" which seek to anticipate and counteract negative trends. Mr. Butler believes that "until forecasts can be made with greater reliability than at present, attempts to use the tools of the 'new economics' as if they were micrometers can produce deeply damaging results."

Among the most dynamic prophets of the U.S. economy is Dr. Theodore Levitt, a member of the Graduate School of Business of Harvard University and a business consultant. Dr. Levitt, author of *Innovation in Marketing*, is a caustic, no-nonsense scholar, who does not hesitate to depreciate his own forecasting ability. He told *Business Week* that "in the academy you can sit back and be irresponsible," and "you can be a prophet; it's easy to be a prophet—you make twenty-five predictions and the ones that come true are the ones you talk about. When running a company, you have other things to consider; you can't be irresponsible."

In international economics, the well-known management specialist Peter F. Drucker published an article in *Harper's* (June 1965) under the heading, "A Crash Next Year? Why It's a Real Danger, and How It Can Be Avoided." His forecasts, covering a specific twelve-month period, could be checked out retroactively. How did they measure up to the actual economic developments, even allowing for the author's skilled hedging?

Speaking of the international monetary situation, he stated categorically that "in one way or another, the American payments deficit will be ended within twelve months." This did not happen, even in twenty-four months. But Drucker had hedged: "At the least it will be reduced sharply from the annual rate of over four billions, at which it ran last fall, to something approximating one billion a year." This also did not happen, either in 1966 or 1967. In fact, the whole basket of eels that makes up the role of the U.S. dollar in world-wide financing was left untouched during and after the period to which Mr. Drucker's forecast applied—exclusive of such time-honored rituals as international financial meetings in Washington, Rio de Janeiro, and several

European capitals. Devaluation of the British pound, late in 1967, merely dramatized the continuing imbalance of the U.S. balance of payments.

Small wonder, then, that the *Wall Street Journal* (May 25, 1966) carried this headline: "Cloudy Crystal Ball: A Mixed-Up World Troubles Forecasters." Underneath, in a dispatch from New York, the paper said: "What's happening? Well, there's a bear market—or a bull market. And business is in for a period of expansion—or contraction. Or something like that." The gist of the article was that political and economic events were "making it harder than ever to predict what will happen" on the stock market.

To members of the computer generation, who might assume that political and economic variables, if programmed correctly into sophisticated apparatus, should yield accurate economic prophecies, the *Wall Street Journal*'s conclusions probably seemed unsettling. Yet one might find solace in a sober, detached analysis of economic trends that appeared, of all places, in *Your Personal Astrology* (January-February-March 1966), written by Lieut. Comm. David Williams. The author, a retired businessman and one of the most respected U.S. astrologers, reviewed the role of current and projected company earnings in relation to past performance in investment forecasting; he examined the relation of current stock prices to current or projected earnings, statistical data, and various systems of mechanical forecasting, such as the Dow Theory.

After giving each of these methods their due, Mr. Williams observed that "the astrological approach to stock-market forecasting is believed by this writer to represent a more positive, although admittedly not infallible method," and noted that the stock market is "not only governed by statistical factors, but also by psychological factors," which may be subject to planetary influences. Mr. Williams, the author of *Astro-Economics* (New York, 1959), has studied the relationship of planetary cycles to the U.S. economic cycle extensively, going back to 1761. He states that "Neptune—the planet of delusion, inflation, market manipulation, unsound ideas of value, and chaos—is an important significator." In 1929, the stock market reached its all-time peak of 386.1 on September 3, "two days after Neptune crossed the point where it had first turned retrograde." This was followed by the crash.

Mr. Williams considers the period from July 8, 1932, the low point after the crash, up to 1966, as one major bull market, which began "just two days before Pluto, the planet of mass movements, turned direct in the third decanate of Cancer, ruled by Neptune, the planet of inflation." Examining planetary cycles for 1966, he saw indications that this "greatest bull market in history will end during the latter part of 1966," but without "any collapse similar to the 1929–1932 debacle, for the inflationary effects of the Neptune-Pluto sextile will continue for the rest of this century." The stock market did, in fact, suffer a severe setback in the fall of 1966, but made a good recovery through most of 1967.

Mr. Rossant, who became Director of the Twentieth-Century Fund in October 1967, wrote in *The New York Times* on June 21, 1967, "What is most disappointing about the Administration's efforts is that despite its elaborate machinery and its wealth of information it has not done as well in forecasting as some private seers." While Rossant presumably was not thinking specifically of astrologers, their concept that "the stars impel, but do not compel" might easily be adapted to the most sophisticated computerized economic forecasting known to modern economic prophecy.

18 The Washington "Seeress"

Parapsychologists are frustrated when apparently stellar performers in prophecy or telepathy are not available for laboratory testing. The best-known contemporary prophetess is Mrs. James L. Dixon of Washington, D.C., whose reputation was vividly dramatized when, following the assassination of President Kennedy, it became known that she had forecast this event consistently over a period of several years. Jeane Dixon's prophecies had been reported since 1952 by the Washington columnist Ruth Montgomery, first in the New York *Daily News* and later for the Hearst Headline Service. In her book, *A Gift of Prophecy: The Phenomenal Jeane Dixon* (New York, 1965), Ruth Montgomery wrote that Mrs. Dixon, because of her "uncanny gift," had become "almost as much of an institution as the Pentagon."

Mrs. Dixon, an outgoing, graceful, courteous woman, has

found a cordial audience in many parts of the United States. Something of the awe and warmth with which she has been received is reflected in a report in *Cosmic Star,* a bimonthly tabloid published in Hollywood, California. The report (June-July 1966), written by Mrs. Michael Barton, stated that Mrs. Barton and her husband "went to see and hear" Jeane Dixon, "at noon on May 7th" at the Hancock Auditorium of the University of Southern California. The report stated that Mrs. Dixon's upturned hat of white silk ribbon "framed her lovely face like a halo," while "her hands curved around a crystal ball, and that great circle of white light around her seemed like something a little more than just the TV spotlight which kept her in its beam. . . ." Mrs. Dixon, according to this report, addressed the audience in a "vibrant, melodious voice." Among the great variety of questions on national, international, ethical, and religious matters answered by the Washington seeress, as she is often termed by Mrs. Montgomery, was "How long will the war in Vietnam last?" The answer, as recorded in *Cosmic Star,* was: "It will be over in ninety days. Ended, but not on our terms."

At various times, Mrs. Dixon has explained that prophetic impressions come to her directly from God, and that she is merely an instrument of undistorted transmission. The report on the Los Angeles appearance stated that telepathy is one of her methods, "meditation another, psychic channeling, and of course the crystal ball," are others; of these, the "truest and most apt to be fulfilled to the minutest detail is the clairvoyant vision," which "has terrific meaning and comes from God. Such was her vision of the Kennedy assassination."

While the President's violent death has continued to absorb much of the nation's and the world's attention in past years —involving much controversy and ambivalently distasteful overtones—Mrs. Dixon's role has seemed to fulfill a need, within herself as well as within her public, that has gained momentum because of the assassination. The degree to which her public has fastened on her forecasts that were or seemed to be, confirmed by events, while virtually ignoring such casually erroneous prophecies as the Hancock Auditorium prognosis on the Vietnam war, illustrates a mass desire for prophetic certainties. There is no doubt that a number of Mrs. Dixon's forecasts have, in startling instances, been borne out by events. But then, she has been quite generous with her prophecies. Questioners could usually count on her to provide one or several predictions during any radio, television, or newspaper interview.

One need not be overly critical to observe that some of her forecasts were mere dramatized projections of developments already well under way. She had preceded her Los Angeles remarks on Vietnam by a forecast quoted by Ruth Montgomery in her column "Washington Wonderland" on January 2, 1966, stating that peace negotiations would "begin early in the year." Peace efforts of one sort or another had, of course, been made for several years; they lasted through 1966 and continued, without success, into 1967. But negotiations were not achieved, and President Johnson told a press conference in February 1967 that there had been no serious response from Hanoi. The Hanoi regime released an exchange of letters with Washington, leaving no doubt that it would not negotiate unless the United States had agreed to such preconditions as a cessation of bombing in North Vietnam. All through the year, events in no way reflected any realistic interpretation that might be made of Mrs. Dixon's prophecy.

Mrs. Montgomery has stated in her book that Jeane Dixon had made "a few forecasts" that failed to occur. She listed an early prediction that "Red China would plunge the world into war over Quemoy and Matsu in October of 1958." In the case of such errors, Mrs. Montgomery writes, Jean Dixon believes that "she was shown correct symbols but misinterpreted them."

Neither outright error nor notable accuracy can be seen in Mrs. Dixon's forecast that "President Sukarno will be out of office before the end of 1966, and Communists will sharply lose ground in Indonesia." This statement followed a wave of anti-Communist riots and executions that had begun in Indonesia in September 1965 and had already caused the death of hundreds of thousands. The Indonesian Communist movement had not merely lost ground "sharply" before the prediction was made; it had been decimated. As for President Sukarno, his star declined sharply after the Communist takeover attempt in 1965, but he managed to remain in office, although with reduced powers, into 1967. In this case, a not-too-expert projection of past and current events into a future pattern could well have formed the framework of Mrs. Dixon's forecasts.

Among the misses that Mrs. Montgomery may have had in mind were several Dixon prophecies she recorded in her column in the New York *Daily News* on January 1, 1953. She then quoted Mrs. Dixon as follows: "President Eisenhower may not know it yet, but he is about to appoint five-star General Douglas MacArthur to an exceedingly important post, probably an ambassadorship!" The columnist, on the basis of her consultation with Mrs. Dixon, also wrote: "The astrological numbers of Generals Al Wedemeyer and Patrick J. Hurley are clearly intertwined. They should combine forces and solve the China problem. MacArthur will be given an important post—either an ambassadorship or an important advisory position where he will prove very helpful. . . ." If such a position was offered to General MacArthur, it was not accepted. He remained Chairman of the Board of the Remington Rand Corporation until his death on April 5, 1964.

The foregoing suggests that then, at least, Mrs. Dixon was supplementing her other forecasting methods with astrological calculations, either by herself or by others. There has since then been no notable reference to astrology in Mrs. Dixon's own statements or in those of her admirer-biographer, Ruth Montgomery. At any rate, whatever intertwining astrological numbers may have linked General Albert C. Wedemeyer and General Patrick J. Hurley, they did not affect them strongly enough to enable them to solve the difficult Chinese situation. Wedemeyer, after retiring from active service in 1951, served successively as Vice President of the Avco Manufacturing Corporation and of the Rheem Manufacturing Company. Hurley had retired to Santa Fe, New Mexico; he ran unsuccessfully for the U.S. Senate in 1952, and died on May 23, 1963, without reentering public life.

Another instance of apparent projection into the future from a past crisis was contained in the same 1953 column. Mrs. Montgomery quoted Jeane Dixon as saying that "one of Russia's allies" would "turn against her after the Soviet armies have pushed through Iran and into Palestine." The columnist added: "Jeane predicts that Russia will move into Iran in the fall of 1953. The bear will not move on to Palestine until 1957. Then comes the deluge. . . ." The Red Army had temporarily occupied parts of Iran at the closing of World War II and withdrew in 1946 after considerable delay, under the terms of the 1943 Teheran Declaration. They did not return, and did not invade Palestine.

One gains the impression that Mrs. Dixon is occasionally influenced by political anxieties. For a number of years, Walter Reuther, President of the United Auto Workers and a high AFL-CIO official, has at times been viewed by some conservatives as a man with presidential ambitions. On October 23, 1954, Mrs. Montgomery quoted Mrs. Dixon as saying that "in 1963, CIO President Walter Reuther will make known to his Union followers that he intends to run for President of the United States the following year." She was quoted on December 31, 1955, as repeating the forecast, stating that "Walter Reuther will make his first bid for the Presidency in 1960, but will not win his heart's desire until 1964."

As one looks back, some of Mrs. Dixon's forecasts, which must have sounded very striking at the time they were made, now appear rather incongruous. On October 23, 1954, Mrs. Montgomery wrote of the seeress: "By 1964, she insists, one man—a swarthy-skinned part-Oriental—will rule the combined countries of Russia and China. . . ." In her forecast column for 1956, the writer said: "Jeane who knows less about politics than the proverbial newborn babe, was puzzled to find ex-Governor Thomas E. Dewey looming so prominently in her crystal ball. 'I don't understand,' she mused. 'Is there anybody between the President and the Vice President in Government, but much more important than the latter? It seems to be a powerful new post at Ike's side that Dewey will have next year.'"

Mrs. Montgomery then told Mrs. Dixon that there had been "speculation about the possible creation of an executive post or assistant president" and noted that "Jeane excitedly assured us that this was it." Mrs. Montgomery quoted her as saying that "Dewey and Senator William Knowland seem to be vying for it in my crystal ball, but Dewey will get it, and Knowland will also become much more important and prominent." History did not find Dewey an "assistant president," though, and Senator Knowland returned to Oakland, California, to take over the administration of his family's newspaper, the *Oakland Tribune*.

In the summer of 1966, Premier Fidel Castro of Cuba temporarily disappeared from public view. This caused a good deal of speculation concerning his health and his position in the Cuban hierarchy, as well as his political and personal fate. Asked in New York, while autographing copies of Mrs. Montgomery's book, what Castro's position was, Mrs. Dixon said, "My vibrations now tell me that he's nowhere around. He's either in China or he's dead." She added, as quoted in the *New York Post* (May 17), "I haven't been able to pick up his vibrations for a week or two." In this case, of course, Jeane Dixon did not suggest that she was engaging in prophecy, only clairvoyance. At any rate, Castro surfaced soon afterward, somewhat less ebullient than before. Considering his government's quarrel with the Peking regime, which had cut back its sugar purchases and rice exports, it seemed unlikely that Castro had been in China. At any rate, he was alive.

Mrs. Montgomery's "Washington Wonderland" column, containing the Dixon predictions for 1967, summarized them as follows:

"Mysterious satellites and UFO's, a 'sixth column,' diabolical blackmail, a mystery woman in the Oswald case, Republican trials and Democratic tribulations all share the spotlight in Jeane Dixon's crystal-ball forecasts for 1967. Even William Shakespeare gets into the act." She provided the following details:

"The famous seeress, whose annual New Year's predictions are as eagerly awaited as election returns, sees little to cheer about in the year immediately ahead.

"Although Red China's Mao Tse-tung and North Vietnam's Ho Chi Minh will soon be gone from the 'world power arena,' she says, the Vietnam war will 'continue unabated until we settle on Russia's terms, not ours.'

"She foresees frightening instruments of blackmail, already in Russia's possession, that will be used as a threat against the United States and Western Europe to force a 'sudden peace,' but more devastating wars are to follow.

"Mrs. Dixon psychically sees the 'door wide open' for a GOP victory in 1968, a troublesome challenge for Governor George Romney late this fall [1967], and increasing headaches for President Johnson.

"The famed capital seeress, who has received a half-million letters and telephone calls since publication of the best-selling book about her, entitled *A Gift of Prophecy*, does have one happy forecast: a cure for cancer that will grow out of research interrupted by World War I."

Later in her column, Mrs. Montgomery again referred to cancer research interrupted by World War I, saying that Jeane Dixon saw "psychically that some European scientists" began work on a theory designed to correct "the vibrations of sick cells and bringing them into harmony with the whole." Perhaps these scientists, Mrs. Dixon now maintained, according to Mrs. Montgomery, were "killed in that war, but their theory will soon be brought to this country." Mrs. Montgomery added that Mrs. Dixon also warned that President Johnson should "guard against bad advice" and saw "a real threat to our country" from three men, with the initials K, T, and H, but emphasized that she was not referring to Kennedy or Humphrey. The most specific of Mrs. Dixon's forecasts was that of a "troublesome challenge" for Romney, whose September remark that he had been "brainwashed" on the Vietnam situation seriously endangered his presidential chances.

The difficulty of weighing Mrs. Dixon's forecasts fairly was explored by Hugh Tyler in his article "The Unsinkable Jeane Dixon" (*The Humanist*, May-June 1977). The author noted that Mrs. Dixon avoids quantitative experiments, so that one has to fall back on "scouring the record of her forecasts and checking her prophecies, one by one." This is made difficult by the elusive nature of most of them. Tyler added: "I suppose one could feed all of Jeane Dixon's prophecies into a computer and categorize them in terms of specificity, giving them a range of one to ten, and tossing out all those that are too vague to amount to much. But that calls for subjective judgments and selection, plus a fairly substantial research grant, independent judges, and a few years of data collection, calculation, and evaluation."

Mrs. Dixon's forecasts are widely scattered, and her earlier predictions are not easy to trace. In the autumn of 1966, a New York researcher, unable to locate some of Mrs. Montgomery's columns on Mrs. Dixon, asked Mrs. Montgomery for photocopies of her key syndicated columns quoting Mrs. Dixon in preceding years. She was advised that Mrs. Montgomery was too busy writing a book on her own increasing involvement in psychic phenomena, and therefore could not find the time for such research. Her book, *A Search for the Truth* (New York, 1967) recorded Ruth Montgomery's mediumist experiences, mainly "messages" from alleged spirit entities.

Public figures, including prophetesses, always become subject to inquiries that tend to bring out shadows as well as highlights. Mrs. Dixon, with Ruth Montgomery's help, has encountered a mixture of awe, good-natured tolerance, curiosity, and much genuine admiration concerning her prophecies. Yet little material is available concerning the personality and outlook of the Washington seeress. This gap was partly filled by an interview she had with the magazine writer Jerome Ellison, entitled "Jeane Dixon Talks About God" (*The Christian Herald*, March 1966), who described the subject of his article as "probably about the nearest thing to an authentic but untypical Old Testament-style prophet our generation of Americans is likely to see.". After describing Mrs. Dixon as "a deeply devout, bright, quick, daintily built woman, perhaps five-foot-three, with blue eyes and brown hair," Mr. Ellison noted that "she never uses her prophetic gift for business or personal profit" and asserted that "probably no prognosticator in history has been attended by a larger cloud of reliable witnesses."

Born Jeane Pinckert in 1918 in Medford, Wisconsin, she is the daughter of a German family that eventually settled in California, Mr. Ellison reported. As she recalls it, a gypsy fortune-teller said to her when she was eight years old that there were "star" lines in her palm; the lady in fact gave her a crystal ball. Jeane married James Dixon, owner of a large automobile agency, at the age of twenty-one. As a Catholic, she received a special church dispensation; Mr. Dixon is the son of a Methodist minister.

In reply to the magazine writer's questions, Mrs. Dixon said that her spiritual life includes an "evening self-examination," although she does not bear down too hard on herself: "I place my life and my day squarely before God." She looks for divine protection "from all negative influences—jealousy, malice, and the like," as "there is much jealousy around me, not of my accomplishments—what is given one cannot be considered an accomplishment of one's own—but of my faith."

Asked about her prophecies in relation to vision, Mrs. Dixon replied:

"Visions have nothing to do with extrasensory perception or with psychic work. I've had people ask, 'Why does God give you visions and not give them to other people?' A vision can be given to anybody God decides to give it to. I do not think I am favored; other people are given visions. But the reason He has given me these visions, I like to think, is that He gives me these visions knowing that I will blurt them out like a child, and tell the world I have seen them. I know the world will be given the message." She emphasized that the crystal ball she uses "has nothing to do with the religion," but "is a convenient device for concentrating one's mind for purposes of mental telepathy, and nothing more. Meditation is prayer. A vision is a gift of God."

Reviewing the Montgomery book in the *Journal* of the American Society for Psychical Research (July 1966), Miss Rhea White noted that while some of Jeane Dixon's political predictions "could have been intuitively—if not rationally—inferred," others "are hard to account for except in terms of ESP." Miss White, an experienced parapsychological researcher, concluded that Mrs. Dixon would seem to have "psychic ability, and she certainly merits the serious attention of parapsychologists." She cited Mrs. Montgomery, too, as having written that the Washington seeress "fascinates investigators of psychic phenomena because her precognition reveals itself through so many different channels." Miss White observed that this sentence "conjures up a vision of swarms of 'investigators' hovering around Mrs. Dixon, marveling at the multiplicity of ways in which her ESP is expressed," whereas it remained to be hoped that "a qualified parapsychologist will be able to study Mrs. Dixon and make his findings known."

Miss White's review was followed by a letter in a later issue of the American Society for Psychical Research's *Journal*, written by Mr. W. H. W. Sabine of Hollis, New York, who shared Miss White's "regret that an expert study of her powers [had] not been made," and added: "Mrs. Dixon's personal character as it is depicted in the book—religious, charitable, and unmercenary—certainly is not one that should impede her in satisfying scientific interest as well as that of the general public and her acquaintances." Mr. Sabine recalled Mrs. Dixon's prediction, published in the Sunday supplement *Parade* (May 13, 1956), which read as follows: "As for the 1960 election, Mrs. Dixon thinks it will be dominated by labor and won by a Democrat. But he will be assassinated or die in office 'though not necessarily in his first term.'" He added the following provocative speculation:

"The publication in *Parade* is not only an impressive piece of evidence for Mrs. Dixon's precognitive powers; it also raises a momentous question: Could the publication have contributed to cause the event? When an event depends on human activities, and when publication has taken place a considerable time before fulfillment, causation by the percipient is obviously one of the possible explanations of an apparent precognition." As a supplement to the *Baton Rouge Advocate*, the magazine *Parade* circulated in New Orleans where, at the date in question, Lee Harvey Oswald was living as a youth of sixteen (*The New York Times*, September 28, 1964). If Oswald saw the article—its reference to a Kremlin shakeup might attract the attention of a young Marxist—the idea of the assassination of a future President could thus have entered his mind.

"In any case, it is evident that the idea of such an assassination, and even a measure of expectation of it, was thus implanted in numerous minds all over the country; while in Washington, Mrs. Dixon, according to Mrs. Montgomery, was constantly reiterating her warning. Thus it may not be necessary to suggest even a telepathic influence in theorizing that Mrs. Dixon's widely known prophecy could have been causative in the events leading to the assassination."

Mr. Sabine's thoughts, with their grave implications, are sobering to any consideration of prophetic function. Expressing concern over a possible danger must have the impact of spurring the public imagination concerning that danger, even if it does not directly serve to create it. Economists know from experience that nervous talk about a setback is likely to create the very crisis of confidence that will bring about a recession. Even unfounded rumors about a bank's alleged liquidity problems may cause a "run" by worried depositors withdrawing their funds, which will then result in the bank's running out of cash.

Dr. Marshall McLuhan, the Canadian sociologist whose ideas have given birth to the concept that "the medium is the message," suggests that communications media strongly influence the very events they record, communicate, and analyze. The practicing prophet, in our time, is a "medium" in more than one meaning of this word. The speaker who warns of urban riots during a "long, hot summer," unless action is taken to prevent or assuage, may by his very remarks add to pressures likely to cause the riots he hopes to prevent. When Dr. Martin Luther King, winner of the Nobel Peace Prize, warned in April 1967 of possible "violence in the streets" in major U.S. cities during the summer, a number of Harlem residents acknowledged the delicate interrelationship of forewarning and event. Interviewed in the weekly New York *Amsterdam News* (April 22, 1967), John D. Silvera noted that there was "danger in making predictions of that sort, because the prediction itself might create an awareness in the potential troublemakers. . . ." Another resident, Will George, spoke of Dr. King's warning as "one of those potentially self-fulfilling prophecies." A third, Davis Fields, said that "sometimes when one predicts dire consequences, it is almost like wishing and willing them to happen." The summer of 1967 was, of course, filled with riots in many U.S. cities.

While there can be no certainty about it, virtually any warning forecast may unleash the actions that it is designed to counteract. Prophecy of disaster has traditionally tended to involve the prophet himself. Kings of ancient Greece at times executed messengers of ill tidings. In mythology, Cassandra, the Trojan prophetess of doom, was disbelieved, hated, and murdered. In Nazi Germany, as we have seen, the astrologer Krafft was arrested when he correctly warned of an attempt on the life of Hitler, because the Gestapo assumed that he might be one of the conspirators.

The prophet does not exist in a vacuum. He is involved. His prophecy is an event in itself; not necessarily or even probably decisive, but a factor that cannot be disregarded. Going back to the Kennedy assassination, so much speculative material has been published on this matter, and so many hypotheses have been offered and fought over, that Mr. Sabine's observation on the appearance of Jeane Dixon's prophecy in a Louisiana paper, where it might have been read by Oswald, constitutes of course just another piece in a gigantic puzzle. It does, however, hint substantially that, in the delicately balanced pattern of public events, a publicized prophetic vision—whether believed to be inspired by God or obtained through more mundane channels—carries with it a serious responsibility.

Mrs. Dixon's responsibility is particularly great, because her other, correct prophecies have brought her a wide following.

19 "Who Is Dead in the White House?"

A hero must die a violent death. To die in old age, peacefully, is unheroic. That, at least, is in accord with the popular image of a hero in mythology, legend, and life today. The contemporary hero par excellence who died a violent death was President John F. Kennedy. A similar pattern emerged with the assassination of President Abraham Lincoln and the death in an airplane of United Nations Secretary-General Dag Hammarskjöld in Africa. History, ancient and contemporary, is littered with similar tragedies.

The death of President Kennedy sparked a world-wide reaction of unique emotional shock. It was also one of the most extensively predicted personal disasters of our time. We have noted that Mrs. Jeane Dixon spoke of an assassination here as early as 1956. She did not waver from this prophecy, which she repeated many times—up to the day of Kennedy's violent death on November 22, 1963, in fact.

As recounted in Ruth Montgomery's book, Mrs. Dixon had an engagement a few days before to dine with Mr. John Teeter, executive director of the Damon Runyon Memorial Fund, the Vicomtesse Fournier de la Barre, of Paris, and Miss Eleanor Bumgardner, in a suburban Washington restaurant. As their conversation was recalled later by Miss Bumgardner, Mrs. Dixon seemed distraught en route, driving her car at a snail's pace. When asked what was troubling her, she replied, "I just can't get my mind off the White House. Everywhere I go I see the White House with a dark cloud moving down on it. Something tragic is going to happen very, very soon." The next day, Miss Bumgardner visited Mrs. Dixon in her husband's real estate office. She found her in an agitated state of mind: "Dear God! In a very few days the President will be killed. I see his casket coming into the White House...."

On November 20, at a luncheon with Mrs. Harley Cope, widow of a rear admiral, and Charles Benter, who had organized the U.S. Navy Band (and was then retired and working for Mr. Dixon's real estate firm), Mrs. Dixon was again extremely self-absorbed, missed part of a conversation, and said, "I'm sorry, but I can't hear what you say, because the President is going to be shot." As Ruth Montgomery narrates this incident, Mrs. Cope, thinking that she had misunderstood, asked, "Who did you say was going to be shot?" Mrs. Dixon answered, "Our President, President Kennedy."

On November 22, after attending Mass, she met Mr. Benter at a coffee shop, where she told him, "This is the day it will happen!" Later, at lunch with Mrs. Cope and Mrs. Rebecca Kaufmann, Mrs. Dixon did not touch her food. When Mrs. Kaufmann urged her to eat, she said, "Mrs. Kaufmann, I just can't. I'm too upset. Something dreadful is going to happen to the President today." The news of the shooting of President Kennedy came over the radio very shortly afterward.

Mrs. Dixon had also expressed premonitions concerning Dag Hammarskjöld. Again, part of the supporting testimony comes from Miss Bumgardner. Jess Stearn, in his book *The Door to the Future* (New York, 1963), quotes Miss Bumgardner as recalling that she was planning a flight abroad just before Hammarskjöld's crash, and that Mrs. Dixon then advised her, "Whatever you do, don't get on the same plane with Dag Hammarskjöld." Stearn interviewed a vice president of the American Security and Trust Company, who admitted that Mrs. Dixon had at that time warned him, too, not to share a plane with Mr. Hammarskjöld.

Stearn asked the bank official, "How did she say it?"

He answered, "She told me not to go up in a plane with Hammarskjöld for the next couple of weeks."

"How long ago was that?"

"A couple of weeks ago."

"Did she give you any reason?"

"She said it wouldn't be healthy, and—I guess she was right. . . ."

Jeane Dixon's prophecy of President Kennedy's death was correct, repeatedly correct. Yet, she shared an objective or subjective concern about the life of President Kennedy with millions of people. Dallas, on the eve of Kennedy's tour of the city in November 1963, was a city fraught with tension. Adlai Stevenson, U.S. Ambassador to the United Nations, had shortly before been threatened by a crowd. Emotional concern for the President and his immensely popular family was shared by people in many walks of life all over the world.

Since the assassination, there have been numerous indications that Kennedy himself was concerned, but fatalistic, about the danger to his own life. An undefinable aura of strain had built up even before the Dallas visit. Predictions of his violent death—revealing ambivalent degrees of concern and sensation-mongering as well—were expressed by many people who were less prominent and less well connected than Mrs. Dixon. Two telephone operators at the Oxnard, California, division of the General Telephone Company recalled that twenty minutes before the assassination, an unidentified woman's voice told them, "The President is going to be killed."

The Oxnard incident was later reported to the Federal Bureau of Investigation. The local telephone manager, Ray Sheehan, said then that the woman's voice appeared to have "stumbled into our operator's circuit," possibly through misdialing. The call could not be traced beyond the fact that it must have originated in the Oxnard-Camarillo area, fifty miles north of Los Angeles. Two telephone supervisors confirmed that the mysterious call was received at 10:10 A.M. Pacific Standard Time, just twenty minutes before the fatal shots were fired at the President.

Numerous similar instances were compiled by John C. Ross, and published as "Premonitions of Kennedy's Death" in *Fate* magazine. The magazine's editor, Curtis Fuller, listed,

among others, predictions made by the British astrologer
John Pendragon, and even one by Billy Graham. From
Glendive, Montana, it was reported that a freshman at Dawson County Junior College, Donna Radin, was leaving a class
as the noon bell rang. She suddenly stopped and cried out,
"The President is dead." Telepathy or precognition—her cry
was confirmed very shortly afterward. Miss Radin had not
heard a radio broadcast. She merely said later, "A queer feeling went through me. Before I realized what I was saying,
it just came out."

Mr. Ross described what he called "one of the saddest of
the premonitions of President Kennedy's death." It was made
by an eight-year-old boy, Ricky E. McDowell, confined to
Doctor's Hospital at Columbus, Ohio. Dying of leukemia,
Ricky had been in a semicoma for two days before the assassination. He woke up at 7 A.M. on November 22. His mother,
Betty McDowell, was sitting by his bed, and he told her of
a strange dream: President Kennedy had died. The mother
reassured Ricky that the President was alive and well. The
boy himself died on December 28; he never knew that his
dream had anticipated reality.

Astrological forecasts dealing with the lives of prominent
persons frequently contain warnings that they are in danger.
This can be viewed with skepticism; is there a national figure,
from Castro to de Gaulle, from Sukarno to Mao, who is not
in constant danger? But some of the references to President
Kennedy's death were specifically striking, even if viewed by
very rigid standards. A professional astrologer of long standing and high repute, Dal Lee, wrote in the *Astrological
Guide*, on sale in October 1963 and prepared months in
advance, what he then called "a word of caution to the President," urging him to "guard his health and safety" and adding: "We wish we could tell the President that November
will be an easygoing month for him, but the aspects forbid it."

An eminent European astrologer of long standing, Countess
Zoë Wassilko-Serecki of Vienna, told the author of this
volume that Kennedy's horoscope had "revealed clearly and
without a doubt—even to a beginner!—that he would have a
short life and die a violent death." She added: "We all knew
this, immediately after his election, when the dates became
known. But we did not publicize it, so as not to spoil people's
enthusiasm from the start. Anyway, fate cannot be changed.
Those in the know included my pupils and some fifty members of the Austrian Astrological Society. And it was easy

enough to pick up such astrological conclusions and to pass them on as 'clairvoyant' prophecy."

In Germany, *Huters Astrologischer Kalender,* published in 1961, stated: "The horoscope of U.S. President Kennedy shows health defects and at one time the danger that a fanatic is preparing his assassination." In addition to the German astrological calendar just cited, the weekly Munich astrological tabloid *Das Neue Zeitalter* carried a report by Gunnar Hellqvist (on December 10, 1960), headlined "Uncanny Prognosis: Will Kennedy Be Murdered? To Die in Service or Become a Murder Victim!" The editors state that the article came to them without the question mark in the headline. They added it, as they were reluctant to carry such a disturbing and sensational forecast as if it were a matter of fact.

The November 1963 issue of *American Astrology* contained an article by Leslie McIntyre, written in May, stating that certain constellations envisaged for the month had in the past "coincided with personal danger to the head of state," and that for President Kennedy "November is obviously fraught with perils of several varieties." One of America's most respected astrologers, the economics specialist David Williams, made an extremely well-documented forecast. Before the 1960 elections, on a boat trip with six other business executives, he was asked whether his astrological knowledge was good enough to enable him to make a specific forecast on the outcome of the presidential election. He dated a slip of paper, "Aug. 4/60" and added the notation "Abd. *Inspiration*" (indicating that it was prepared aboard the *Inspiration,* owned by Henry Fried, President of Mackay Construction Corporation). He then wrote:

"Prediction by D. Williams.

"Kennedy will be elected and will die in office and will be succeeded by Johnson."

Williams signed his full name. The statement was attested to by the signatures of two of the men aboard. Four others casually added, "We heard it too," and signed their names as well.

Astrologers do not always agree in their interpretations, but several recalled a compilation made in November 1901 by John Hazelwigg in the *Astrological Herald* of New York. Jerry Klutz, writing in *American Astrology* shortly after the 1960 elections (in December), recalled that Hazelwigg had "related the twenty years periodicity of the conjunction of

Jupiter and Saturn with deaths of presidents in office." Klutz explained it as follows:

1840	Harrison	died in office
1860	Lincoln	murdered
1880	Garfield	murdered
1900	McKinley	murdered
1920	Harding	died in office
1940	Roosevelt	died in office

Now, of course, it would be possible to add:

1960	Kennedy	murdered

Also in *American Astrology* (March 1961), the Australian astrologer Arthur de Dion, analyzing John F. Kennedy's horoscope, stated that the position "Mercury adverse Venus" presented "as deadly an aspect in private life or politics as is ever known," and that "the United States will surely have to keep him well guarded."

Dr. Stanley Krippner, Maimonides Medical Center, Brooklyn, N. Y., dealt with the death cycle in an address to the Society for the Investigation of Recurring Events, New York Academy of Medicine, in November 1966. He cited his own prevision of Kennedy's death while under the influence of a psychedelic drug, psilocybin, in 1962, when "Lincoln's features faded and those of Kennedy's appeared," and his own eyes opened, "filled with tears." But Krippner had known about the twenty-year cycle and "could have unconsciously used this knowledge in structuring his psychedelic impressions." Speaking of the twenty-year cycle, he found "only about one chance in 100 that this situation could be due to chance." He listed "causal and acausal" explanations, including synchronicity, expectancy set, and "the gradual buildup of hostility among paranoid schizophrenics which is assuaged vicariously (for about two decades) by the presidential death."

It might be well at this point to examine an hypothesis that has significance to any serious evaluation of astrology. It is a concept that has been advanced consistently by Dal Lee, whom one might well call an elder statesman of U.S. astrologers; he has repeatedly written that astrologers, involved as they are in charts and mathematical calculations, might indeed be practicing unconscious extrasensory perception. We have dealt with this idea earlier in this volume; certain cases of apparent precognition could easily have been instances of telepathy. Could it be that the astrologers and others had sensed a strong unease within President Kennedy himself—a fatalistic sense of danger that prompted him to rule out the protection that the famous bubble top might have given to the presidential limousine as it passed slowly through the streets of Dallas? Was it Kennedy, not they, who proved prophetic?

That Kennedy had premonitions about his fate seems fairly well documented. Washington columnist Drew Pearson reported that Kennedy spoke very seriously to the then Secretary of Labor, Arthur Goldberg, whom he was about to appoint to the Supreme Court. Kennedy said to Goldberg, "It's like cutting off my right arm to have you go." Goldberg said that he might fill another Supreme Court vacancy later on, but the President expressed his doubts, saying at first, "I don't know that another opportunity will present itself," and then adding gloomily, "And you'll be here a long time after I'm gone."

During the summer of 1963, when President Kennedy was leaving Mass at Hyannis Port, at one point he said to a newspaperman, who was also a family friend, "I wonder if they'll shoot me in church. . . ."

Lincoln's death premonitions have been recorded by a former law partner, Ward Hill Lamon, in his *Recollections of Abraham Lincoln* (Dorothy Lamon, ed.; Chicago, 1895). During the Civil War, Lamon was Marshal for the District of Columbia. He took notes immediately after hearing Lincoln narrate the following prophetic dream, and observed that the President had been deeply, almost fatalistically impressed by it. Here is Mr. Lamon's account:

"The most startling incident in the life of Mr. Lincoln was a dream he had only a few days before his assassination. To him it was a thing of deadly import, and certainly no vision was ever fashioned more exactly like a dread reality. . . . After worrying over it for some days, Mr. Lincoln seemed no longer able to keep the secret. I give it as nearly in his own words as I can from notes which I made immediately after its recital. There were only two or three persons present. The President was in a melancholy, meditative mood, and had been silent for some time. Mrs. Lincoln, who was present, rallied him on his solemn visage and want of spirit. This seemed to arouse him, and without seeming to notice her sally he said, in slow and measured tones:

" 'It seems strange how much there is in the Bible about dreams. There are, I think, some sixteen chapters in the Old Testament and four or five in the New in which dreams are mentioned; and there are many other passages scattered throughout the book which refer to visions. If we believe the

PROPHECY IN OUR TIME

Bible, we must accept the fact that in the old days God and His angels came to men in their sleep and made themselves known in dreams. Nowadays, dreams are regarded as very foolish, and are seldom told, except by old women and by young men and maidens in love.'

"Mrs. Lincoln remarked, 'Why, you look dreadfully solemn; do *you* believe in dreams?"

"'I can't say that I do,' returned Mr. Lincoln, 'but I had one the other night which has haunted me ever since. After it occurred, the first time I opened the Bible, strange as it may appear, it was at the twenty-eighth chapter of Genesis, which relates the wonderful dream Jacob had. I turned to other passages and seemed to encounter a dream or vision wherever I looked. I kept turning the leaves of the old book, and everywhere my eye fell upon passages recording matters strangely in keeping with my own thoughts—supernatural visitations, dreams, visions, etc.'

"He now looked so serious and disturbed that Mrs. Lincoln exclaimed, 'You frighten me! What is the matter?'

"'I am afraid,' said Mr. Lincoln, observing the effect his words had upon his wife, 'that I have done wrong to mention the subject at all; but somehow the thing has got possession of me, and, like Banquo's ghost, it will not down.'

"This only inflamed Mrs. Lincoln's curiosity the more, and while bravely disclaiming any belief in dreams, she strongly urged him to tell the dream which seemed to have such a hold upon him, being seconded in this by another listener. Mr. Lincoln hesitated, but at length commenced very deliberately, his brow overcast with a shade of melancholy:

"'About ten days ago I retired very late. I could not have been long in bed when I fell into slumber, for I was weary. I soon began to dream. There seemed to be a death-like stillness about me. Then I suddenly heard subdued sobs as if a number of people were weeping. I thought I left my bed and wandered downstairs. There the silence was broken by the same pitiful sobbing, but the mourners were invisible. I went from room to room; no living person was in sight, but the same mournful sounds of distress followed me as I passed along; every object was familiar to me, but where were all the people who were grieving as if their hearts would break? I was puzzled and alarmed. What could be the meaning of all this? Determined to find the cause of a state of things so mysterious and so shocking, I kept on until I arrived at the East Room, which I entered. There I met with a sickening surprise. Before me was a catafalque on which rested a corpse wrapped in funeral vestments. Around it were stationed soldiers who were acting as guards; and there was a throng of people, some gazing mournfully upon the corpse whose face was covered; others weeping pitifully.'

"'Who is dead in the White House?' I demanded of one of the soldiers.

"'The President,' was the answer; 'he was killed by an assassin!' There came a loud burst of grief from the crowd, which woke me from my dream. I slept no more that night, and although it was only a dream, I have been strangely annoyed by it ever since.'

"'That is horrid!' said Mrs. Lincoln. 'I wish you had not told it. I am glad I don't believe in dreams or I should be in terror from this time forth.'

"'Well,' responded Mr. Lincoln thoughtfully, 'it is only a dream, Mary. Let us say no more about it and try to forget it.'"

Mr. Lamon's account concludes with some comments of his own:

"This dream was so horrible, so real, and so in keeping with other dreams and threatening presentiments of his that Mr. Lincoln was profoundly disturbed by it. During its recital he was grave, gloomy and at times visibly pale, but perfectly calm. He spoke slowly, with measured accents and deep feeling. . . ."

According to Lamon, when Mrs. Lincoln heard of the President's assassination, her first words were, "His dream was prophetic!" And his body did then lie in state in the East Room, with soldiers guarding it.

Lincoln's dream, even allowing for basic weaknesses in Lamon's narrative—the obviously contrived after-the-fact dialogue; the self-conscious air of doom—is a striking incident of precognition. And it did occur very shortly before the President's death; the details about the East Room and the guard are added premonitory evidence. Yet, it is well to keep in mind that President Lincoln was a more complicated man than popular history suggests. He had a keen sense of his own "destiny."

Abraham Lincoln had dreamed of his future before. He wrote, under the impact of the Civil War: "I had my ambitions—yes—as every American boy worth his salt has. And I dared to dream this vision of the White House—I, the humblest of the humble, born in a lowly pioneer's cabin in the woods of Kentucky. My dream came true, and where is its glory? Ashes and blood. I have lived with aching heart through it all and envied the dead their rest on the battle fields."

Writing in the psychoanalytic quarterly *Imago* (June 1940), Dr. George W. Wilson of Chicago has suggested that Lincoln virtually set the stage "to get himself murdered," that his premonitory dream and his persistent failure to keep himself properly protected could be traced to the same impulses. Lincoln, Wilson recalls, "had been warned, coaxed, and cajoled by his friends and political associates for the utterly careless manner in which he exposed himself to physical attack." Wilson recalls that Secretary of War Edwin M. Stanton once took Lincoln to task for this carelessness, threatening to send in a whole company of infantry to guard the President wherever he went. Lincoln countered by asking Stanton that he send his own aide-de-camp, a man who had a fixed assignment elsewhere, to guard him at Ford's Theater that evening. This was quite impossible, and an obvious rebuff to Stanton. Lincoln's supposed guard was a notoriously unreliable ex-policeman, who was not even at his post when John Wilkes Booth forced his way into the presidential box.

Dr. Wilson views Lincoln's final premonition of death as the last of many presentiments and dreams that the President had mentioned to friends and even strangers; he states that Lincoln "claimed by inference that he could foretell the future," including presentiments that "revealed to him the probable outcome of state problems and impending battles." Concluding that "he attributed a prophetic quality to all his dreams," Wilson feels that the President claimed omnipotence for himself and that his death dream accurately "portrayed the unconscious wishes of Abraham Lincoln," revealing "his exhibitionist and self-destructive impulses."

Lamon has written: "Assured as he undoubtedly was about omens, which to his mind were conclusive—that he would rise to power and greatness, he was firmly convinced by the same tokens that he would be suddenly cut off at the height of his career and the fullness of his fame. He always believed that he would fall by the hand of an assassin: and yet, with that appalling doom clouding his life, his courage never for a moment forsook him."

The hero must die! Do men live out the symbols that they have created of themselves? And do their dreams, therefore, anticipate their destinies, often with striking accuracy and detail? Or do their fears and wishes communicate themselves to others who thus become prophets?

These are esoteric questions, and one hesitates to put them, as they cut across several areas of the unknown. Still, some serious attempts are now being made to answer questions of this nature. In his essay on "The Integrity of Life and Death," the psychologist Dr. Ira Progoff (*Eranos Jahrbuch*, Zurich, 1965) deals with the symbolism associated with the deaths of Kennedy, Hammarskjöld, and Lincoln. Dr. Progoff notes that it was typical of "the attitude of bravado on the part of Kennedy" that he had ordered to leave the bubble top of his car open, without protection against a sniper's bullet, a "gesture that is characteristic of the hero type of personality." The strength of this hero image, Progoff says, "filled him with so great a sense of inner presence, that he felt he did not need to take protective steps of a simply physical nature." Although this sense of power may have sustained him from time to time, Progoff adds, "it was a totally unreasonable thing for Kennedy to die for, but it is in precisely this area that we must look for the meaning of his death. . . ."

In the cautious language of the professional, Progoff narrates what he calls "a traditional story about Lincoln, that as early as 1850 when he was still a country lawyer with few tangible expectations of success, a fortune-teller made a prediction that impressed Lincoln and his friends strongly:

"The fortune-teller was an old Negress who practiced her craft according to the voodoo arts. The story is that when she turned her attention to Lincoln and focused her spirit on his, psychologically, in order to give him a reading, she became startled and excited by the feelings, or vibrations, that came to her. She apparently sensed—as a sensitive mediumistic type is bound to do—that there were extraordinary qualities in the person before her. She responded to this feeling and made a bountiful prediction. She knew that the man before her was an attorney and perhaps that he was in politics, so she made a prediction that was enthusiastic but not unnatural under the circumstances. She prophesied that Lincoln would one day be President."

Progoff adds: "Understandably, Lincoln's friends and some of his biographers have made quite a fuss over this event, interpreting it ex post facto in the light of the rapid political successes that came to Lincoln in the intervening decade, culminating with his nomination and his election in 1860. Some enthusiasts take it as a sign of the supernatural working in his life. Others, who are sceptics, take it as a shrewd guess— one that happened to be remembered because of the unusual events that followed it—but they see it as no more than a guess on the part of an old woman who knew how to flatter her customers. . . ."

Progoff feels that Lincoln himself "responded to occurrences of this type with serious attention, but he regarded them in a quiet and certainly not in an enthusiastic way. He accepted the prophecies to the degree that he believed that something important lay in store for him." Lincoln does indeed then seem to have had a strong sense of inevitability in life. At the time of the premonitory dream, Progoff believes, there was fear in Lincoln and also resignation. In the case of Lincoln, again, as in the case of Kennedy, protection failed or was even discouraged by the President. Progoff agrees that "with all his psychic presentiments and his conscious acceptance of their message for him, Lincoln did nothing—and we can truly say that he deliberately did nothing—to improve the police protection that might have saved him." He was even reluctant to attend the performance at Ford's Theater; his feeling ran against it, but he went, nevertheless. (Kennedy, too, apparently had misgivings about his Dallas tour.)

Lincoln may well have come to a point, at that particular moment in his career, of accepting, as Progoff puts it, "The whole train of events, the future equally with the past, as part of his unfolding and necessary destiny; whatever it was, that was it." Was he, indeed, living out an image of himself? He had turned to the Bible after his premonitory dream, and found passage after passage of direct significance to his own deep concern. In the Old Testament, often, when the servant of God has served his purpose, he is sent off into the mountains and disappears.

Leo Tolstoy, himself a man of self-doubts and deeply struggling with the meaning of death, said in an interview after Lincoln's assassination: "Lincoln was a Christ in miniature. . . ."

Dag Hammarskjöld, whose world outlook and fate Progoff categorizes within "the road of the suffering servant," died in what is believed to have been an airplane crash while he was on an official United Nations peace-enforcing mission in Africa. As his journal, published under the title *Markings* (New York, 1964), indicated, he saw himself virtually as a sacrificial offering in a service performed for the Divine; a brief poem of his put this image of his fate, as he envisaged it, with simplicity and clarity:

> I have watched the others:
> Now I am the victim
> Strapped fast to the altar
> For Sacrifice.

Progoff comments on the theme of the sacrificial victim in Hammarskjöld's writings: "This was the background of it in the life and psyche of the man. There were many thoughts of death, even poetic descriptions of violent death, as though the psyche were evoking the fatal event that lay ahead—not so much predicting it as evoking it. . . ."

These three men were symbols in their lifetimes. Yet their violent deaths were, somehow, needed to complete and heighten this symbolism. All three anticipated possible or probable violent death, and so did others about them. All three remain as symbols of themselves and of the images they embodied.

20 Ever Since Dodona

Its very name is like the sound of thunder. Dodona. Long before the classic age of Greece, long before Homer or the Delphic Oracle, men and women consulted this most ancient of known oracles. Perhaps as long as 4,000 years ago, an oak stood at Dodona, today a part of the mountainous area in northwestern Greece. *Was* it the very sound of thunder, heard frequently in the sky above Dodona, which at times seemed to speak there with the voice of an oracle? We know too little and too much about this place. The simplicities and complexities of man may well have first merged at Dodona. Men certainly want to know what the future will bring; but what they truly want, and always wanted, to know is: What am I to do?

This tree, this cove, this sky, this stone, this cauldron, this grotto, this rippling lake, this whisper of leaves, this hallowed ground, this molten lead, this mirror, this fleeting cloud—they have all been asked these questions: Tell me what to do? Tell me what the Gods want of me? Tell me what sacrifices I must make, what roads I must travel, what words I must speak, what rituals perform, what masters obey. What blessed or frightful thing must I do?

The simple man asks simple questions. Thousands of years ago, as recorded on stone tablets, Agis asked at Dodona whether he had lost his blankets and pillows, or whether "someone outside has stolen them." A certain Lysanias asked the oracle whether he was the father of the child carried by his wife, Nyla. And Evandrus and his wife wanted to know, so a tablet tells us, "by what prayer or worship they may fare best, now and forever." There is a broken plate of lead, on which the Corcyreans, forever fighting among themselves, asked the oracle "to what god or hero, through offering prayer and sacrifice, they might live together in unity."

Plato reminds us that to "the men of that time, since they were not wise as ye are nowadays, it was enough in their simplicity to listen to oak or rock, if only these told them true." Ah, how wise we are nowadays! Our Presidents, with no oracles to call upon, no court astrologers to tell them what days are propitious, turn toward, or away from, public opinion polls that have tabulated a million anonymous voices saying yes, no, or I don't know.

Mrs. Jeane Dixon has told of her visits with President Roosevelt a few months before his death, her crystal ball tucked under a silver-fox fur piece. As she recalls their two meetings, President Roosevelt asked her assurance in answer to the question, "Will we remain allies with Russia?" To which Mrs. Dixon recalls having replied, "The visions show otherwise, but we will become allies again later on, against Red China." The President did not think China would go Communist, Jeane Dixon has stated. She also says that when he asked her how many years he had to live, Mrs. Dixon answered, "Not years. You can't measure it in years, Mr. President, but in months. Less than six months."

Prophecy in our time. What is "our time?" We wonder whether it moves backward as well as forward, whether it is "relative" or "serial," whether it stands still or expands, and we wonder about the laws of the natural sciences, of philosophy, of that oracle of oracles, our own soul. The Dodona oak, silhouetted against the blue Greek sky, stood as a symbol of all that prehistoric man hoped and feared. It must have been a place for communing with spirits of the dead; its soil must have tasted the blood of human and other sacrifices; its bark must have been hollowed by the touches and kisses of supplicants; its acorns must have been carried away as omens of strength and good fortune.

Superimposed on its original animistic symbolism, dedication to Zeus eventually transformed Dodona. The temples built around it were ravaged time and again by one tribe after another. Frederic W. H. Myers, in his *Classical Essays*

(London, 1883), tells us that "so long as the oak was standing, the temple rose anew"; but: "When at last an Illyrian bandit cut down the oak, the presence of Zeus was gone, and the desolate Thesprotian valley has known since then no other sanctity, and has found no other voice."

Cutting back and forth across millennia, we exchange the ridiculous and the sublime—but nowhere are the two more mixed than in man's efforts to "make sure" of things, to find "something to hang on to," be it cosmic faith or a good-luck charm. The urge for prophecy is as near as the corner newsstand with its astrological pamphlets, or the evening paper with its columns of "advice" to the bewildered millions. And we may classify the politico-economic soothsayers with those who minister to the so-called lovelorn. Man's confusion about the world and himself is being dramatized as he turns to his doctor, his stockbroker, his clergyman, his psychiatrist —anyone with the trappings of knowledge: a law diploma, a witch-doctor's mask, a clerical collar, or a wall chart of commodity prices.

And how important trappings are, and have been! The woman acting as the Delphic Oracle, we are told, would receive a question and then step down into the bowels of the earth; there, she would seat herself on a three-legged stool and bow her head over the chasm, from which intoxicating vapors arose (caused, mythology alleged, by the decomposition of the python slain by Apollo), which inspired her to utter weird and fateful words. More often than not, these words had to be, as it were, "translated" by the attending priests, the *Prophets* who were, of course, accused of intruding with their own ideas on the original.

Even these settings involved no more than poetic license. Serious scholars are virtually unanimous in agreeing with A. Oppé, who wrote on "The Chasm of Delphi" (in *The Journal of Hellenic Studies,* London, 1904) that the chasm and the "mephitic gas" emerging from it were both the inventions of guides who showed awed country bumpkins around the oracle site at a time when Delphi's influence had badly sagged. Oppé feels strongly that the chasm-and-vapor story was spread by "the wild accounts of the Latin authors," providing a version which was most agreeable to the Stoics, who were "delighted with an explanation of a divine manifestation which was compatible with their general notion of a deity acting by natural means."

And there goes the decomposing-python legend—to which the Pythian oracle of Delphi owed her very name. Words, indeed, handed down to us from classical or even archaic Greece are virtually covered with barnacles of meanings. Myers mentions that "oracle" in Latin points especially to cases where the voice of God, or a spirit, was actually heard "whether directly or through some human intermediary." But the corresponding Greek term merely "signifies a seat of soothsaying, a place where divinations are obtained by whatever means."

Our own very current word "enthusiasm" strikes me as one of the most vividly meaningful terms of them all. Its center is the Greek word for God, "Theos"; its first syllable conveys "entering into"—and the total meaning concerns someone who has been entered into by the gods, who is "possessed" and therefore either inspired, controlled, uplifted, transformed, or turned into an instrument of knowledge, or passion, beyond his normal human limits. The oracles, in this sense, were originally seen as "enthused," mouthpieces of the gods, of dead ancestors, or of a cosmic force—not unlike Jung's "collective unconscious"—that holds knowledge greater than the individual's in all directions, including the future.

Such magnificent images, and often such trivial applications! Would not the petals of a flower do, to answer whether "she loves me . . . she loves me not . . .?" *Must* man seek his hoped-for knowledge in what Freud called the "black mud" of the occult; among voracious gypsy fortune-tellers; from half-mad and certainly homosexual shamans all through Northern Asia and into the South Pacific; from greedy and manipulative priests forming the entourage of successive Delphic oracles?

Socrates wrote that "Our greatest blessings come to us by way of madness, provided the madness is given to us by divine gift." Plato regarded Apollo as the patron of a divine madness which controlled the two Apolline oracles, the Pythia and the Sibyl, as well as the priestesses of Zeus at Dodona. The German scholar, Erwin Rohde, in his key work *Psyche* (New York, 1925), contradicts general Greek classical tradition with the finding that Apolline religion had been "hostile to anything in the nature of ecstasy," and that only the intrusion of Dionysian ideas forced divine madness on the Pythia. (Rohde was a life-long friend of Friedrich Nietzsche, and it was his research on Dionysus that contributed toward giving Nietzsche's thought its final twist against what he regarded as Christian meekness in favor of Dionysian exuberance.)

Professor E. R. Dodds, in his magnificent work *The Greeks and the Irrational* (Berkeley, 1959) states that "prophetic madness is at least as old in Greece as the religion of Apollo," and probably older, because "the association of prophecy and madness belongs to the Indo-European stock of ideas." He notes that most Apollonic oracles, such as the Delphic one, did not rely on "vision" but upon "enthusiasm" in its original and liberal sense, in that the god "entered into her and used her vocal organs as if they were his own."

The history of prophecy is studded with the mad, the odd, the tragi-comical. In 1485, one Robert Nixon, in England, known as "the Cheshire idiot," was heard talking to his horses while plowing, calling them "Dick" and "Harry." And while neither of the horses was so named, lo and behold, Richard III had, or so it appeared afterwards, been killed in battle on Bosworth Field, and Henry VII named King of England—at precisely that time. Obviously, the locals concluded, their village idiot was a prophet, or something like that. Henry VII then heard about "the Cheshire idiot" and brought him to his palace. To test him, Henry is supposed to have hidden a diamond and to have told Nixon that he had lost it; could Nixon find it? No fool, then, as legend has it, Nixon came up with something appropriately oracular, such as "those who hide can find." But the Court tired of the Cheshire lad, locked him in a closet, and forgot all about him until several days later, when everyone returned from a hunt. He was dead. A toy; a court jester; a prophet; a madman; or just a plowboy who had spoken to his horses at the right—or wrong—time.

The peasants of Cheshire had been looking for something miraculous, or wild, or mad, and they consequently found it. Just as those who will look long and hard enough at a cloud formation or at a Rorschach test ink blot can find almost anything. This is timeless and universal: the ancient Greek practice of foreseeing the future from molten lead is still retained in much of Western Europe; on New Year's Eve, one melts a bit of lead in a spoon, throws it into cold water—and reads the events of the future from it. Not much different from the egg-throwing practices in Assam, of which D. C. Becker wrote in *Anthropos* (Vienna, 1917–18) on "Das Eierwerfen von Khasi" ("Egg Throwing in Khasi"). Becker there described a local fortune-telling custom, using eggs and unboiled rice. The eggs are painted red, so that it is easily possible to tell the outside and inside of the shell apart, after they are broken. The eggs are hurled down, and their shapes then read oracularly. Being realists, according to Becker, the Khasi repeat this procedure until the omens are just right; then, all the ingredients are cooked into scrambled-eggs-with-rice à la Khasi.

In his thoughtful study of the psychological aspects of myth, *The Hero With a Thousand Faces* (New York, 1949), Joseph Campbell observes that the dominant motivation of traditional ritual is not the manipulation of life events, but an effort to integrate them. There are no festivals to prolong summer or hold back winter, because, Campbell writes, "the dominant motive in all true religious (as opposed to black-magical) ceremonial is that of submission to the inevitable of destiny." I think we have found that one of man's most consistent motives in pursuing prophecy is his desire to comprehend, and anticipate, this destiny.

Campbell feels that contemporary civilization has lost the unity that existed in earlier mythology and religions; man's traditional fears, of animals and natural disasters, have been eliminated. But the original effort to comprehend the incomprehensible, man's fate, his future, his destiny, has taken on different meaning. He states: "Today, no meaning is in the group—none in the world: all is in the individual. But there the meaning is absolutely unconscious. One does not know toward what one moves. One does not know by what one is propelled. . . ." The hunger for prophecy in our time may well be an expression of the need for new hope. The prophetic image can marshal the unconscious forces of human strength and optimism, offering a set goal, attainable despite man's knowledge of his limitations.

Generally speaking, psychological aspects of prophecy have been explored within rather narrow limits. The reasons for this can be found partly in the quite natural concern of psychologists with mental illness and partly in the fact that the larger case-history collections of prophetic experiences are either too new or, for one reason or another, not accessible enough. In addition, few incidents of precognition include all the criteria that a truly thorough examination would demand.

First of all, the ideal case would be at least as fully documented as those especially selected by the American Society for Psycical Research under the direction of Dr. Gardner Murphy. In addition, a series of in-depth interviews should take place with the person who has perceived a future event, with those who observed the perception and event or participated in them, and with others who may have been close to the total development. Naturally, the psychologists engaged in these investigations should be open-minded but meticulous. Ideally, the number of cases studied should be large enough to permit quantitative as well as qualitative evaluation.

Now, all this is simply not possible. At one or several stages, these much-desired links either do not exist or fall apart. Freud wrote his paper "A Premonitory Dream Fulfilled" as early as 1899. But he lived, in subsequent years, in a world that was peopled either with patients or with colleagues who were trying to pull him too hard hither or yon, toward or away from things that smacked of the "occult." When he encountered "premonitory" feelings or dreams among patients, Freud was inclined to attribute them to the overt or covert desires of these men and women, to find them symptoms of the emotional disturbances that he set out to cure.

A striking contemporary event illustrates this orthodox point. On August 1, 1966, Charles J. Whitman, a student at the University of Texas, in Austin, killed fourteen persons and an unborn baby. All told, he shot more than forty persons from his position on the university tower, which to many who attended the university's mental-hygiene clinic has the aura of a "mystic symbol." This very wholesale slaughter had been forecast by the killer in a conversation with a staff psychiatrist of the university, Dr. Maurice D. Heatley, on the preceding March 29. As Dr. Heatley noted: "He readily admits having overwhelming periods of hostility with a very minimum of provocation. Repeated inquiries attempting to analyze his exact experiences were not too successful with the exception of his vivid reference to 'thinking about going up on the tower with a deer rifle and start shooting people.'"

Whitman's image of his own action was, in a popular sense, prophetic. In Freudian terms, it may be linked directly to the man's death wish toward his father, whom Dr. Heatley noted, he regarded as "brutal and domineering and extremely demanding of the other three members of the family." The father admitted, "I did and do have an awful temper." Whitman's murders from the tower coincided with a severe family crisis involving his father and mother. The mother had left the father, who lived in Lake Worth, Florida, when, in early March, Charles had gone to Florida to bring his mother to Austin. The father then telephoned almost daily to ask that she return to Lake Worth. In the interview with the psychiatrist, Whitman "admitted that his tactics were similar to his father's and that on two occasions he had assaulted his wife physically." In a note he left behind, he said that he hated his father with "mortal passion." A fellow student in architectural engineering, Larry Fuess, recalled that "his whole life was an escape from his father." Another friend was quoted in *The New York Times* (August 3, 1966) as saying that "he hated himself when he did something like his father." The father's home in Lake Worth was decorated with guns in virtually every room.

Even a non-Freudian would acknowledge the Oedipal situation underlying the Whitman case. In the end, the young man's vision of his "shooting people" began with the murder of his mother and his wife and was followed by the death and wounding of the people he shot from the university tower. Of those whose lives touched him directly, only his father remained alive.

Charles Whitman had translated his own prophecy into reality. He had, as it were, "seen" himself standing on the tower, with godlike omnipotence, dealing out death; he outdid his father in this violence, as he had not succeeded in doing in other spheres of life. The mountaineer who told his dream to Jung, and who turned it into reality by falling to his death, did not consciously admit his suicidal intent. Whitman told the psychiatrist of his idea of shooting people from the tower, much in the manner in which one might relate any dream-like fantasy.

Granted, there is much that separates the type of precognitive dream reported to psychical researchers from the ultimate violence of Whitman's mass murders—but granted, too, we are dealing with widely varying degrees of prophetic utterances and experiences. Freud, from his particular vantage point, most frequently encountered the kind of "premonitory" cases that were akin to Whitman's death wishes. But the range that separates one category of prophecy from another should not give way to all-too-neat subdivisions that virtually ostracize one or another subcategory.

It seems proper to ignore the neat subdivisions of prophecy, premonition, precognition, predeterminism, etc., at this point —and to admit as well the terminological limitations of such words as "normal" and "abnormal." Mrs. Rhine, in her book, *Hidden Channels of the Mind*, notes that "psychiatrists are concerned with those hidden aspects of the mind that become unhealthy," while "the forms of expressions of ESP—dreams, hallucinations, compulsions, automatisms—perfectly healthy and normal forms of expressions as they are, may also be used by the mind in morbid states." And it would be hard to dispute this point. The fact, then, that precognition may be claimed, or experienced, by the mentally ill does not necessarily make it a symptom of illness.

The range of the prophetic, including the pseudoprophetic, is too wide and the documented material available too limited to permit definitive psychological conclusions. The "death wish" label may apply to certain people and in certain situations, but it cannot cover everything. The "synchronicity" hypothesis is still fluid. The basic concept that a deep emotional factor, or need, is involved is by now almost self-evident, except when precognition is so apparently trivial that emotional involvement would have to be well and deeply hidden.

The very nature of the prophetic experience, notably the precognitive dream, seems to correspond to the personality traits and life situations of the persons involved; no two cases are truly alike, although similarities always exist. A prophetic vision may be vague, couched in elusive oracular language or images, or it may be as clear as the image on a well-tuned television screen.

Let us be honest: We cannot answer the question as to why, exactly, a prophetic experience takes place. It is easy enough to apply one or another psychological dogma to the case material available—but that means, given what we know, reducing the data to a Rorschach image, onto which each school of psychology can simply project its particular brand of ideas.

There is enough smoke, though, to merit much further investigation. And the next steps seem perfectly clear. The collection of cases must go on, including that of cases observed by psychologists of various schools. Documentation should take place, wherever possible. And then, the material should be allowed to tell its own story. The researcher dealing with prophecy is much like the sculptor who has to decide to carve a specific image, or to let a particular piece of wood or stone suggest outlines by its own contours, texture, and internal quality. I would urge the latter choice in the assessing of prophetic case histories.

Whatever else the present and future role of the computer may be, it has provided us with a handy analogy. We feed a wide variety of information into it—we program it, to use the technical term—and then, when asked a question in which all or part of this information can be utilized, the computer provides us with a quick answer. A good deal of human prophecy is certainly based on integrated knowledge of the past, as in the computer; but an elusive element of actual foreknowledge remains uniquely human. One of the simplest analogies, but at the same time one of the most sophisticated, is that of Dr. Joost A. M. Meerloo; he believes that a tennis player anticipates—forecasts, prophesies, use any word you think appropriate—the point at which his opponent's ball will hit the court, from a great variety of information pieces. He draws, of course, on his own conscious and not-so-conscious memories of previous games with other opponents, or even with the same one. He not only observes consciously, and mainly by sight, just how the opponent stands, performs, places his feet, holds his racquet—he also takes in a variety of possibly subliminal factors. And then, with all this information instantly "programmed" within himself, he forecasts the point of impact of the ball, and seeks to interrupt its course.

If the player did not interfere with the ball's course in order to reverse it and smash it back across the net, the anticipated event would probably come about. But so many rapid calculations and observations are involved, so many virtually simultaneously received and recorded impressions are at play, that the recordable conscious actions are probably in the minority. The player would no more benefit from knowing intellectually what, exactly, he is doing, than would our old metaphoric friend, the centipede, benefit from knowing which of his numerous feet to move first.

We are justified, I think, in adding additional likely pieces of information in order to attempt an explanation of more dramatic prophetic conclusions. If those who anticipated President Kennedy's assassination did not actually "see" the event itself, in the future, chronologically set later in time, then just what did they see? They saw a pattern of events emerging, blending with emotional elements within Kennedy and those close to him. Did they, in the old-fashioned sense of these words, "read Kennedy's mind?" And if not in this old-fashioned sense, did they perhaps record subliminally an attitude, a fatalism, a fear, a trait of derring-do, a self-image of the Young Hero Destined for Death? Astrologers who say that the stars "impel" but do not "compel" us are using two highly appropriate words. The life style of John F. Kennedy, his public image, and the image he had of himself (let the people see me—let's leave the bubble top off—you can't run away from death) had emerged strongly in the public mind; it could be sensed on many levels, more by some than by others.

Those who anticipated Kennedy's violent death, allowing for the confusion of emotional response known as ambivalence, fall perhaps into the categories of those who "feared" his death and those who "wanted" his death. But the boundary line between fear and wish is a theoretical one, virtually erased often by conscious or unconscious hypocrisy, self-deception, sensationalism, and a panorama of guilt feelings. The post-mortem Kennedy cult, which feeds upon itself, can easily be described in the most archaic images of guilt and atonement, endlessly repeated.

Franz Werfel, best known for his novels *The Song of Bernadette* and *The Forty Days of Musa Dagh*, once wrote a book in German entitled *Not the Murderer, the Victim Is Guilty*. Indeed, there are people who are not only accident-prone but death-prone. And while death strikes only once, with irreversible finality, a personality pattern emerges, not only in daredevil sportsmen such as Donald Campbell, but in many others less prominent than a youthful, heroic figure who is head of the most powerful nation on earth. These men, in the extraordinarily perceptive meaning of the phrase, are "courting death" through many of their actions or omissions.

They signal this attitude to the world around them, and these signals are recorded in sensory and quite possibly in extrasensory ways as well. And those who record these signals most fully are men and women who, for individual reasons, are highly sensitive to them. This sensitivity may express itself in the fairly obvious fashion of their either wanting or fearing (or both) the death of The Hero, in the psychological-mythological meaning of this concept. They may also be extrasensitive to such signals because their own fear of or desire for death has heightened their sensitivity, rather in the manner in which a safecracker increases the sensitivity of his touch by sandpapering his fingertips.

A complex constellation of overt and covert emotions, consciously observed or subliminal, are thus "programmed" within a "prophet" who, like the rest of us, is much more complex than the most intricate of computers. And then, these "data are processed," a forecast is made, and a prophecy reflecting the dramatic elements within the individual "prophet" is placed before the world. At that, the prophecy may be way off the mark. But if it is on target, the public impact can be momentous.

The accumulated case histories and laboratory tests of extrasensory perception are too numerous to be ignored. Among the clues recorded by a particularly sensitive, particularly "impression-prone" individual, telepathically or clairvoyantly perceived slivers of information must be included. In the terminology of the Institute of Parapsychology at Durham, North Carolina, precognition is defined as "cognition of a future event which could not be known through rational inference." Where, then, does the "rational" end, and where does the "nonrational," in its manifold guises, begin?

We do not know. John F. Kennedy, on the morning of his assassination, spoke of the ease with which he might be assassinated in the streets of Dallas. He knew the risks he was running, but he did not play it safe. Indeed, he dared fate. To the degree that he knew or felt that he was driving into "kook" territory, as he had put it to his wife a few hours earlier, the President *was* tempting fate, courting death, challenging the gods.

President Kennedy followed yet another well-known psychological pattern, which a sensitive, recording his attitude through the antennae of the sensory or extrasensory, might easily have noted. He had been used to a pattern of success, of overcoming personal handicaps in his health, of defeating political opponents by the score, of triumphing again and again over adversity, and adversaries. In a nonliteral sense, Kennedy in Dallas was acting like a tribal African warrior who, following a reassuring ritual, believes himself to be protected by a magical shield stronger than any bubble top. To be, as it were, untouchable, not quite like other mortals, the inhabitant of a glamorous, partly make-believe "Camelot" —all that had gone into the man's make-up, together with charm, riches, intellect, masculine as well as political triumph, and the heady self-assurance that must come with being a powerful and popular leader of millions.

Ambivalence, contradictions, cross currents of self-assurance and fear, daring fate while wary of it—these coagulated into a crisis atmosphere in the city of Dallas. William Manchester, in *The Death of a President* (New York, 1967), virtually sees Dallas as a death-dealing entity. It is perhaps more correct to speak of this city, that November day, as *symbolizing* the forces within and without President Kennedy himself that made up a fateful constellation. These forces had been at work long before. When Mrs. Dixon told her Washingon friends that she saw a "dark cloud" over the White House, she had the sense of the dramatic, the freedom from inhibition, and the child-like nerve to put into words what others felt only vaguely. Doom is an easy prophetic theme;

death is easily foretold. But the ancient fear that "the gods may be jealous" of the baby that is too perfect, of happiness that is too great, of triumph that is too magnificent, is our persistent human heritage. Prophecy goes against the grain of our time-space oriented civilization. But this very civilization is in ferment; it wakes up each morning, bewildered and still more ignorant than knowing.

Prophecy in our time competes with the vast number of items of information we perceive through our known senses. With instantaneous information transmission, computerized data retrieval, and myriad items of human, social, political, and economic information at hand, we have so much consciously perceived knowledge at our disposal that prophecy might seem out of date. Yet the basic human need for guidance through the jungle of supposedly well-established facts all around us has not diminished since Dodona. As myth and legend have faded and science has asserted itself, we have narrowed down the area in which prophecy seems to happen. Still, as in atomic physics, certain events can never be perceived at the time or place they occur, so our experience of prophecy is still elusive, and we remain in pursuit of ultimate proof and understanding.

There is a simple analogy about prophecy. If you are in a helicopter, circling over a mountain, and you can see two trains on opposite sides of the mountain but heading toward each other—you can then foresee a collision as if you had superhuman knowledge, at least in contrast to the passengers and engineers on the two trains. It is a neat analogy. It does not demand basic readjustments of traditional concepts of time and space. But can we achieve helicopter-like perception of our own future? Yes, certainly, to the degree to which each of us gains greater insight into himself—because we are not so much masters as, unconsciously, the magnets of our fate.

Author's Note

The subject of this book, prophecy in our time, is part of an area of long-standing interest to the author: the psychology of public affairs. But what, exactly, is prophecy? How does its meaning compare to that of precognition, foreknowledge, forecasting, anticipation, and related concepts? Prophecy, a highly subjective experience, is too much in flux, too alive, for rigid categorization. I have sought to avoid a dogmatic definition of my subject matter, thus gaining freedom to select and explore.

Taking advantage of this freedom, I have included prophetic efforts in modern economics (Chapter 17, "Toward the Year 2000"), because forecasting techniques in this field are closer to traditional oracular methods than is commonly realized; I hope to examine this topic in greater detail in future writings. On the other hand, I have refrained from detailed treatment of current debates on the philosophy and psychology of time, mathematical-statistical theories of probability, and the deeper psychodynamics of individual prophetic experiences; these subjects demand special interest on the part of the reader. An excellent starting point for psychological study is the symposium *Voices of Time*, edited by J. T. Fraser (New York, 1966); serious inquiry into philosophical and physical aspects might begin with H. A. C. Dobbs' paper, "Time and ESP" (*Proceedings*, Society for Psychical Research, London; Vol. 54, Part 197, August 1965). Additional reading suggestions may be found in the "Selected Bibliography."

Selected Bibliography

The listings in this Selected Bibliography serve to supplement and amplify references contained in the text of this volume. In addition, the reader may refer to periodicals in the field of parapsychology, which are, for the most part, well indexed and contain relevant entries in such categories as "Precognition," "Prediction," "Prophecy," and "Premonition." Of specific interest are the *Journal of Parapsychology*, P. O. Box 6847, College Station, Durham, North Carolina 27708; the *International Journal of Parapsychology*, 29 West 57th Street, New York, N. Y. 10019; the *Journal*, American Society for Psychical Research, 5 West 73rd Street, New York, N. Y. 10023; and the *Journal*, Society for

Psychical Research, 1 Adam and Eve Mews, London W. 8. A number of journals in the field of psychology and allied disciplines may also be consulted, among them the *American Psychologist*, 1200 Seventeenth Street, N.W., Washington, D. C. 20036, and the *Psychoanalytic Review*, 29W East 10th Street, New York, N. Y. 10003.

BALTZER, ARMIN, *Philosoph oder Prophet? Oswald Spenglers Vermächtnis und Voraussagen.* Neheim-Hüsten (Germany), Verlag für Kulturwissenschaften, 1962.

BARRETT, W. F., "Premonition." *Journal*, Society for Psychical Research (London), Vol. I, 1884–85.

BELL, DANIEL, and others, "Toward the Year 2000: Work in Progress." *Daedalus*, Journal of the American Academy of Arts and Sciences, Vol. 96, No. 3, Summer 1967.

BENDER, HANS, *Parapsychologie: Entwicklung, Ergebnisse, Probleme.* Darmstadt, Wissenschaftliche Buchgesellschaft, 1966.

———, "The Gotenhafen Case of Correspondence Between Dreams and Future Events: A Study of Motivation." *International Journal of Neuropsychiatry* (Chicago), Vol. 2, No. 5, 1966.

BESTERMAN, THEODORE, *Crystal-Gazing.* New Hyde Park, N. Y., University Books, 1965.

———, "Report on an Inquiry into Precognitive Dreams." *Proceedings*, Society for Psychical Research (London), Vol. 41, 1933.

BROAD, C. D., *Lectures in Psychical Research.* New York, Humanities Press, 1963.

———, "Knowledge and Foreknowledge." *Proceedings*, Aristotelian Society (London), Vol. XVI, 1937.

———, *Religion, Philosophy and Psychical Research.* New York, Harcourt, 1953.

BUTLER, WILLIAM F., *How Business Economists Forecast.* Englewood Cliffs, N. J., Prentice-Hall, 1966.

CAYCE, HUGH LYNN, *Venture Inward.* New York, Harper & Row, 1964.

CLARK, ARTHUR C., *Profiles of the Future.* New York, Harper & Row, 1963.

COURNOS, JOHN, *A Book of Prophecy.* New York, Scribner, 1942.

DEVEREUX, GEORGE, ed., *Psychanalysis and the Occult.* New York, International Universities Press, 1953.

DODDS, E. R., *The Greeks and the Irrational.* Berkeley and Los Angeles, University of California Press, 1963.

DUNNE, J. W., *An Experiment with Time.* London, A. C. Black, 1927.

EBON, MARTIN, "Parapsychological Dream Studies," in G. E. von Grunebaum and Roger Caillois, eds., *The Dream and Human Societies.* Berkeley and Los Angeles, University of California Press, 1966.

———, "The Second Soul of C. G. Jung." *International Journal of Parapsychology* (New York), Vol. V, No. 4, August 1963.

EHRENWALD, JAN, *Telepathy and Medical Psychology.* New York, Norton, 1948.

ELLISON, JEROME, "Jeane Dixon Talks About God." *The Christian Herald* (New York, March 1966).

FESTINGER, LEON, with RIECKEN, HENRY W., and SCHACHTER, STANLEY, *When Prophecy Fails.* Minneapolis, University of Minnesota Press, 1956.

FORDHAM, FRIEDA, *An Introduction to Jung's Psychology.* Baltimore, Md., Penguin Books, 1953.

FORMAN, HENRY JAMES, *The Story of Prophecy.* New York, Tudor, 1939.

FREI, BRUNO, *Hanussen: Ein Bericht,* Strasbourg, Brant-Verlag, 1934.

FREUD, SIGMUND, *A General Introduction to Psychoanalysis.* New York, Garden City Publishing Co., 1938.

———, *Studies in Parapsychology.* New York, Collier Books, 1963.

FREY-WEHRLIN, C. T., "Ein Prophetischer Traum," in *Spectrum Psychologiae.* Zurich, Rascher & Cie., 1965.

GARRETT, EILEEN J., *The Sense and Nonsense of Prophecy.* New York, Creative Age Press, 1950.

GREEN, CELIA, "Report (1959) on Enquiry into Spontaneous Cases." *Proceedings,* Society for Psychical Research (London), Part 191, Vol. LIII, November 1960.

GREY, E. HOWARD, *Visions, Previsions and Miracles.* London, L. N. Fowler, 1915.

GUARIGLIA, GUGLIELMO, "Prophetismus und Heilserwartungs-Bewegungen als völkerkundliches und religionsgeschichtliches Problem." *Wiener Beiträge zur Kulturgeschichte und Linguistik* (Vienna), Vol. XIII, Verlag Ferdinand Berger, 1959.

HAMMARSKJÖLD, DAG, *Markings.* New York, Knopf, 1964.

HANUSSEN, ERIK JAN, *Meine Lebenslinie.* Berlin, Universitas-Verlag, 1930.

HOWE, ELLIC, *Urania's Children: The Strange World of the Astrologers.* London, William Kimber, 1967.

JACOBI, JOLANDE, *Komplex, Archtypus, Symbol in der Psychologie C. G. Jungs.* Zurich, Rascher & Cie., 1957.

JAFFÉ, ANIELA, *Apparitions and Precognition.* New Hyde Park, N. Y., University Books, 1963.

JONES, ERNEST, *The Life and Work of Sigmund Freud.* New York, Basic Books, 1961.

JUNG, C. G., *Collected Works,* Vol. 1–17. Bollingen Series. New York, Pantheon Books, 1957–1965.

———, "Synchronicity: An Acausal Connecting Principle," in *The Interpretation of Nature and the Psyche.* Bollingen Series. New York, Pantheon Books, 1955.

KRIPPNER, STANLEY, "The Cycle in Deaths Among U.S. Presidents Elected at Twenty-Year Intervals." *International Journal of Parapsychology* (New York), Autumn 1967.

LEONI, EDGAR, *Nostradamus: Life and Literature.* New York, Nosbooks, 1961.

LEVITT, THEODORE, *Innovation in Marketing.* New York, McGraw-Hill, 1962.

LEWINSOHN, RICHARD, *Science, Prophecy and Prediction.* New York, Harper & Row, 1961.

LYTTELTON, DAME EDITH, *Some Cases of Prediction.* London, G. Bell, 1937.

MACNEICE, LOUIS, *Astrology.* Garden City, N.Y., Doubleday, 1966.

MANCHESTER, WILLIAM, *The Death of a President.* New York, Harper & Row, 1967.

MEERLOO, JOOST A. M., *Hidden Communion.* New York, Garrett Publications, 1964.

———, *The Two Faces of Man.* New York, International Universities Press, 1955.

MEIER, C. A., "Projection, Transference, and the Subject-Object Relation in Psychology." *Journal of Analytical Psychology* (London), Vol. IV, No. 1, 1959.

MONTGOMERY, RUTH, *A Gift of Prophecy: The Phenomenal Jeane Dixon.* New York, Wm. Morrow, 1965.

MÜNSTERBERG, HUGO, *On the Witness Stand.* New York, McClure, 1923.

MYERS, F. W. H., *Classical Essays.* London, Macmillan, 1921.

———, "The Relation of Supernormal Phenomena to Time—Precognition." *Proceedings,* Society for Psychical Research (London), Vol. 11, 1895.

NOSTRADAMUS (Michel de Nôtre Dame), *Centuries.* Lyon (France), Macé Bonhomme, 1655.

OCHOROWICZ, JULIAN, *Zjawiska Mediumiczne.* Warsaw, Biblioteka Dziel Wyborowych, 1913.

OSBORN, ARTHUR WALTER, *The Future Is Now.* New Hyde Park, N. Y., University Books, 1962.

OSTY, EUGENE, *Supernormal Faculties in Man.* New York, E. P. Dutton, 1923.

PARAPSYCHOLOGY FOUNDATION, "Precognition: Evidence and Methods." Account of conference on precognition. *Newsletter,* Vol. 7, No. 2, March–April 1960.

———, *Ten Years of Activities.* New York, 1965.

PARKE, H. W., and WORMELL, D. E. W., *The Delphic Oracle.* Oxford, Blackwell, 1956.

POLLACK, JACK HARRISON, *Croiset the Clairvoyant.* New York, Doubleday, 1964.

PRATT, J. GAITHER, *Parapsychology: An Insider's View of ESP.* New York, E. P. Dutton, 1966.

PRINCE, WALTER FRANKLIN, "Pseudo-Prophecies and Pseudo-Sciences." *Bulletin XII,* Boston Society for Psychic Research, May 1930.

RAO, K. RAMAKRISHNA, *Experimental Parapsychology: A Review and Interpretation.* Springfield, Ill., Charles C Thomas, 1966.

RHINE, J. B., *The New World of the Mind*. New York, Wm. Sloane Assoc., 1953.

———, and others, *Extrasensory Perception after Sixty Years*. Boston, Bruce Humphries, 1940, 1966.

———, with PRATT, J. G., *Parapsychology: Frontier Science of the Mind*. Springfield, Ill., Charles C. Thomas, 1957, 1962.

RHINE, LOUISA E., *ESP in Life and Lab: Tracing Hidden Channels*. New York, Macmillan, 1967.

———, *Hidden Channels of the Mind*. New York, Wm. Sloane Assoc., 1961.

SALTMARSH, H. F., *Foreknowledge*. London, G. Bell, 1938.

———, "Report on Cases of Apparent Precognition." *Proceedings*, Society for Psychical Research (London), Vol. 42, 1934.

SERVADIO, EMILIO, *Psychology Today*. New York, Garrett Publications, 1966.

SIDGWICK, E. M., "On the Evidence for Premonitions." *Proceedings*, Society for Psychical Research (London), Vol. 5, 1888.

SMITH, SUSY, *ESP*. New York, Pyramid Books, 1962.

SMYTHIES, J. R., ed., *Science and ESP*. London, Routledge, 1967.

SOAL, S. G., and BATEMAN, F., *Modern Experiments in Telepathy*. New Haven, Yale University Press, 1954.

STEARN, JESS, *The Door to the Future*. Garden City, N.Y., Doubleday, 1963.

———, *Edgar Cayce: The Sleeping Prophet*. Garden City, N.Y., Doubleday, 1967.

STEVENS, WILLIAM OLIVER, *The Mystery of Dreams*. New York, Dodd, Mead, 1949.

TENHAEFF, W. H. C., *Oorlogsvoorspellingen*. Den Hague, H. P. Leopold, 1948.

TREVOR-ROPER, HUGH, *The Last Days of Hitler*. New York, Macmillan, 1947.

VARENA, MARCUS, *Gesammelte Prophezeiungen*. Freiburg i. Br., Hermann Bauer Verlag, 1959.

WOHL, LOUIS DE, *The Stars in War and Peace*. London, Gollancz, 1952.

Readers who wish to participate in precognition research by submitting a premonitory experience, a dream, or other prophetic impression, may request a questionnaire and instruction sheet from:

> The Premonitions Registry
> P.O. Box 482
> Times Square Station
> New York, N.Y. 10036

Upon receipt of the instructions, readers may file their premonition for future reference. It is best to enclose a self-addressed, stamped, return envelope.

Index

ALDRICH, JOHN W., 176
American Society for Psychical Research (New York), 10, 19–20, 35, 93, 133–148, 201
AMOS (Biblical prophet), 12
ANDERSON, MARGARET, 167–169, 172–173, 175
Anderson-Gregory precognition experiments, 172–173, 175
Animals and precognitive effects, 176–184
Apparitions, precognitive, 146–148
Aristotelian Society (London), 36
ARMSTRONG, DAISY, 82
ARMSTRONG, THOMAS, 82, 83, 84
"Arrival" cases, 146–148
Assassinations, predictions of
President Kennedy, 9, 204–210, 225, 227
President Lincoln, 210–213
Association for Research and Enlightenment (Virginia Beach), 37–50
Astrology, 11, 15, 67, 193–194, 218
and the death of President Kennedy, 207–210
in Hitler Germany, 61–67
Automatic writing, 81–85

BAJETTO, ALESANDRA, 71
BARRON, FRANK, 170
BARTEL, JANOS, 55
BARTON, MRS. MICHAEL, 195
BECKER, D. C., 220
BELL, DANIEL, 184
BENDER, HANS, v, 67, 68–71, 105, 127–128
BENTER, CHARLES, 205

Billet reading, 56–57
BLUMENTHAL, MORTON, 39
BOLTON, FRANCIS P., v
BOOTH, JOHN WILKES, 13, 213
BOSMIALEK (New Guinea "prophet"), 78–79
BREITBART, "IRON KING," 56
BRETSCHNEIDER, J. H., 71
BROAD, C. D., 36
BROWN, SYBIL, 9
BRUCE, H. ADDINGTON, 98
BUMGARDNER, ELEANOR, 205, 206
BUTLER, WILLIAM F., 192
BUTT, ARCHIBALD, 22
BUTT, CLARA, 22

CAMPBELL, DONALD, 10, 226
CAMPBELL, JOSEPH, 220
CAMPBELL, MICHAEL B., 179, 180
Cancer cures, prophecies concerning, 199
CARINGTON, WHATELY, 163
"Cargo Cult" practices of the South Pacific, 76–87
Cassandra, 203
CASTRO, FIDEL, 198, 207
CAYCE, EDGAR, 37
CAYCE, HUGH LYNN, v, 37, 38–40
Cerebrocentric vs. psychocentric view of man, 166
CERMINARA, GINA, 37, 44, 49
"Chair tests" (Croiset), 67–76, 153
Checking effect (feeling of success) in precognition experiments, 171
Children as ESP subjects, 167–176
CHURCHILL, WINSTON, 66

INDEX

Clairvoyance, 14, 64, 98, 149, 153, 163
  fraudulent, 57
  Pearce-Pratt tests for, 159–160
Classical Essays (F. W. H. Myers), 217–218
Classroom experiments in ESP, 172–176
COATES, J., 21
Collective unconscious (C. G. Jung), 219
COPE, MRS. HARLEY, 205
Creativity and ESP, 170–171
Creativity and Psychological Health (Frank Barron), 170–171
CROESUS, KING OF LYDIA, 12
Croiset the Clairvoyant (J. H. Pollack), 75
CROISET, GERARD, 67–76, 153
Crystal gazing, 195, 200–201, 217

DAGMA, FRAU, 00
DALE, LAURA A., v, 141
Death cycle of American presidents, 208–209
Death of a President, The (William Manchester), 227
Death of self, premonitions of, 9–10, 12, 209–213, 227
DECLE, LIONEL, 28
DE KERLOR, W., 21
Delphic Oracle, 10, 12, 44, 105, 218, 219
DE STEIGER, MRS. I., 21
De Voorschouw (W. H. C. Tenhaeff), 68
DEWEY, THOMAS E., 198
DE WOHL, LOUIS, 63, 65–66, 67
Displacement effects in ESP research, 162–164
Distance and ESP, 159–160, 167–169
DIXON, JAMES, 201, 205
DIXON, JEANE, 194–203, 205–206, 217, 227
DOBBS, H. A. C., 228
"Doctrinal compliance" (Jan Ehrenwald), 35, 120, 128
DODDS, E. R., 220

Door to the Future, The (Jess Stern), 205
Dreams, 98
  precognitive, 17–20, 21, 22–23, 38–40, 93, 94–95, 99–106, 107–118, 148–157, 223
  telepathic, 95–96, 108
DRUCKER, PETER F., 192
DUNNE, J. W., 26–36
DZINO, ISMED, 59

EASTMAN, BOB, 83, 85
EBERTIN, ELSBETH, 61
Edgar Cayce: The Sleeping Prophet (Jess Stearn), 37
EHRENWALD, JAN, v, 32, 35, 120, 128, 131–132
EIDELBERG, LUDWIG, 109
EISENBUD, JULE, v, 120–127
EISENHOWER, DWIGHT D., 196–197
ELLIS, HAVELOCK, 98
ELLISON, JEROME, 200
ESP: A Scientific Evaluation (C. E. M. Hansel), 164
EVANS, EDITH, 22
EVARA (New Guinea "prophet"), 79
Experiment with Time, An (J. W. Dunne), 26
Extra-sensory Perception (J. B. Rhine), 159
Extrasensory perception, 15, 67, 158–166, 167–175, 225–227; see also Clairvoyance; Precognition, experimental; Telepathy

FAHLER, JARL, 73
Far Memory (Joan Grant), 20
FARRA, MARTHA, 56
Feeling of success, see Checking effect
FERENCZI, SANDOR, 92
FERNSWORTH, ISABEL, 24
FESTINGER, LEON, 81
FIELDS, DAVIS, 202
FITZGERALD, ROBERT, 90
"Flying saucers" and prophecy, 81–84, 104
FORDHAM, FRIEDA, 100

INDEX

Forecasts, technological, 184–194

Foreknowledge (H. F. Saltmarsh), 181

Foundation for Research on the Nature of Man (Durham, N. C.), v, 10, 93, 158, 165, 173–174, 227

FRANCO, FRANCISCO, 47
FRASER, J. T., 229
FRASER, TOMMY L., 79

Fraud hypothesis (as related to ESP research), 164

FREDERICK THE GREAT, 65
FREEMAN, JOHN A., 173–175
FREUD, SIGMUND, 12, 88–98, 99, 100, 108, 119, 120, 121, 131, 219, 222, 223
FREY-WEHRLIN, C. T., 105–106
FRIED, HENRY, 208
FUESS, LARRY, 223
FULLER, CURTIS, 206

GARBUTT, J. T., 169
GARRETT, EILEEN J., v
GAYN, MARK, 87
GEORGE, WILL, 203

Gift of Prophecy: The Phenomenal Jeane Dixon (Ruth Montgomery), 194, 199, 201, 205

GLANDECK, ADAM, 61
GOEBBELS, JOSEPH, 52, 59, 62, 64, 65
GOLDBERG, ARTHUR, 210
GOLDNEY, K. M., 162–164
GÖRING, HERMANN, 60–61
GRAHAM, BILLY, 207
GRANT, JOAN, 20

Greeks and the Irrational, The (E. R. Dodds), 220

GREENBACK, R. K., 111–119
GREGORY, ELSIE, 173, 176
GUARIGLIA, GUGLIELMO, 85
GUBISCH, WILHELM, 52
GUILFORD, J. P., 171
GURNEY, EDMUND, 142

HAMMARSKJÖLD, DAG, 204, 205, 214, 215
HANSEL, C. E. M., 164
HANUSSEN, ERIK J., 50–61, 67
HARMON, COUNT, 21
HASLAM, PROFESSOR, 181
HAVLICEK, GENDARME, 57
HAYS, CHARLES M., 20
HAZELWIGG, JOHN, 208
HEATLEY, MAURICE D., 222
HELLDORF, WOLF H., 51, 52, 58, 59, 60
HELLQVIST, GUNNAR, 208

Hero with a Thousand Faces, The (Joseph Campbell), 221

HESKETH, J., 24
HESS, RUDOLF, 60, 63, 64
HEYWOOD, ROSALIND, v

Hidden Channels of the Mind (L. E. Rhine), 149, 223

HIMMLER, HEINRICH, 63
HINDENBURG, PAUL VON, 51, 65
HITLER, ADOLF, 46, 50–67
HITSCHMANN, EDUARD, 94, 95, 108, 119, 121
HO CHI MINH, 199
HODGKINSON, LEONARD, 23
HOMER, 216

Horse races and spontaneous precognition, 179–184

HUGENBERG, ALFRED, 51
HUGHES, MRS. CHARLES, 23–24
HUMPHREY, HUBERT, 200
HURLEY, PATRICK J., 197
HYNES, ROSE, 167–168
Hypnosis, 61

IIDA, K. K., 41

International Conference on Spontaneous Phenomena (1955), 142

Interpretation of Dreams, The (Freud), 88, 93

"Intervention" and precognition, 149, 151

Introduction to Jung's Psychology (Frieda Fordham), 100

ISHII, I., 41

JAFFÉ, ANIELA, v, 107
JAMES, WILLIAM, 133
JARMAN, A. S., 179–180
JENSEN, WIERS, 146

INDEX

JOHNSON, LYNDON B., 77, 78, 199
JONES, ERNEST, 91
JUHN, ADOLF E., 56
JUNG, C. G., 92, 99–107, 119, 131, 219, 223

KAHN, HERMAN, 185, 190–191
KAUFMANN, REBECCA, 205
KEECH, MARIAN (pseudonym), 80–85
KENNEDY, JACQUELINE, 9
KENNEDY, JOHN F., 12, 13, 194, 195, 200, 204, 214, 215, 225, 227–228
  predictions of his assassination, 9, 204–210
KING, MARTIN LUTHER, 203
KLUTZ, JERRY, 208
KNAPP, R. H., 169
KNOWLAND, WILLIAM, 198
KORODI, WALTER, 00
KRAFFT, KARL E., 62–64, 66, 67, 203
KRIPPNER, STANLEY, 209

LAMON, DOROTHY, 210
LAMON, WARD HILL, 210–212, 213
LAWRENCE, PETER, 79–80, 86
LEE, DAL, 207, 209
LEHRER, ELISE, 65
LEMON, A. KENT, 182
LEVITT, THEODORE, 192
LINCOLN, ABRAHAM, 12, 13, 204, 214–15
  dream of his assassination, 210–212
LINCOLN, MARY TODD, 211–212
LINDBERGH, CHARLES, 25
LONGWELL, C. R., 41–42
LORD, WALTER, 20
LOUWERENS, ANNET, 73
LOUWERENS, NICOLAUDA, 71, 73
LUBBE, MARINUS VAN DER, 61
LYTTELTON, EDITH, 182

MACARTHUR, DOUGLAS, 196
MCCAHEN, MR. AND MRS. PAUL H., 145—147

MACDONALD, COLIN, 24
MCDOUGALL, WILLIAM, 157–159
MCDOWELL, RICKY E., 207
MCINTYRE, LESLIE, 208
MCLUHAN, MARSHALL, 203
MACNEICE, LOUIS, 62
MANCHESTER, WILLIAM, 227
Many Mānsions (Gina Cerminara), 37
MAO TSE-TUNG, 199, 207
MARSHALL, MR. AND MRS. JACK, 20
MATHEWS, NORAH K., 24
Mediumship, 21, 66–67, 158–159, 183
MEERLOO, JOOST A. M., 225
MEIER, C. A., 106
MENOZZI, TINO, 71
Mental retardates as ESP subjects, 173–175
MIDDLETON, J. CONNON, 20
MIYABE, N., 41
Modern Experiments in Telepathy (Soal and Bateman), 162
MONTGOMERY, RUTH, 194–203, 205
MORRIS, ROBERT, 177–179
MURPHY, GARDNER, v, 141, 142, 221
MYERS, F. W. H., 217, 218

NASH, MR. AND MRS., 147–148
NEBELMEIER, FELIX, 63
NIETZSCHE, FRIEDRICH, 219
Night to Remember, A (Walter Lord), 20
NIXON, ROBERT (the Cheshire "idiot"), 220–221
NOSTRADAMUS, 12, 49, 62, 64

O'DONNELL, KENNETH, 9
O'DONNELL, KITTY, 83–84, 85
Oedipus complex, 88–98
OHST, HERBERT VON, 51, 58, 60
OPPÉ, A., 218
OSWALD, LEE HARVEY, 200, 202, 204

Pain, telepathic sharing of, 151

INDEX

Parapsychology: An Insider's View of ESP (J. G. Pratt), 160

Parapsychology Foundation (New York), v, 14, 142, 221

Parapsychology Laboratory (formerly of Duke University), 13, 158–166, 167–170, 172–175

Patient-therapist relationship, 114–115

PEARCE, HUBERT, 159–162, 163
PEARSON, DREW, 210
PENDRAGON, JOHN, 207
PERRONE, V., 71

Personality characteristics and ESP success, 000–000

Phantasms of the Living (Myers, Gurney, and Podmore), 142

Physics and paranormal phenomena, 35, 166

Photography, paranormal, 120

PINCKERT, JEANE, see Dixon, Jeane
PLATO, 217
POLELESI (New Guinea "prophet"), 80
POLLACK, JACK H., 76
PORTALES, MARIA, 51
PRATT, J. G., 159–162, 163

Precognition, experimental, 12, 13, 103, 105, 158–166, 167–176, 226; see also Clairvoyance; Extrasensory perception; Telepathy

involving animals, 176–179

Precognition, spontaneous, 17–25, 26–36, 130–148, 149–158

involving animals, 176–184

Precognitive telepathy, 162–164
PRICE, GEORGE R., 164
PRIESTLEY, J. B., 26
PROGOFF, IRA, 213–215

Prophecy; see also Dreams, precognitive; Extrasensory perception; Precognition, experimental

in ancient Greece, 10–11, 12, 217–220

Biblical, 12
and the "Cargo Cult," 76–87
concerning world events, 44–49, 194–204
in Croiset's "chair tests," 67–76
of Edgar Cayce, 37–50
in Hitler's Germany, 50–67
involving animals, 176–184
of Jeane Dixon, 194–204
philosophical implications of, 165–166
psychological aspects of, 221–228
self-fulfillment in, 201–204, 212–216, 225–227
and the *Titanic* disaster, 13–14, 17–25

Psi trailing, 177

"Psychic shuffle" experiments, 161–162

"Psychic surgery" in the Philippines, 67

Psychoanalysis and paranormal phenomena, 32, 35, 88–98, 99–107, 108–118, 119–133

Psychokinesis ("mind over matter"), 159–162

Psychological factors, role of in ESP success, 169–172

Psychology and psychical research, 166

RADIN, DONNA, 207

Recollections of Abraham Lincoln (W. H. Lamon), 000

Reincarnation, 18, 77
REUTHER, WALTER, 197
RHINE, J. B., v, 12, 103, 105, 148, 158–162, 163, 164–166, 167, 172, 177
RHINE, LOUISA E., v, 12, 93, 148–157, 223
RICHARDS, PHYLLIS, 182
RICHET, CHARLES, 161
RICHTER, C. F., 42
RIECKEN, HENRY W., 81
ROBERTS, MARY K., 24
ROBERTSON, MORGAN, 18
ROHDE, ERWIN, 219
ROMNEY, GEORGE, 199

INDEX

ROOSEVELT, FRANKLIN D., 65
  prophecy of his death, 217
ROOSEVELT, THEODORE, 98
Rorschach test, 17, 220, 224
ROSS, JOHN C., 206
ROSSANT, M. J., 191, 194

S., MRS. (Polish blindfold medium), 183
SABINE, W. H. W., 202–203, 204
SALTMARSH, H. F., 161, 181–182
SCHACHTER, STANLEY, 81
SCHMEIDLER, GERTRUDE R., 169–171
SCHRENCK-NOTZING, ALBERT VON, 64
SCHULTE-STRATHAUS, ERNST, 63–64
"Scientific prophecy," see Forecasts, technological
Search for the Truth, A (Ruth Montgomery), 200
SEBOTTENDORF, R. F. VON, see Glandeck, Adam
SEGALL, MRS. ROY J., 136–137
Self-fulfillment in prophecy, 201–204, 212–216, 225–227
SERIOS, TED, 120
SERVADIO, EMILIO, v, 107–110, 142
Sex differences in ESP scoring rates, 173–175
SHACKLETON, BASIL, 162–163
SHEEHAN, RAY, 206
"Sheep-goat" differentiation in ESP research, 169
SHELEPIN, ALEXANDER N., 200
SILVERA, JOHN D., 203
SMETANA, FRIEDRICH, 57
SMIT, J. A., 71
SOAL, S. G., 162–163
Soal-Goldney experiments, 162–163
Society for Psychical Research (London), 10, 93, 141–143, 180–182
SOCRATES, 219
Some Cases of Prediction (Edith Lyttelton), 182
SOPHOCLES, 88–91
Spiritualism in Brazil, 67

STALIN, JOSEPH, 45
STANTON, EDWIN M., 213
STEAD, W. T., 21–22
STEARN, JESS, 37, 40, 44, 46, 49, 183, 205
STEINSCHNEIDER, HERMANN, see Hanussen, Erik J.
STEINSCHNEIDER, SIEGFRIED, 54
STERLING, ADAM, 183–184
STERLING, JAN, 183–184
STEVENSON, ADLAI, 206
STEVENSON, IAN, v, 18–25
STORRS, MRS. R. B., 142–145
STRICKLAND, HIRAM D., 9
SUGRUE, THOMAS, 37
Suicide and paranormal experience, 115–118
SUKARNO, 196, 207
Survival of bodily death, 158–159
SUSLOV, MICHAEL A., 200
Synchronicity (C. G. Jung), 103–104, 224

TAFT, WILLIAM HOWARD, 22
Targets, selection of in precognition experiments, 161–162
TAYLOR, SALLY, 39
Teacher-pupil relationship and ESP success, 172–175
TEETER, JOHN, 205
TEGOBORZA (Polish medium), 65–66
Telepathic leakage, 120–128
Telepathy, 25, 76, 77, 90–92, 98, 104–105, 108, 116, 131, 149, 150–151
TENHAEFF, W. H. C., v, 67, 72–74
TERLINGO, ANTOINETTE, 138–142
Testimony, psychology of, 14
There Is a River (Thomas Sugrue), 37
TILEA, VERGIL, 62
TILLOTSON, E., 43
TOLSTOY, LEO, 215
Time
  attitude toward by ESP subjects, 169–171
  theories of, 13, 26–36, 130–131, 155, 166

INDEX

Time Metaphor Test (Knapp and Garbutt), 169–170
Titanic disaster, premonitions of, 14, 18–25
TREVOR-ROPER, HUGH, 65
TURVEY, V. N., 21
TUYTER, A., 73
Twenty Cases Suggestive of Reincarnation (Ian Stevenson), 19
TYLER, HUGH, 200

Unorthodox healing, 67, 76

VANN, VELMA C., 142, 145
Vardøgr (human double) cases in Norway, 146–147
Venture Inward (Hugh Lynn Cayce), 37
VETTER, KARL, 59

WADA, T., 41
WALTHER, GERDA, 64–65
WASSILKO-SERECKI, ZOË, 207

WEDEMEYER, ALBERT C., 197
WEREIDE, THORSTEIN, 147
WERFEL, FRANZ, 226
WHITE, RHEA, v, 141, 168, 202
WHITMAN, CHARLES J., 222–223
WIENER, ANTHONY J., 185
WILLIAMS, DAVID, 193–194, 208
WILLIAMS, JOHN H., 181–182
WILSON, GEORGE W., 213
WOHL, LUDWIG VON, *see* de Wohl, Louis
World of Dreams, The (Havelock Ellis), 98
World of Ted Serios, The (Jule Eisenbud), 120
Wreck of the Titan (Morton Robertson), 18

ZABRISKIE, MR. AND MRS. G., 134–135
ZORAB, GEORGE, 142
ZULLIGER, HANS, 94–98, 108, 121